Beyond "BARN FINDS"

THE BARONESS
AND THE MERCEDES

and 49 other Entertaining True Tales
From the World of Rare and Exotic Car Collecting

Wallace A. Wyss

Enthusiast Books

Enthusiast Books
1830A Hanley Road
Hudson, Wisconsin 54016 USA

Visit www.enthusiastbooks.com

Enthusuast Books are offered at a discount when sold in quantity for promotional use. Businesses or organizations seeking details should write to the Marketing Department, Enthusiast Books, at the above address.

Library of Congress Control Number: 2014935631

ISBN-13: 978-1-58388-312-6
ISBN-10: 1-58388-312-9

14 15 16 17 18 19 6 5 4 3 2 1

Printed in The United States of America

Cover images: Courtesy Gooding & Co.

Beyond "BARN FINDS"...

THE BARONESS
AND THE MERCEDES

and 49 other Entertaining True Tales
From the World of Rare and Exotic Car Collecting

TABLE OF CONTENTS

ACKNOWLEDGEMENTS

The author would like to thank Skip Marketti of the the Nethercutt Museum in Sylmar, California, and Gary Fisk of the Automobile Driving Museum in El Segundo, California, for allowing me to peruse their library. Also thanks to Richard Bartholomew and Eric Mussara for graphics advice. And let's not forget my sister April and brother Warren, who are not "car guys" per se but are owed thanks for advice on wordage. A special thanks to Tom Cotter for inspiration—for building the model in his "Barn Find" books for what I think could be a new literary arm of the car book world, for those who have longed for an entertaining read along with their facts and pictures.

FOREWORD

Terry Michaelis is owner of ProTeam Corvette and has bought and sold more than 10,000 Corvettes in his storied career. Terry is considered an expert on all things Corvette. He is much in demand as an interview subject for countless radio shows, TV shows, and buff book articles. Terry continues to lobby for the collector Corvette community with the same passion and affection for over-the-top marketing that he first displayed back when he parted out his '61 Corvette in 1974.

A COLD TRAIL CAN TURN WARM… THAT'S WHAT WE LIVE FOR.

Wally Wyss and I struck-up a friendship in the 1970s when he was a beat reporter for *Motor Trend* and I was on the West Coast promoting the World's Largest Gathering of Corvettes and the world premiere of the movie Corvette Summer starring Mark Hamill and Annie Potts. It was a relationship forged by our mutual passion for these cars. We did not know then just how deeply the Corvette was woven into America's car culture, as its allure had not yet hit its stride. It would be a decade or more before we understood just how entrenched the passion for the Corvette was. At that time, we drove them purely for the joy of a hot ride and as an extension of our own personality.

Working on a hunch backed by intuition has been my calling card since those early days. Whether it was an entire collection or a 1958 retractable hardtop, I learned to follow my instinct. There were plenty of wild goose chases but every once in a while a tall tale became truth hidden under a tarp in an out-of-the-way garage. Long hours, hundreds of miles and years melted away when the jewel was unearthed. When opportunity knocks, it is important to open the door.

Wally has put together a book that works to capture the thrill of the chase and the importance of doing your homework. It is something we in the hobby continually wrestle with. We understand the real value of "The Find" comes only after forensics and research validate the hunch. Only then can the conversation began about restoration versus preservation. Only then can we consider historical importance as opposed to watching these cars run the course in freshly restored brilliance. *The Baroness and the Mercedes* gives the reader a look into the frustration or pay-off that comes with each roll of the dice.

What has struck me most within these pages is Wally's ability to bring these barn find cars to life all the while knowing their real worth lies in the people who found them first. Their lives—however briefly they are attached to the car—are often interwoven in the cars' histories as well.

Terry Michaelis
ProTeam Corvette, Napoleon, Ohio

AUTHOR INTRODUCTION

"BARN FIND"...the two most exciting words in the car hobby. Why? Because just the words bring visions of rusty hulks that, once restored, will be great cars.

Now there is one school of thought that says that a car can't be classified as a "barn find" unless the finder finds it in an actual barn. Well, there's damn few barns available now, what with corporate farming, so I'm hereby exercising "author's privilege" to expand the definition to include "any collector car found derelict, ignored, apart or generally in circumstances not worthy of its pedigree until recognized and saved by a discerning enthusiast." This could include cars parked in fields, under trees, in cellars, left in parking garages or even (horrors) under a pile of other cars in a junkyard.

A second old-fashioned definition of "barn find" that needs to be retired is that the car has to be bought at a bargain price; i.e. the owners don't know its historical significance and sells it cheap. In this book, for my definitional purposes, I respect that point of view but, after researching more than 100 great finds, that purchase-price-only definition is way too confining. On the high end, you will find some cars in here that were bought by the barn finder for anywhere from a quarter-million to a million dollars. How could that, under the old definition, be a "barn find"? Because some of these cars are going up in value as the ink dries on these pages. They were a million last month and will be a million more next year. So I use the phrase common in Keith Martin's *Sports Car Market* magazine, "well bought," meaning there's enough space between what it was bought for and what it could sell for in case you, the new owner, ever decide to bail out, you can still make a profit.

Another area where, begging your indulgence, I would like to push the envelope a bit on the definition of "barn find" is to include "pushmobiles." I sometimes recognize them as real cars. These are concocted out of plaster, wood, plastic, fiberglass, metal and such by automakers to put on the stage at major automobile shows. Some of them are built on the bones of real car chassis, but just weren't made operational. There are those enthusiasts who fell in love with a prototype so much that they hunted it down and bought it and spent hundreds of thousands making them into running driving cars. (Didn't we see movies about this where a guy would fall in love with an actresses' portrayal of a character on screen and fall in love with the actress only to find out she wasn't the same in real life as she was on screen?) So I'm throwing in some pushmobiles that almost made it to a real car including the very first Lamborghini ever made.

One final category of "barn finds" I include under my tent are racecars converted for the street. But, as you will read in this book, it's also one of the most controversial areas. Why? Because racecars are, with astonishing regularity, bashed, burned, and crashed; and engines, chassis and bodywork are not only changed from season to season but sometimes several times a season. Result: there's lots of room for fraud. Yet, ironically, in my research for the first book in this series (*Incredible Barn Finds*) I found that cars in that category of used and abused racecars represent some of the largest increases in value percentage-wise of all the cars I write about. Take the Ferrari 250GTO sold by *Road & Track* writer Henry Manney III for $8,500 in 1971. Last time I looked, word was that a 250GTO topped $50 million in a private sale. What's that percentage-wise? Way past my mathematical ability. Almost incalculable (and you will kick me again when you read the 250GTO chapter in this book wherein you find out I turned down Manney's GTO at $18,000 two years earlier).

You'll note that this is a different sort of car book than you are used to. No charts with specifications. No long lists of colors, upholstery choices, final axle ratios, carburetor CFMs, engine choices, comparisons of production numbers, yadda-yadda. That's because, with the advent of the internet search engine, you can find all that out on almost any production car in seconds. I prefer to concentrate instead on the drama of how these cars were hunted down; how they were bought and what passion drove the barn finder to persist in their quest through thick and thin? In other words, the human story behind all that metal, rubber and glass. Occasionally I was lucky enough to find stories about the people who ordered special one-off cars or the people who engineered or designed them or the barn finders who hunted them down even though their targets were "missing, presumed lost." Even better, sometimes I met these people in person or talked to them on the phone, a fact that has made working on this series far more enjoyable than any book I ever worked on. It's made me an enthusiast all over again. I consider myself a "gearhead reborn."

I had to draw one line in the sand, though, just for practical purposes. Near where I live, every day I see dust-covered '65 Mustang notchbacks in driveways, parked, I presume, to gather value with age like vintage bottles of wine. I have no doubt if I bought one I would not lose a dollar and would probably see it appreciate $1,000 to $2,000 a year. If I include all the cars I could find for under $5,000 and still make a profit on, this book would be 1,000 pages thick. So, for practical purposes alone, I had to decide on a basic parameter and that is that any car included here, when sold, has to be worth what one acquaintance termed "a life-changing amount," which he defined as $100K. In Kansas that amount can probably still buy a nice little 2-bedroom house. I know it's unfair to you working with low-investment cars but this book is all about chasing dreams, some of which can be bought for the prices of those low-dollar cars because you—and you alone for one shining moment in time—have the eye, and the talent, for spotting the barn find.

Another difference between this and other car books is pictures. I love color pictures of cars shot right before sunset or at sunrise. I can recommend books with world-class car photography (Randy Leffingwell's books, Dennis Adler's books), but this book is about the hunt, before the cars were rescued and restored. Often they weren't pretty when found. I decided early on in this project that I could either spend a lifetime taking pretty pictures or I could instead track stories of the hunt. I chose to track the hunt. So think of this as a book of short stories. True short stories. And how many short story books have any pictures at all?

Finally, in the last chapter I outline some strategies on how I used to go about finding cars. In the '80s, between writing books, I would trot about the country looking for this or that car for moneyed clients. I'm talking Ferraris, Rolls Royces, Bentleys, even Italian oddballs like Bizzarrini and Iso Grifo. I would say, based on the value of all the collector cars I bought for myself and others, it's easily $5 million worth of cars.

Now I already anticipate critics loading their blunderbusses to snipe at me regarding the whole concept of this book. I expect to get carping comments like "All the good ones have been found," or another favorite, "Hey, loan me a time machine and I'll go back and buy that car at that 1971 price." I say balderdash to those comments because although the prices have risen in general, and car owners, through internet search engines, can check in seconds what their model of car is selling for at auctions, the one thing that hasn't changed is the constantly changing circumstances of the car owners.

While the cars are sitting there gathering dust, the owners are getting married, getting divorced, being incarcerated, going bankrupt, getting sick, even dying or, at the other end of life's scale, getting married, having babies born. The cars sleep on, unaware. So considering car owners' life circumstances are changing continuously, cars do on occasion become available. And if you did your research, and kept your powder dry (i.e. by keeping your funds what bankers call "fluid"), you can be there to buy the car you want when the owners are thinking of selling.

So that's the reason for this book. I've missed many a car (ah, that Henry Manney Ferrari 250GTO still hurts the most). But I've succeeded just enough times in buying cars for myself (two Mercedes gullwings, a 12-cylinder Ferrari, a 356 Porsche Convertible D, etc.) to know that rare cars with appreciation potential can be found by your ordinary working class bloke with a discerning eye and a bit of entrepreneurial blood in his veins.

Now in some other books they quote great philosophers, Plato, etc. But this is a car book. So maybe you won't mind if I quote a fellow Michigander, comedian Tim Allen. He wrote in an *AARP* magazine article that his old cars add value to his life. "You don't want the end to come and say, 'I wish I'd loved more. I wish I'd smelled more roses.'" I say the same thing about just one time letting go of all those practical considerations that normally dominate your life. Letting go just enough to allow an interesting car to come into your life. I remember driving my first gullwing on Woodward Avenue, and, two decades later, blasting my first 12-cylinder Ferrari through the Malibu tunnel at 7,500 rpm while upshifting to third. So I've had those moments of glory, too few of them if you must know the truth. You'll see by my own car adventures, mixed in with the great finds in this book, that I regret not having the nerve to snag some other cars I found that would have provided memorable moments as well.

In my current life, between writing car-oriented mysteries, learning the thoroughbred horse trade from the ground up and honing my fine art brush techniques, I don't have much time to barnsearch. It's time to let younger, more ambitious folks continue the hunt, benefiting from my experience and the stories of all of those other successful barn hunters described in this book. So let's hope you have the "eye" for what's good, the stamina to stay the hunt and the follow-through to do your own great barn find.

Good hunting.

Wallace Wyss
Cobra Ranch
Mendocino, California

Chapter 1
THE SPLIT GRILLE FERRARI
(1962 FERRARI SWB 250GT)

Okay, it's weird looking but hey, there's only one of them.

Ferrari builds exciting cars. You could argue that even just show-ing the chassis of a new Ferrari is enough to generate sales (or just showing the engine). Of course most of the sales are motivated by the performance, the link with racing and the styling, almost always ahead of the curve, so to speak.

Back in the early '70s, while a spear carrier for *Motor Trend*, I did a little photography on the side and managed to get an assign-ment from Chuck Queener, the assistant art director at *Motor Trend*, and a Ferrari fanatic, to help *Automobile Quarterly* find some Ferraris to photograph for a story they were running. So off I went, from one owner on the list supplied by Queener to another. Most of the cars were impressive (the GTC/4 inspired me to buy one decades later), but I wasn't prepared for the singular beauty of the one-off Bertone short wheelbase berlinetta.

First let me go back and say who Bertone is…Bertone was in the Sixties one of the great Italian coachbuilders. They designed cars and on occasion even won the contract to build the production versions of some of the cars they designed, while others of their designs were farmed out to other coachbuilders. Though they didn't succeed in getting many Ferrari contracts, there was an early car, then one 250GT, and then this one before they finally got the production contract to do the 308GT4 (alas one of the most "knocked" of all Ferraris).

The name of Bertone is more linked with Alfa Romeo, which is more the pity because this car is so singularly beautiful. I should add that the young designer on the boards at Bertone was Giorgetto Giugiaro, later to become the most famous car designer of the 20th Century.

A lot of the design of SN 3269GT picks up some of the design cues from the DB4 Bertone Jet, a one-off Aston Martin done by Giugiaro for Bertone during the same time period, even down to vents in the side and a similar roofline. The "split" front grille of the Bertone Ferrari remains controversial in that it has a Pontiac resemblance. Pontiac came out with this on the '61 models so there's a chance GM could have copied it, but maybe it was coincidence, unless a GM designer happened to be visiting Bertone's carrozzeria when the car was still being built.

One operating theory of historians for the car's raison d'etre is that Nuccio Bertone wanted to tool about in a Ferrari, but being a coachbuilder himself, it just wouldn't do to drive one with a design by his archrival, Pininfarina, who had done most Ferraris since the other companies like Touring, Ghia, Ghia-Aigle, etc. began closing their doors.

You would think, when getting the benefit of a great design house wanting to clothe one of your chassis, you would get the chassis for free. But that was not the case—he had to buy the car though Ferrari reportedly wrote a nice note to the effect of "your thoughts and words are the unmistakable signs of a man gripped by the same passion that has led me to where I am today." The one-off car made its debut at the 1962 Turin Motor Show.

When I saw the car in 1972, I vaguely remember the price being the same for this ten-year-old car being equal to a new Ferrari. Some four decades later I found the owner from the '60s on a Ferrari website, remembering the price he was asking at the time being over a million dollars. But I beg to differ—back then, though it's hard to believe, no old Ferrari was worth that much. Even Steve

Earle, the founder of the Monterey Historics, sold his 250GTO in the early '70s for less than $100,000 (I know, I introduced him to the Japanese customer).

The Bertone split-grille one-off owner then wasn't really a Ferrari guy as far as driving to club events, but he knew he had something special.

Following the trail of the Ferrari, according to Alan Boe, a prominent Ferrari historian, the car went from Bertone to SR. Musico, in Milan, a music company and from there to Lorenzo Bandini the race driver. And from there it went to Pete Civati, a mechanic who I met when he was buying old Ferraris three at a time to vend to dealers in Los Angeles. He bought it in December 1964 and then in 1966 it went to the Hollywood jazz musician who had it when I photographed it sometime between '70 and '72. The musician apparently kept it all the way to 1990 when it went to Mexico's premier collector Lorenzo Zambrana. The car has been dark blue, silver, and dark blue again.

Zambrano bought it and had an independent Ferrari shop (not an authorized dealer) restore it to its present splendor. Ironically it was sold to John Mecom, a famous Texas oil man and car enthusiast, but he sold it right back to Zambrano who maybe missed the car just too much. In 1988 it was offered by Forristal's cars in Houston, an independent Ferrari sales source, but as far as this writer can determine, it's still in Zambrano's hands.

Lessons to be learned here? 1) Listen to the experts. If Chuck Queener, the first art director of *CAVALLINO* magazine and an expert on Ferrari, told me it was the "ultimate swb 250GT," it was (though he did keep talking about the SEFAC hot rod swb-250GTs and 250GTOs, so he had me thoroughly confused as to which was the most desirable car). 2) I should have made an offer. I didn't ascertain how much of a hurry the owner was in to sell it. Sometimes you can get a whiff of divorce, lawsuits, etc. that could make the seller more motivated. 3) I should have realized it as a "one-off" that is an "in period" (done when the car is new) vehicle from a recognized name coachbuilder like Pininfarina, Zagato or Bertone. For instance, coating the car with gold likely means there is only one. If someone wants it, they want it and there's no alternative. Plus add that as Giugiaro grows more and more famous, each of his early achievements (the cars he designed at Bertone and Ghia) receive added luster as well. I would say, side view, this is the most beautiful Ferrari road car (while the P3/4 racecar still is the most beautiful Ferrari ever).

Today the car is in the multi-million dollar class and its record of wins at concours like Pebble Beach, the Cavallino Classic, etc. is among the best of any Ferrari. Whoever passed this car up when it was kicking around the West Coast in the early '70s because "it looked different than other Ferraris" was passing up a great opportunity for appreciation. Sure it looked less pugnacious than the regular swb 250GT, but in the end, its curvaceous looks are what make it appreciated today.

Chapter 2
AN ODE TO SUPER SLUG
(1965 COBRA DAYTONA SUPER COUPE)

Brock's Last Folly at Shelby-American.

When Pete Brock, the young designer and race driver, designed the Cobra Daytona coupe for his employer, Shelby-American, in '64, the wizened mechanics back at the shop were a bit skeptical and called the car "the slug." When it subsequently went 180 mph in its first run at Riverside as Brock had promised, the guys at the shop expressed grudging admiration.

But not for long.

In the '65 season Brock was back with another coupe design, this time for the 427 Cobra chassis, which had larger diameter frame tubes, spread wider apart, and coil spring suspension all around. Not to mention the humongous 427-cubic-inch (7-liter) "side oiler" engine rated at about 485 hp in racing trim. This time Brock was promising 215 mph, and predicting that his so-called Type 65 (Europeans called their cars "Type" so this made it seem oh-so-European) would beat the GT40s, even though it had the "obsolete" configuration of being front-engined, which even Ferrari was abandoning for in favor of mid-engined layouts in the prototype class.

Brock thought that his boss, Carroll Shelby, could field the 427 coupes in addition to the 289 Cobras for the 1965 season. Shelby was lukewarm on the idea. He liked the idea of preparing an "ace in the hole" car in case the mid-engined high tech GT40s failed to win at Le Mans (and they had flopped big time in '64, not winning a single race), but didn't want to accord much budget for it. So what did he do? He did a Shelby—he horse-traded. He went to a British coachbuilder, Radford, who was actually an upholstery shop with the account to upholster the GT40s; and they lowballed an offer and got the job. They might have even done it for free, for fear of losing the GT40 upholstery contract.

A special competition chassis, CSB3054 (Carroll Shelby Britain were what the initials stood for, and only on right hand drive cars), was built by AC Cars Ltd and the chassis sent over to Radford. They dragged their heels on completing it so at one point Phil Remington, Shelby's ace development engineer, dropped in on them and came back with a negative report on how it was going. Brock ragged on Shelby so much that Shelby arranged to ship the uncompleted car back to Shelby-American for completion.

Brock's hopes were buoyed, but meanwhile Ford had seen how fast the GT40 could be with the same 427 big block engine (the car that became the Mk.II). Ford had absolutely no interest in backing or developing a big block front engine car, and Shelby, maybe with too many balls in the air at once, had dropped the ball on making the necessary hundred big block 427 Cobras needed to meet the FIA's requirement for homologation. So as a result of his goof, the '65 big block Cobra roadsters could only be run in FIA races as prototypes, which was hopeless since they could usually only reach 180 mph where the Ford GT40 and Ferrari prototypes were topping 200 mph.

Fortunately for the reputation of the Cobra, Shelby had ordered more small block 289 Daytona Coupes but the small block coupes escaped the "minimum 100" requirement because Shelby had sneakily classified them as "mere body variations" on the roadster, saying they were the same underneath (funny, he forgot to mention the added sub-frame). The chances that he could repeat that same miracle all over again with a big block

Cobra coupe body were slim, the FIA getting wise to the "variation of body" subterfuge.

Now back in Dearborn, in the "Glass House" (the nickname for Ford World HQ) they looked askance at any monies not being spent on the GT40 because you could have the fastest front engine Cobra in the world and it wasn't going to put a Ferrari prototype on the trailer. They discouraged Shelby from spending any more on the big block Type 65 Super Coupe which of course the wise guys in the shop, on seeing the car for the first time, were now calling it "Super Slug." Brock went away mad. He could have embraced the GT40 era at Ford, but he told your author in an interview that he came from a different era—the "by guess by gosh" era of fabricators. When Ford started the GT40 program they began to send engineers from Dearborn out to Shelby-American and Brock could see that he no longer had a significant role to fill. He went on to start his own firm, promoting Datsun racing cars and was very successful there.

The Type 65 Daytona Super Coupe was sold; thrown in with several other cars and uncompleted projects in a package deal when Shelby-American closed its doors. No doubt it was pennies on the dollar, but Shelby didn't mind. He was itching to go big game hunting in Africa (for more background, see the author's book *SHELBY: The Man, the Cars, the Legend*) and didn't have any place to store many tons of obsolete racing machinery.

There were several subsequent owners, some known to the car collecting community and some not. For instance, the first owner after Shelby may have been a Kansas collector, whose name has escaped this author. However, the first "known" collector was Craig Sutherland of Colorado who brought in Mike Dopudja of Englewood, Colorado, a skilled bodyman who could work aluminum, to complete it in 1980. While the car was being refined, many race drivers tried it out, including Dick Smith, Bob Bondurant, Brian Redman, and Bob Hindson.

The completed Super Coupe was unveiled at the Riverside vintage races in April of 1981. It was then vintage raced for a number of years with Dick Smith as the primary driver, Smith being the owner of a famous 427 roadster that was actually clocked at 199 mph at Daytona. The interesting thing is that Pete Brock was available to guide the restorers, even recommending some small updates, something that rarely happens when you are restoring a car, having the original designer around to guide you.

By the way, it never was taken to Le Mans so it never was able to prove Brock's contention that it could outrun a GT40. In terms of its original history, if completed in 1965, it would have been akin to being the fastest prop plane in WWII—a good claim to be able to make, but one that would have been a little too late in the game, as the fastest prop plane in WWII (said to be the Hawker Sea Fury) was overshadowed in 1945 when the Germans began to field jets (Messerschmitt Me-262).

The 427 Daytona Super Coupe was later purchased by George Stauffer, a Wisconsinite who further refined the car and put it on the track at vintage events. After Stauffer sold it, it once again went through a comprehensive restoration. Finally, in January 2007, at the Russo & Steele auction in Scottsdale, it sold for $1,320,000 while over in the other side of town at another auction Shelby's own twin Paxton-supercharged 427 Cobra fetched over $5 million and change. Why the big difference in price? Well, you can look at it two ways. The Daytona Super Coupe was sold by Shelby-American as an unfinished project, and it was, in truth, a car that never ever ran a race under the Shelby-American flag during the firm's original era (Shelby-American has since been reconstituted and is making cars today). The twin-Paxton 427 was never in a race either but was actually driven by Der Snakemeister on many an occasion and gained some notoriety (this car profiled in Incredible Barn Finds, the preceding book to this one). Hence its appeal is in its specialness, i.e. it was the boss' own creation for his own use.

Lessons to be learned here? That one of the best times to buy a one-off prototype is when the automaker themselves have given up on it or, worse yet, are hanging up their shingle as an automaker. It was obvious Shelby was going to get out of the car business in the late '60s—he had asked Ford permission to dissolve their partnership in 1969 after seeing the sad sales figures of the '69 Shelby (some were renumbered so they could sell the leftovers in 1970 as new models) so enthusiasts who went down to Shelby's facilities with cash in hand got bargains on the leftovers in racecars and unfinished projects.

A second lesson is: buying an unfinished car is always a bit of a "pig in a poke" (meaning you buy it sight unseen, or that you are buying without knowing much about it) so it took several owners, lots of shakedown development, and engine and chassis tuning before the car's basic merits were recognized. Even finely fettled, you have to realize that this car may never be a great driver, nor recognized as a significant contribution to engineering, not like the GT40 anyway. No, its significance is more the sheer notoriety of it being both a "Shelby project" and a "Brock Project" that makes it collectible, and those two pedigrees are responsible for getting it over the million dollar hump.

Plus it has the ace-in-the-hole of having a real 427 chassis. Hey, it could always be rebodied as a 427 Cobra roadster if the roadsters ever go much past $1 million!

Chapter 3
HEY, GOOD LOOKIN'
(1971 MASERATI BOOMERANG)

From the International Car Show Stage to a Nightclub in Spain...

Some concept cars are meant only to be concept cars, to strut their stuff on a rotating stage at a major auto show and then POOF, they disappear into some warehouse; or worse, are junked. Well, that was the plan for the Maserati Boomerang, one of Giorgetto Giugiaro's first designs after he left Ghia to start his own design house, Ital Design.

The Boomerang is perhaps the ultimate expression of Giugiaro's "wedge" period when a lot of the cars he designed looked, from the side view, like wedge-shaped wooden doorstops. It is much flatter planed than the production Bora which he did at the same time, a car which still has sensuous curves. Aside from the extreme wedge-shaped body, it had a new steering wheel concept in which all the instruments were contained inside the wheel's circumference: speedometer, tach and gauges. Of course this wouldn't last long in real production, as air bags were coming along and they commanded the center of the steering wheel. Another thing that made it unique was the windscreen rake. Giugiaro raked it over at a 13-degree angle but in mass production that wouldn't have made it. Even on the similarly shaped Lotus Esprit that Giugiaro did for Lotus head Colin Chapman, the windscreen was raked at a more reasonable 24.5 degrees to meet the laws of the time.

The Boomerang was first displayed as a non-functional push-mobile at the Turin Motor Show in 1971. By the Geneva Salon in March 1972, it had been transformed into a fully operational vehicle complete with chassis number (identified as No. 081). All the running gear was lifted basically from the production Bora, also designed by Giugiaro. The Boomerang's V8 engine was like the Bora, 4.7 liters, and it was rated at 310 hp, good for an indicated top speed of 300 km/h. It had a rather long life for a show car, lasting until 1974, having been shown at the Paris, London and Barcelona motor shows.

Ital Design was a young coachbuilder and design house back then, so perhaps that is why the Boomerang was sold. It was apparently Ital Design's four-wheeled calling card, meant to promote Giugiaro's availability to any automaker. And it did well in that function. It achieved its purpose after Volkswagen, impressed by its originality, retained Ital Design to do the VW Golf (decades later Volkswagen would buy Ital Design and bring the Giugiaros, father and son, in house).

NIGHT CLUBBIN'

After the Barcelona show, the Boomerang remained in Spain in the hands of a cabaret owner in Benidorm who no doubt wanted to park it outside his establishment to draw crowds. He did drive it on the road, however, and it was while he was on the road that it was seen by a German tourist who subsequently bought it around 1980.

The German tourist was not your ordinary tourist. First of all, he knew Maseratis and wasn't scared of their complexity. Secondly, though he was on vacation, he was ready to buy, if the car was available. But first he had to catch up with it! He was in a rental car and couldn't hope to catch it, though he gave chase. But Lady Luck smiled at him and following the road where it disappeared to, he saw it parked at a grocery store. He staked out the car until a young man appeared and went up to the car with the key. It turned out he worked for the nightclub owner and, yes, the car was for sale and he even added the fact that the nightclub owner needed money.

Negotiations went on for several months but eventually they reached a mutually beneficial deal and the car was flat-bedded back to Germany. The new owner restored it and was able to enjoy that extremely rare and pleasurable moment that comes to few barn finders of having the original designer of his car judge it at its first concours, in this case the 1990 Bagatelle Concours in Paris. Giugiaro also graciously hand-signed the rear panel for him. The car was later sold and taken to Paul Grist's Traction Seabert Company. It was there that, over the next 18 months, it was refurbished. Every mechanical and electronic part was replaced. Those who aren't familiar with stringent TUV regulations for registering a car in Germany should know if a car passes TUV, it's a reliable car mechanically.

The Boomerang has gone across the auction block at least twice since then as far as this author can determine. The first time was in 2002, when Christies sold it for 721,750 Euros and the second time in 2005, when at the Retromobile event in Paris. It sold for 781,250 Euros, which is just over one-million U.S. dollars today. Marc Sonnery, author of the book entitled *Maserati, the Citroen Years* says, "The current owner bought a prototype that is more fettled (ready to drive) than most other concept cars; in fact he drove it from the south of France to Villa d'Este in Italy 2006."

The Villa is the site of a well known concours d'elegance, one on the level of Pebble Beach as far as quality.

That German buyer, and the Spanish one before him, were both fortunate in being able to buy an early Giugiaro design marking the point where the young designer had broken free of just being a designer on the boards at a long established design house so he could have a design house of his own. By the way, Giugaro told Maserati historian and author Marc Sonnery, that there was never any intention of the Boomerang being the basis for a production model. It was just a way for him to push boundaries.

Lesson learned? Yes, once again I'm here to tell you that concept cars, despite everything you ever heard about them not being able to be sold, are in fact sold on occasion. The Boomerang got to the road where we can see it at various concours (and what a blast it would be to take it on a tour like the Colorado Grand!) today. Too bad Maserati didn't go for it.

Chapter 4
THE WORKING MAN'S LAMBO
(1975 LAMBORGHINI URRACO P250)

Yes, it's an 8-cylinder Lambo marketed well before the Lamborghini-Audi connection.

Let's say you are a connoisseur of exotic cars. You know your Daytonas from your Dinos and your Miuras from your Countaches. That's the way Dr. Gene Ondrusek, a psychologist in the north San Diego area is. He knows his cars. Even when he is away on business, he can't help but look through the local classifieds. So it was that he, a few years ago, came across an ad in the classified section of a Dallas newspaper offering a Lamborghini P250 for sale.

First some background about the model is in order…Almost from the day he opened the doors of his plant in 1963, Ferruccio Lamborghini spoke of a smaller, cheaper, higher-volume car to bolster his factory's financial security; though in the meantime kept building super exotics, with V12 power for the high end of the market. It wasn't until seven years after he opened his doors that he finally got his "people's car" prototype, the P250 Urraco, unveiled in 1970 at the Turin auto show to compete with the likes of the Porsche 911 and Ferrari Dino.

Named in Spanish slang for "little bull," the Urraco packed four seats and a mid-mounted, transverse 220-hp, 2.5-liter V8 all packed into a compact wedge whose most distinctive feature was the louvered rear window.

Bertone's Marcello Gandini, who also designed the Lamborghini Miura and Countach, drew the shape. The car boasted a four-corner strut suspension, and all-steel body. Lamborghini confidently predicted sales of 1,000 cars per year.

The company didn't predict labor strikes, management changes (Lamborghini sold half his stake in the company in 1972, the rest in 1974), and mechanical problems, including cataclysmic failures of the V8 engine's timing belts. This all delayed the Urraco's launch to 1973, just in time for the first oil crisis and a global recession. From January to April 1974, the company sold just 19 cars. Federal emissions regulations kept the later 250-hp, 3.0-liter DOHC (now with chain drive) engine upgrade from landing in America, the Urraco's prime target market. It was hardly a Lamborghini as far as power, burdened with smog equipment and able to crank out just 175 hp. The stateside price in 1975 was $22,500, more than twice the cost of the faster Porsche 911. Worse, the Urraco was a dog; needing 10.1 seconds to reach 60 mph and 17.9 seconds for a quarter-mile, slower than today's Saturn Ion. Weeds grew at dealers.

In all, Lamborghini built just 776 Urracos before it was redesigned into the two-seat Lamborghini Silhouette in 1976 (52 built), which morphed into the Lamborghini Jalpa in 1982 (about 300 built).

THE FINDING

The red 1975 example shown here belongs to Gene Ondrusek of San Diego, California. He rescued what was a worn-out beater in 1983 and spent three years restoring it to near-original condition. Dr. Ondrusek thought when he read the ad, "this car could be in bad shape" because Dallas, Texas, is not known as a great exotic car heaven; it's more a "run what you bring" town populated by muscle cars and pickup trucks. He went to look at it anyways. It was indeed in sorry shape. The engine was barely running, the car had been upholstered wrong, and the paint was wrong. It was a beater. Now if you were looking at say, a 1965 Chevy you might think "Why bother," but this was a Lamborghini, and a rare model at that (less P250s were produced than Miuras, for instance).

So he wrote out a check somewhere under $30,000. He tried

to drive it a little after buying it but then discovered the problem with the timing belt as he blew the engine. He had it shipped back to California and that began a three-year ordeal refurbishing the car. "It wasn't easy," he says. "I had to order parts from Italy and even have some fabricated from scratch because they were no longer available." One of the toughest parts was getting the "mouse fur" dash material. Today the car is thriving, and Dr. Ondrusek takes it to many events, as far up North as Los Angeles.

With a small, deep-dish steering wheel at the end of your reach and the minuscule V8 buzz-sawing behind your back, the Urraco feels like a Baja bug. Your legs slant to the right in order for the driver's feet to reach the miniscule pedal box. The rectangular dash is low, the most important gauges pushed out to the edges. But Ondrusek's Urraco puts on a good show pulling like a pit bull on a leash and making menacing sounds in the meantime. He attributes that to fine tuning of the four Weber IDF 40 carbs. But it's not going to set any cornering speed records with its narrow tires and softly sprung chassis.

"I was chastised by those who knew Lamborghinis that it was going to be a big expense for a car of unknown value," he says, "but since I did much of the work myself, I like to think I saved money." Now he has one of the few Urracos around, most of the restoration on Lambos being done on Miuras.

Lesson to be learned here? You can make out on an exotic car by picking a model to buy that is not at the top of their model lineup in desirability. Lesson No. 2? Trying to buy one in San Diego or nearby Orange County would have put him up against competition who knew the brand but in Dallas, there were fewer buyers, giving him more bargaining power.

Chapter 5
THE CAR IN THE CAVE
(1953 FERRARI 375PLUS)
Well, maybe not a cave, but damn well hidden.

Okay, let's say you are a Ferrari guy in SoCal. You want an old Ferrari; maybe a racing Ferrari. And then you hear there's this guy from Northern California who periodically comes to down to Los Angeles and schleps around, shopping this old racing Ferrari his dad left him.

But the amounts he is offered never seem to be enough, so the guy goes back to the woods, wherever he is from, in East Podunk.

The car is an oddball with not only a driver fairing (sort of an elongated hump going from the drivers head down to the rear deck of the car) but a big ol' tailfin coming out of that, Jaguar D-type style. But, on the plus side, it was driven by some famous racers, like Carroll ("Mr. Cobra") Shelby, before he ever thought of the Cobra. Rumors abound about why no one has seen it—dark rumors that the car is a.) buried in a gold mine or b.) hidden in a cave, which is booby-trapped.

But finally in 1995, it breaks the light of day and is sold at a huge price, over a million dollars.

That's the story in a nutshell of 0286AM, a 1953 Ferrari Spyder that started out as a 340 MM with Spyder coachwork by Vignale. It was built to be a factory racecar. Soon after it was built, the engine was enlarged to 375 Plus specs. It was entered in the GP Senigallia, piloted by Luigi Villoresi, but failed to finish.

It made up for it 21 days later when it won the 1000km Nurburgring race with Alberto Ascari and Giuseppe Farina driving.

It then went to Franco Cornacchia of Milan and then the same year to Luigi Chinetti. Chinetti was not only a dealer but Ferrari's North American distributor, plus a race driver. He entered the car in 1953 in the 1000-mile long road race through Mexico called the Carrera Panamericana, where it was piloted by himself and the infamous playboy, Count Alfonso de Portago. They didn't finish. It was then sold to a Mexican named Carlos Braniff and raced in the U.S. to a second place overall at Bergstrom AFB. The races were sponsored by Gen. Curtis LeMay, head of the Strategic Air Command who was also a sports car racer, driving a Cad-Allard (all the while puffing on a cigar—probably against safety regulations but when you are the same General who commanded all the Allied Air Forces in WWII, you make the rules).

In 1954 a Texas-based racing sponsor named Allen Guiberson bought the Vignale Spyder and treated it to a total rebuild. According to Ferrari historian Mark Savory he sent it to his Carson City, California, workshop where Lugie Lesovsky, a legend in Indy car building, and another mechanic prepared it for the fifth running of the Carrera Panamerican Road Race. The car was taken down to the frame and rebuilt, extending the tail for two spare tires, while the front spindles and brakes were replaced. The engine got new "hot rod" camshafts, valves, springs, and new bearings throughout the engine.

Guiberson got the best up-and-coming drivers including future F1 World Champion Phil Hill who, as his driver, finished 2nd overall in a race at March AFB in Riverside and 14 days later finished the same in the harrowing Carrera Panamericana race with his high school buddy Richie Ginther serving as co-driver.

In 1955 Guiberson hired failed chicken farmer but up-and-coming race driver Carroll Shelby out of Texas, and Shelby added several podium finishes to the car's resume including the Fort Pierce, Florida, race where he finished second. Shelby was a bit battered though, having flipped an Austin Healey end over end several times in the Carrera Panamericana. Guiberson had a great talent for spotting drivers, also employing Ken Miles to drive the car in the Seattle Seafair NSCR where Ken took third overall. Ken of course went on to work for Shelby-American and helped develop the Cobra into a winning car.

Then Guiberson offered the finned Ferrari for sale in August 1955 for $6,000, which could've bought a small one bedroom house at the time.

On the website marksavory.com, Mark says that Lou Brero Sr., who has been described as either a trucking firm owner or a lumber company owner from Arcata, California, bought it for $3,500 including many spares. Brero, with his son, Lou Jr., raced some great cars and was prominent in West Coast racing in the mid-1950s.

He's best known for the fabulous Ferrari 375MM (SN #0286AM) but also raced a Jaguar D-Type XKD 509. Together the Breros, father and son, raced their iconic Kurtis 500S-Cadillac and the son is also listed on some records as racing an MG, a Kurtis-Kraft and a Maserati.

Brero Sr.'s high point in the Ferrari was when he took it to Nassau in the Bahamas and participated in several events, his highest finish being a third overall in the Ferrari race. That was his swan song in the car.

On April 22, 1957, the senior Brero died in a racing accident at Dillingham Field, Mokuleia, Oahu, Hawaii. *Road & Track* briefly mentioned it:

"The untimely death of Lou Brero, Sr., cast a gloom over the scene. Lou's D-Jaguar had blown up earlier and on Saturday he was practicing in a borrowed Chevrolet-powered Maserati. Booming along at 130 mph, the car suddenly caught fire. The driver slowed to about 40 mph and leaped out, tearing off his burning clothing. He died that evening. Later reports from qualified observers indicate that a broken U-joint had split the gas tank and flooded the cockpit."

His son went back to California, stored the Ferrari in a tractor trailer, while the engine and transmission were stored someplace else. The Ferrari engine's heads were said to have cracked from overheating and were never repaired. There was a start on replacing the engine in the Ferrari with a Jaguar engine but that conversion was never completed.

THE BIG SLEEP

The car entered the period I like to call "The Big Sleep." In this case it snoozed for nearly 40 years. There were no gold mines, caves or booby traps, but suffice to say that it was not something you could see easily if you drove by the house in Arcata, a small quaintly Victorian-style town in Northern California. There was a forest behind the house and in those forests tractor trailers.

Finally, after decades of shopping the car around, Brero's son met a salesman from San Diego, who came up with the magic number and the car was sold. I'd identify the dealership but the salesman who found it proved un-co-operative when contacted. Too bad. He cinched the deal on a barn find that remains legendary in Ferrari circles, maybe in the same league as the buy of the Ferrari 250GTO that was parked in an Ohio field for nearly a decade.

After the San Diego salesman found it, the new buyer sent it to Pete Lovely's racing shop in Redmond, Washington, where it was rebuilt and driven down the road under its own power for the first time in roughly four decades. In a really touching gesture its new owner graciously invited a former pilot of the car, Phil Hill, to take the wheel at the Monterey Historic races in 1997. Hill cinched himself in, and raced it, taking first, and even lapping the whole field.

It is now owned by one of the most well-monied teams in vintage racing, whose equipment includes dozens of racing Ferraris, some of equally legendary status.

Lesson to be learned? That car was out there for decades, never really "lost." To the contrary, all the Ferrari insiders knew exactly who owned it and even what city it was in, but until the salesman from San Diego cracked the impasse, nobody could come to terms with the younger Mr. Brero. But don't let this discourage you—first lesson: the car was exactly where it was parked for nearly 40 years—so, if there's a car you want, and all you have is old, old information on the address, go to that location and check if the object of your affection is still there. In the case of the Brero Sr. car, it was.

Second, find out what it will take for the owners of the car to release it? A new car? A suitcase full of cash? A bathtub full of diamonds? A condo in Monte Carlo? Something swung the deal but, until that salesman decides to talk to yours truly, we'll never know exactly what that was. One Ferrari collector in Los Angeles—who has had 100 Ferraris pass through his hands—and who had tried to buy it several times but was always "priced out" (the price kept rising every time the car was for sale) said the reward in this case "went to the most tenacious." But the point is that some cars—even factory racing Ferraris driven by America's greatest drivers—are still exactly where they were parked decades ago. It's up to you to come up with an offer that turns "no" to "yes."

Chapter 6
THE CHANGELING
(1952/'57 MERCEDES 300SLS ROADSTER)
And what, you ask, is an SLS?

Not all barn finds are of intact cars. Sometimes you have to buy the car with a chassis here, a body there and all the parts in boxes.

It can be risky. The sellers always say all the parts are there, but after you buy, some tiny items may be missing—items you'll have to have fabricated at great cost.

That's the story of this car, which turned out to be a '52 Mercedes 300SL coupe (yeah, I know they didn't make the gullwing until '54 but keep reading…it's all explained).

First a little history on Mercedes after WWII ended…You have to know that Mercedes, when their factory was bombed out, was itching to show that once again they could be a power in both luxury cars and in sports cars. They got the luxury cars going first, the 300 series, and in the early Fifties began building racing prototypes.

Rudolph Uhlenhaut, Mercedes' head of racing, saw Jaguar C-types win Le Mans in '51 and figured that Mercedes had the technical ability to beat the Jaguars. He went back to Stuttgart and developed some racecars built around the 300 engine, an inline overhead-cam six, developed for the luxury car, the 300S. One of the first racing prototypes was a series of 300SL ("SL" for super-light) roadsters and coupes, the coupes with distinctive gull wing doors cut into the roof.

Originally it was the gullwing coupe that went into production in 1954 as a 1955 model. They were continued to 1957 when the roadster was introduced. This is the story of a 300SL that started out as a racing roadster, became a coupe and then became a roadster again. Weird but true. It started out as chassis 00009/52, one of eight 300SL prototypes raced by Mercedes-Benz in 1952. Those had different styling than the production '54 gull-wings, more akin to a Porsche 356.

Mercedes began to race the 300SL prototypes in '52 with Karl Kling, driving the 00004/52 prototype coupe, finishing second to Giovanni Bracco's Ferrari in Mille Miglia in Italy. Then they did even better with a 1-2-3 sweep at Berne and a stunning 1-2 at Le Mans in June.

It is a monumental challenge to throw a car into its first race when the race is the 24 Hours of Le Mans but 00009/52's first race was indeed the 24 Hours of Le Mans, where Theo Helfrich and Norbert Niedermayer finished second overall to Hermann Lang and Fritz Reiss in a similar coupe. After the race, four coupes were rebodied into lighter roadsters for the August Nurburgring race, where it finished 3rd behind two other factory 300SLs. Then Mercedes began its assault on the Carrera Panamericana in Mexico, a huge race of thousands of miles across Mexico. With American John Fitch driving, and taking a riding mechanic along, it was disqualified due to a technical infraction. Mercedes was still happy as two other roadsters finished 1-2.

This was a really remarkable record—the 300SLs finishing first or second in every race they entered and yet the car had only been thought of 11 months before! With all this racing having honed the car, now it was time for production; plus the racing department was busy developing an all-new Grand Prix racecar for 1954.

NEW BODY, NEW LIFE

But then Mercedes decided to mass-produce the 300SL roadster. This is while the gullwings were already being made in '54. So the old mule chassis 00009/52 was then pressed into service by being fitted with a close approximation of what would be the production roadster body that wouldn't be sold to the public until '57.

It became world-famous when a famous *Colliers* magazine photographer, David Douglas Duncan, went along with a group of Mercedes test drivers in three identical 300SL prototype roadsters, called "SLS," from Germany over the alpine passes to Italy. He photographed the whole trip and the pictures appeared in the October 12th, 1956 issue of *Colliers* magazine. They really made the new cars look exciting as the drivers were wearing old-time cloth helmets and goggles like prewar Mercedes drivers.

Then the car was used again when Mercedes wanted to back a 300SL roadster in American sports car racing. So this *Colliers* magazine car was used to test parts being developed for what would become the car available to racers in America. Now let's be clear here. This chassis of 00009/52 was not the racecar that was sent to America—those cars would have new chassis using the single-point swing-axle chassis. No. 00009/52 was the team's "mule" test car, the one they tried out different parts on, such as windscreens, wheels, tires, etc. It was heavier than the actual racecars and had the old-fashioned (and some say dangerous) gullwing-type swing-axle. It was not raced, being only the unglamorous "mule."

Finally, its usefulness to the factory at an end, Mercedes sold the car with the body it had on it when it was an SLS.

AMERICAN ADVENTURE

The car then had a number of owners, including the first one after the factory, Karl Jurgen Britsche of Hamburg, Germany, and then Arthur von Windheim, also of Hamburg. Then the car came to America in 1980 when Lloyd Ikerd purchased it.

Seven years later it was sold to the man who would restore it— Scott Grundfor of central California. Grundfor, specializing in Mercedes Benz, knew Ikerd. He came across the car at Ikerd's shop and decided to buy it because it was labeled a "prototype." He knew it had an early serial number but, at the time, didn't realize its significance as the first prototype 300SL roadster. Many of its parts, as he unboxed them, were identified as special parts different from production 300SL roadsters, such as the magnesium intake manifold, the magnesium oil pan, and a drilled-out, lightweight suspension. It also had early-style Dunlop front disc brakes. Even the headlights were special—one-piece glass head-lamps used to guide the design of the production car.

Many of the interior parts showed that the final design for the production 300SL roadster hadn't been settled on yet, such as having a dished, wood-rimmed steering wheel and indirect interior lighting. The seats were a cross between the coupe's and the Roadster's. Ironically the car came with no side glass. They had been on the car in the Colliers article but disappeared, and weren't replaced. Those who have a fine eye for design realize, while comparing it to a production car, that it has a lot of subtle differences in shape. Inside is a tipoff that this was an early car, as the shift lever is tucked under the dash, being adapted from a 300 sedan. The car has had bumpers for some factory photographs but as a racecar had them removed. The exhausts were racecar-like—two short, un-muffled pipes poking out from the right front rocker panel. Grundfor showed the car at Pebble Beach where its discovery was lauded by 300SL enthusiasts and eventually sold on the car to an owner who continues to show it.

Lesson learned? When you hear of an "early" car of a given model series, even if it is all still in boxes, don't turn down the chance to see it, and be ready to buy. In this case the car turned out to be a famous car in its *Colliers* magazine form, and Grundfor chose to honor that era in the car's life. But theoretically, if you wanted to spend $100,000-$200,000 making an alloy body, it could also be rebodied to be a 1952 Mercedes racecar and be correct in that body too. It pays to be an expert in one model of car and therefore you can be prepared to evaluate the worth of such a barn find, but the general advice here is to be open to unfinished project cars. In this case the car in pieces turned out to be a car with rich history—actually three histories, all in one car.

Chapter 7
THE ITALIAN MUSTANG
(1965 MUSTANG 2-PLUS-2)
Still missing in action?

Ford, back in '64, had an undeniable hit in the Mustang. Right out of the ballpark. There were 22,000 sold the first day.

And yet, in the back of their minds, Ford brass knew hey, you're only as good as your last quarterly sales figure, so they quickly scheduled a 2-plus-2 model for '65.

And lined up Cobra snakemeister Carroll Shelby to build a Shelby version.

And they were even open to oddball promotions, such as the one proposed by publisher L. Scott Bailey, who in 1962 founded a hardbound magazine called *Automobile Quarterly*. The magazine had high printing standards and employed many of the best authors and photographers.

Most of the time Bailey published history but for once he actually made history by commissioning his own Mustang to be built in Italy, a one-off car.

One of the saddest things this author has seen was an ad placed by L. Scott Bailey looking for the lost Bertone Mustang, a car he and Ford had jointly spawned. It was like a father desperately asking if by chance anyone has seen his kidnapped child (now aged in the photographs to compensate for growing up).

Bailey saw that Ford was very bullish on promoting the Mustang, and he knew certain Ford brass (mainly Henry Ford II) loved anything Italian (with prototypes have names like La Aventurra, the Italien and so forth) so he proposed going to Carrozzeria Bertone and having an all-new body designed for one as a promotional vehicle. Ford was all for it, and donated the chassis which was sent to Bertone for an all-new design by Giorgetto Giugiaro, the wunderkind designer who had been hired at Bertone a few years earlier at the age of 19.

The Bertone Mustang made its debut at the 1965 New York Auto Show, where it was hailed as a brilliant design, winning a "best in show" award. The car was an original shape, much more together and integrated than Ford's design. It had retractable headlights and those little side vent grilles Giugiaro liked and used on many of the cars he designed. Since the hoodline was lower than the stock Ford Mustang, he had to design bumps or bulges into it to clear the shock absorber connection points and for the air filter. The whole front of the car was also lower than the stock Mustang.

The odd little side windows could be opened electrically. The roof was still very light-looking, adopted almost whole by the Mazda RX4, a car that might have been secretly designed by Carrozzeria Bertone though, at the time, Italian coachbuilders were saying they would never help the Japanese auto industry for fear it would drive the Italian-building working class out of business. The nay-sayers were right, the Japanese cars drove the lower-priced Italian cars like Fiat from the U.S. but it wasn't the styling that did it, it was the reliability that sold Toyotas and Datsuns in the U.S. and drove the shoddily-built Fiats and Renaults out of the country.

In an AQ edition published just after the car was built, Bailey even ran a picture of himself with Bertone's hotshot "young designer-in-charge" Guigiaro, both standing next to the wood "former" for the car, the wood buck guiding the panel beaters who beat out each body panel by hand. This author doesn't recall when he saw the ad where Bailey was looking for the car, but rumors abound where the car went to after its show career.

MISSING—PRESUMED LOST

One story is that it was in a Ford showroom in Monte Carlo and it disappeared from there. Another is that a journalist borrowed it, never to return (sounds improbable but I can tell you that, as a journalist traveling in Europe, Once I walked into a showroom in Italy, pointed at a mid-engined Lancia, said I was going to photograph it and drove off in it, no papers signed, no showing of a driver's license, not even leaving a card. I could have, I think, kept going…).

I saw the Bertone Mustang parked once at the Ford World HQ so I know they had it for a while. Other journalists have also seen the ads run by Bailey. A real puzzler is a display ad printed in the Sept. 1967 issue of *Road & Track*, offering the car for sale for a mere $10,000 (still about twice the price of a fully-loaded Mustang back then). The seller? None other than Bertone themselves.

That ad brings up new questions. It could be Bailey never owned it but Bertone did. Maybe the fact is that Bailey decided in his later years that he had made a mistake not buying it when he had the chance, and wanted it as a golden memory of his publishing career. He set out to find it (much as it resembles the plot of a 2013 film where a woman who gave up a child for adoption sets out to find that grown child 50 years later). Bailey died in 2012 while in his '80s, never to see his baby again.

The value of the car, in my opinion, has appreciated tremendously owing to the fact that Giugiaro, after founding his own firm, Ital Design, is arguably the world's most famous Italian car designer. The downside is the subsequent Mazda RX-2 had a nose very similar. That design too might have emerged from Bertone Carrozzeria. And even the Mazda RX-4 (nee Cosmo) had a similar roofline. The truth is coachbuilders sometimes recycle designs—Ford obviously wasn't going to pony up for a production version, so, hey, maybe Mazda would want that design and Mazda was writing checks to Bertone at that point.

One thing is sure: one-off coachbuilt cars by famous coachbuilders are soaring in value as sort of four-wheeled souvenirs of great designers. The Tom Tjaarda-designed Corvette Rondine done for Carrozzeria Bertone for instance. Or the Giugiaro design for the Alfa Canguro, a one-off car built on a genuine racecar TZ chassis. If you can tie the design into a famous coachbuilder and a famous designer, you've got a double whammy going. If its built on a factory racecar, you can add another few 100K to the assessed value.

POTENTIAL SUPERSTAR

Your author predicts that the Bertone Mustang, if found, could allow its owner to "write his own ticket" as far as entering a prestige event like Pebble Beach or the Amelia Island concours. Hell, Ford might even pay the owner to bring it to Ford events (unless of course there's too much of a chance it could outshine any new Mustang they have just introduced).

Now, I know, to most people who aren't car enthusiasts, what's the big deal that this car has disappeared? Hey, an old car, who cares? (Sacrilege to say that to enthusiasts...I know!) But I, as an enthusiast, I stay awake nights wondering if there's answers to such questions as: where is it now? When this author posted a query about it on a Mustang-oriented forum another forum poster cheekily replied it's been found but the owner doesn't want to talk about it. Well, la de da, when you own a legend, word has a way of getting out.

This writer is talking about it, feeling that the Bertone Mustang is far too much a part of the rich legacy of Mustang history to be hidden away forevermore. And that, in a sense, we enthusiasts—we who enjoyed *Automobile Quarterly* for all those decades—owe it to ol' L. Scott Bailey to find his baby...if you have it, please let your presence be known.

Chapter 8

THE THROWAWAY CORVETTE
(1963 CORVETTE STINGRAY COUPE)

Why you should say "yes" even if it's not your favorite marque.

There are times when you take a car just to do a buddy a favor. You really don't want the car. It's not your type of car. All your car buddies are tied up with another make. But damn it, your buddy needs you to take the car off his hands.

This is the story of a '63 Corvette Stingray that was going to be a throwaway car, unless the guy offered the car skedaddled over there and picked it up.

First, a little background on the car...It involves Mickey Thompson, an outsize figure in building racecars in the '50s and '60s. He was a tough scrapper of a competitor, willing to build a car for every form of racing from off road racing, to Indy, to sports car racing to Bonneville land speed attempts.

In late 1962, Chevrolet chose Thompson to head up one of their "cover" race teams (because GM was telling the public they weren't in racing as a sponsor) with the job of entering one of six of their new aerodynamic irs-equipped Corvette Stingrays at Riverside in October '62 with the sole purpose of humbling Shelby's new Cobra sports car. Though six of the Stingrays with the Z06 suspension and other racing equipment were built, this particular car never saw Riverside.

Instead, this car—30837S100787—and one other of the six were diverted to a NASCAR-sanctioned event on the famous Daytona Oval in Florida. The cars had to meet the NASCAR rules that applied to stock cars so further modifications were made. Though the production 1963 Stingray coupe did not have a big block option, this particular one got an experimental big block 427-cubic-inch Chevrolet engine, one that was not even out on the market yet. It was called the Mark I and was basically the 409 with two-piece intake and heads.

More particularly it was called the "Mark Is" Z11 engine, the small "s" meaning it was stroked from its 409-cubic-inch displacement. This was the same basic engine used in 51 Z-11 Chevrolet Impalas destined for NASCAR. An even later development of that was called the Mark II, a.k.a. "the Mystery Motor," and only a handful of those were made (most experts say nine).

Next was the Mark III which only existed on paper as a design. The engine that finally reached the showroom was the Mark IV 427 available as a Corvette option from 1966 thru 1969. In '65 the production big block Corvette was the 396-cubic-inch V8.

This Corvette, before its race at Daytona, was lightened in every way possible until it tipped the scales at just over 2,800 pounds, roughly 1,000 pounds less than a showroom stock Corvette. Extra fuel was carried in a specially fabricated tank occupying the area behind the driver.

Driven by Junior Johnson, this special car was the fastest qualifier at over 162 mph. On race day, though, substitute driver Billy Krause from California (hired away from the Shelby team much to Shelby's chagrin) drove through the rain to finish third behind Paul Goldsmith's Pontiac and A.J. Foyt in another standard 1963 Z06 Corvette 327 fuel-injected Corvette. (Ironically Foyt later drove a Mk. IV Ford GT for Shelby's team and, with Dan Gurney, won the 24 Hours of Le Mans in '67.) Special features of the Mickey Thompson NASCAR Corvette according to the registryofcorvetteracecars.com, include: special 427 engine, adjustable front sway bar, three-speed transmission, adjustable rear suspension, magnesium differential, flat aluminum floors, two shocks per wheel, special exhaust system, special axles, lightweight fiberglass seats, 4 wheel disc brakes, 50-gallon gas tank, engine oil cooler, plexiglas windows, differential oil cooler, full roll cage, fully welded frame, and aluminum instrument panel.

After Daytona, both of Mickey Thompson Corvettes came back to California where the big block engines were removed and the silver Corvette was sold to a Southern California road racer with a 327 engine installed. The car was once again reunited with Billy Krause in the Los Angeles Times Grand Prix in October, 1963. Other racers associated with it during its regional racing career in California were Doug Hooper and Andy Porterfield.

Around 1979, Tom McIntyre, a Burbank, California, manufacturer of car emblems and a well-known car collector and vintage racer, purchased the car, not too sure of its provenance, buying it more or less as a favor to his buddy who needed the space. The fact he bought it at all came as a surprise to many because Tom was known as a Ford guy through-and-through. He didn't think of Chevys. When you're racing Fords, Chevy owners are your enemies.

THE GREAT GARAGE CLEAN-UP

"But then a friend called me and told me he was cleaning out a garage down in Orange County and had a Corvette Stingray he wanted to get rid of and he thought of me. I remembered seeing it before, a rough looking car that had been through a lot of owners and a lot of races. I turned him down—I was a Ford guy and knew where to get Ford parts, etc. All my connections were in the Ford world. But he kept saying, "I'm going to clean out this warehouse," with the subtle implication that it could go to scrap if I didn't want it so I drove down there in my truck towing a trailer, loaded it up and took it home and parked it in back of my business for the next five years."

That could have been all she wrote. Meanwhile he kept racing his 427 Cobra in vintage racing. By the early '80s, though, there was a problem in that arena. "Steve Earle—the creator of the Monterey Historics—kept putting me in the class with prototypes and I couldn't win against them," recalls McIntyre. "So I thought, hey, I got this Corvette, I'll prepare that for racing in D-production."

When he was done preparing it, which involved a lengthy rebuild and installation of a blueprinted engine, McIntyre wrote a little blurb about the car's history for the event program and mentioned "Mickey Thompson" because he had heard the famous car builder had been involved with the car sometime in the past.

DISCOVERING THE PEDIGREE

"When I got to the races there was this little contingent waiting for me of Corvette people," McIntyre recalls. "They began asking detailed questions about the car's serial number and finally I gave them permission to unbolt part of the body and look and they found the number they were looking for under some other parts. With that information, they ascertained that my car was the third of the Z06 Corvettes that had been built to fight the Cobra and the only one of the long lost Z06s that had not been located."

Tom was eventually able to find a big block engine at Smokey Yunick's shop. Smokey Yunick was the famed engine tuner who used to have a shop in Daytona Beach (his slogan painted on the building was "The Best Damn Garage in Town") and was a favored mechanic of GM brass like Semon "Bunkie" Knudsen.

Tom recalls: "Smokey had been told, after the car raced at Daytona, to take the engine out and it was one of two special big blocks in his garage. I bought one."

Tom did not install that engine, though, as he prefers racing his Stingray in its present small-block form. He has raced it in vintage events since 1983. "That engine allowed me to be back in D-production racing against my Cobra buddies," he recalls.

Lesson learned? People collect things and people throw away things. Everyone's got their own priorities in life that lead to unanticipated changes in plan. When Tom McIntyre got that phone call, he was dubious. He was a blue oval Ford guy through and through. But a small part of his brain said "RACECAR, RACECAR" so he took it. But buying an old thrashed racecar can be akin to buying a pig in a poke. Some are purely amateur in construction and don't have much of a history but others, if you dig deep enough, may have a storied history. Tom lucked out—he did a pal a favor and got a legendary car in return. It was a good thing his previous 100-percent allegiance to Ford could be bent enough to allow him to consider owning a Chevrolet or the car would have never reached his collection....

Chapter 9

THE ULTIMATE WEDGE
(1965 BIZZARRINI MANTA)
You just never know what you'll find trapped in Customs.

When Giorgetto Giugiaro, arguably the most influential Italian car designer of the 20th Century, decided to leave Carrozzeria Bertone in 1968 and start his own design firm (Ital Design), he knew he had to make a very dramatic car to capture the attention of the media.

He succeeded, with his mid-engined Manta, based on the chassis of a retired racecar, a Bizzarrini P538 (that name is pronounced BITH-UH-REEN-E). The car was totally radical, almost too radical for the street, in that the windshield angle was only 15 degrees when most street cars have windscreens that are around 40 deg.

Also it was a three-seater, very unusual, and had the gauges clustered under the center-positioned steering wheel. The engine was a 327 Chevy V8 with four sidedraught Weber carbs, basically the same as the racing Bizzarrini engine.

Ing. Bizzarrini, a graduate of the University of Pisa, began his auto career working for Alfa Romeo. His talents were recognized early on and he was recruited by Ferrari, first to improve the short wheelbase

250GT from which he evolved a separate model, the 250GTO—a car that is arguably the *sine qua non* of postwar sports cars.

Bizzarrini was one in the group of Ferrari engineers that revolted against the tyrannical rule of Enzo in 1961, and left Ferrari to work with other firms including the fledgling rival to Ferrari, ATS, which soon failed. But he became a consultant to firms like Lamborghini (designing their first V12) and eventually tied in with Iso of Bresso, a firm making GT cars with Chevrolet V8 power.

Actually Ing. Bizzarrini and Giugiaro were old friends, as Giugiaro, while at Bertone, had designed the front engine Iso A3/C and A3/L and Iso Grifo production cars, as well as the four-seater Rivolta, all for Iso, and all engineered by Bizzarrini.

RACECAR ORIGINS

The Manta is rumored to have been created in a mere forty days (that time frame sounds so biblical!) in order to make it to the revolving stage at the 1969 Turin Auto Show.

The most popular story is that it was built atop a racecar that was no longer eligible for Le Mans because of rules changes. Though the Bizzarrini racecars have simple chassis numbers like 002 and 003, for some reason the Manta has its own number—6901. Some Iso historians say the show car is based on the racing Bizzarrini P538 that was numbered 003. If that's true, it's a car that for one brief shining moment (well, for over an hour anyhow) ran the 24 Hours of Le Mans when it was still a works racer. What put it out of the race was when it was jacked up in the pits, some idiot put the jack in the wrong place and broke a pipe carrying water and there was no replacement ready.

The Manta was a big success for Ital Design—it won Giugiaro attention worldwide when automakers saw that he had the capability on his own, free from his previous employers like Bertone or Ghia, to design a dramatic new car. Soon commissions from automakers poured in.

LOST IN CUSTOMS

But, then Giugiaro was so busy taking on new work that the Manta was left in the lurch. Exactly what happened isn't clear—the car may have been traveling to car shows hither and yon on the "carte" (card of paperwork) of the racecar it was based on. According to a story by Joel Siegfried on the website Examiner.com: "The

Manta was first exhibited at the 1968 Turin Motor Show. Through an unexplained shipping mishap, it was lost in transit after being exhibited in Tokyo and Los Angeles. It was finally rediscovered at a Port of Genoa Customs auction about 10 years later."

Giugiaro might have been relying on its identity as a P-538 racecar whereas what Customs saw before them was a completely different looking car, the Manta. Two cars, in their view, couldn't use the same chassis number, which to them would be like two people traveling on the same passport. At any rate the car was confiscated and Customs charges began accruing from Day One. (God knows how many cars they've confiscated; as racers are notorious for switching number plates to avoid duties as they transport racecars across borders.)

THE RESCUE

A man named Giovanni Giordanengo of Cuneo, Italy, found it in 1978 or 1979 and bought it—a risky venture buying a non-running prototype car, because you never know what it's going to take to get it running. He took it for restoration to SD Carrozzeria, a firm run by Sergio Diomante, who used to work with Bizzarrini on many projects, and then sold it around October 1982 to Ulf Larsson of Switzerland. Larsson then spent all the money necessary to make it a running driving car.

One shouldn't assume that, just because a show car has an engine in it, that the engine is actually connected to anything. Is there a fuel system, an electrical system, a braking system? Buy a car like this and you might end up finishing the engineering that was never done originally because the car's original task was just to be a pushmobile—in this case to boost Ital Design's availability as a new design firm.

Giugiaro must have liked what Larsson wrought. It was during Larsson's ownership that Giugiaro reached out and borrowed it back for a 20th Anniversary party at Ital Design, even repainting the car silver for the show.

According to historian Daniel Vaughn, a few years later, Texas collector Alfredo Brener purchased the car and had it brought back to its original 1968 Turin Motor Show configuration. In March of 2005, near the completion of the restoration, Mr. Brener sold the car to its current caretaker. It finally reached Ron Spindler, a Californian who already owned two front-engined Bizzarrinis (one found by your author as a barn-find!). He brought the car to Rod Drew for restoration and the restored car appeared at many concours, taking first in class at Pebble Beach in 2005 and has since taken awards at Amelia Island, Concorso Italiano and the Villa d'Este. At the last named the car was again reunited with its original designer, Giorgetto Giugiaro, something rare in the classic car world, where a designer can see his old treasure restored! The car went to the Gooding auction in Monterey in 2012 but did not reach the seller's reserve even after a bid of $850,000. The Examiner.com reporter seemed to think the seller had expected it to reach Gooding's pre-sale estimate of $1,000,000-plus.

Lesson learned? First of all, as much as we like to think that a car designer will always keep his first "baby" very much in mind, once the Manta achieved its goal of bringing in customers to his door, Giugiaro moved it far down in priority on his "to-do" list and that explains why it got lost in the lurch.

So, barn-finders, one of the first places to look for a one-off prototype is at the door of the designer who designed it. They may have, as Giugiaro apparently did in this case, plumb lost track of it!

Secondly kudos to the barn-finder who found it in storage at Genoa Customs. Italy is where most truly exotic cars are designed and made, so it makes sense that, at Customs warehouses there, there may be dozens of exotic cars sitting on four flat tires until someone somewhere bellys up to the bar and pays the accrued import duty or proves why a duty should not be paid. (It would seem that a valid argument is that the car originated in Italy so why in blue blazes should a car of Italian origin be charged duty coming into Italy as if it was an import?)

Third lesson: there are hidden costs to making a "pushmobile" into a running driving car. In this case, that cost didn't end with the Swedish man who made it drivable, as subsequent owners spent additional hundreds of thousands to make it more drivable and you can still say it's not as drivable as a production Bizzarrini GT5300 (for instance the windows do not retract—that refinement, of course, would have come in a production version, which never happened).

But just the same, kudos to the fans of Giugiaro design who rescued the car from Customs, and this author hopes the car finds another owner who will cherish the car as a great example of "early" Ital Design.

Chapter 10
THE ITALIAN CORVETTE
(1959 CORVETTE)

*Take three Texans and an Italian bodybuilder
and the inevitable happens.*

In the beginning (don't all great stories start out that way?) there were some Texans who liked Ferraris; but even in the late 1950s, Ferrari parts cost a lot of money. That is why practical folk, those with true grit like Texans Jim Hall, Dick Hall, and Carroll Shelby would sometimes put a Chevy V8 into a Ferrari when they broke a Ferrari engine. One Ferrari crank cost more than a whole Chevy engine. In fact one Ferrari crank often cost more than a whole Chevy!

Now it so happened, back in the Fifties, Shelby—who became America's most famous sports car driver when he won Le Mans in '59—was in the car business with Dick Hall, brother of Jim Hall, the racer. The Hall brothers had parents who were in oil and who had died in a plane crash, and they had inherited a fortune. But rather than be wastrels, they worked, and worked hard! Dick started a car dealership and Jim got a degree from Cal Tech in Engineering (with a little racecar drivin' schooling as well, his teacher being Carroll Hall Shelby) and also worked in oil well engineering.

The dealership was called "Carroll Shelby Sports Cars" in Dallas, and they knew a Chevy dealer/oilman named Gary Laughlin. So they got to talking one day about how Ferrari parts prices were a rip-off and decided to call up Ed Cole, head engineer at Chevrolet and ask for three Corvette chassis right off the assembly line. They sent them to Sergio Scaglietti (pronounced SCAL-YETTI) over in Italy who had started off as a private repair shop fixing smashed Ferraris in the early '50s and segued into building most of the Ferrari racecars in the late '50s to early '60s.

Ol' Sergio got to pounding on the aluminum sheets (using sandbags or tree stumps as a form) and making bodies for them that looked at a distance not unlike his Ferrari long wheelbase 250GTs. Plus they were lighter than production Corvettes—400 pounds lighter! Now the chassis they sent him were not race prepped. Two of them had carbs and only one, chassis no. J59S102405, had the new trick of the week, fuel injection; but these three were just the trial balloons. This writer has not seen pictures of them when new but at least one had a Corvette big chrome tooth grille (which may have been added in America). The others have had various grilles, usually the Ferrari-style eggcrate. At some point, one or more of them had roof vents added and side vents to better copy Ferrari's Tour de France berlinetta coupe.

Inside they had a sort of Italian interior—a black wrinkle-finish dash and leather bucket seats, but the gauges were good ol' Stewart-Warner and the shift knob on the Borg-Warner T-10, a big old white billiard ball type. Fighting against these American influences was the Italian stuff like Nardi wood steering wheel, twin Ansa exhausts and Borrani cross-laced wire wheels. The badging was a bit confusing too. There was Scaglietti's vertical metal logo badge and then on the nose Corvette's crossed flags.

Working as the man inbetween, or go-between, on this deal was an American living in Modena, Pete Coltrin, who also contributed to *Road & Track*. One thing the cars were was roomy, all three gentlemen in the venture being well over six feet, and the Corvette having a long 102-inch wheelbase.

How come you never heard of them? Well, the whole project died a-bornin' as they say. First of all Ed Cole had siphoned off these three complete chassis without permission of the High Brass at GM. When they found out they told him to forget it, that this lightweight from abroad could undermine the Corvette.

It's possible, too, that Zora Arkus Duntov, the so-called "father of the Corvette" (though he was hired at GM after the Corvette was already in production) might have seen this effort as an end run around his kingdom where he was in charge of all development on the Corvette. He started to exert effort to stop the project. So Cole called Shelby and said, "Forget you ever saw those chassis." Another thing that killed it off was the long wait for the cars to arrive. The first one arrived a full 18 months after the first chassis was sent. That made it a 1-1/2 year old car from the get-go, pushing it into "used car territory" when it was still new.

Jim Hall was the lucky one, he fobbed his off for a reported $3,500, hardly more than you could get for a regular Corvette. If there was a "barn find" moment in the car's existence, this was it, though whoever bought it was taking a chance as Hall was not so famous yet, and only Ferrari fans were aware of the name "Scaglietti."

Shelby was about to become more famous than he already was (his original fame came from winning the 24 Hours of Le Mans in 1959) but he was not yet known as a car builder, the Cobra still in his future.

The Scaglietti Corvettes were not completely unknown. The Scaglietti-Corvette had been on the cover of *Car Life* (which belonged to R&T at the time) in June 1961 and even in R&T a few months earlier. Both articles hyped the ease of repair of aluminum bodies, estimated the costs of running them as half that of a Ferrari with similar performance, and mentioned that the 1956/'57-style Corvette grille had been Laughlin's requirement. Good promo but wrong timing. The project disappeared and the cars kicked around the American car collecting community for decades.

THE REDISCOVERY

Enter, in the late '80s, our hero, one Chuck Brahms. Brahms, who restored Mercedes 300S/SCs, was plunged by his ownership of two of the Scaglietti Corvettes into the world of not-very-exact history such as there exists in the tidy Mercedes world. But he was a perfectionist and persisted in making them as perfect as he could.

When Brahms found his first one, it was rather untidy, an ugly green, no grille at all, and had been converted from a Powerglide automatic to a manual. But he did his research and got it back to the way it was when new.

Brahms found his by showing excellent barn hunting instincts when he followed an old lead but still hit paydirt. He found his first Scagliletti Corvette had been sold just weeks after the magazine stories hit in 1961 to Fred Gifford in the Chicago area and that Gifford had tucked the car away in his garage for the next 26 years. Gifford liked unusual cars—he also had Rust Heinz's (the ketchup guy) Phantom Corsair, a bizarre one-off. Once he bought it from Gifford, Brahms painted the Corvette's Italian body silver gray and kept on the Italian bumpers but put other bumpers over them.

The cars never were intended to be racecars though Brahms did let Len Frank, a renowned wordsmith and talk show host, drive one of his pair at Laguna Seca in the vintage races in 1987. Only one of the three had a high performance 315-hp Rochester f.i. engine and most of the competition options, the other two had Powerglide automatics.

Looking back, Brahms recollects some of the hard parts of rebuilding the cars. He told Len Frank that he only had a few weeks to restore the first car that was entered in the vintage races and even the paint job only took a week. He found when he took off the original paint that the car was mostly filler. "Remove the filler and you have a car-shaped light alloy walnut remaining," wrote Frank. "There was also the matter of fifty or so pounds of Italian bituminous undercoat and the 27 years of dirt that it had collected to remove."

Brahms also built two engines for the car they would take to the vintage races—one a 283 with Rochester injection, Chevy 097 "Duntov" cam, 1.94-inch valve early "fuelie" heads, stock "rams horn" exhaust manifolds, etc., the second what Frank called "a slightly more liberal interpretation of 'vintage.'" The original Warner T-10 four-speed was rebuilt, short track 4.11 gears installed in the rebuilt "posi" rear end, and the Borrani wire wheels rebuilt, re-chromed and re-polished. Original heavy-duty brake components were found and refurbished, the radiator, instruments, steering gear, front end, springs were all either new or rebuilt, new shocks were fabricated for the front, and Konis found for the rear. Brahms had to make changes in the wiring, the original was so badly done.

Getting the Borranis by the race inspectors was dicey, as Frank wrote in recalling the race: "A set of American Racing mags were bought as backup (the center-lock Borranis were adapted with bolt-on hubs—these are frowned on by vintage racing tech inspectors) and a couple of sets of Goodyear Blue Streaks fitted." At some point it had front discs but still drums in the back. Alas the car's debut in vintage racing was not ideal. The fuelie engine took a dump, even after expert Lou Culitta, was brought on board. And he was the man who had designed the system at GM! The car ran out of gas in the race, fuel feed problems the culprit. But it was among the racecars chosen to go over to the Pebble Beach concours in the racing car class and over there, pointed out Frank, "it didn't have to run over 400 yards to be driven over the trophy ramp. Small victory."

Now back to the year 1960. After GM put up the big stone wall to keep interlopers out, Shelby of course never looked back. He got a line on help from Ford by 1961 ("Hey buddy did we tell ya about our new V8 engine?") who linked them up with A.C. Cars Ltd. in England and acted as the go-between long enough to create the Cobra. The rest is history.

Two of the cars went overseas once they were restored and recognized as the rare cars they are. Brahms sold one to Japan. Another went to France. One stayed in the U.S. where it was restored by an Orange County man who sold it in 1997 so he could devote himself to making a one-off Bizzarrini. It next appeared in the Blackhawk Collection in Northern California and from there went to Paul Russell & Co, a restoration shop, for additional mechanical work. It resides today in the Petersen Auto Museum, who bought it from Blackhawk.

At some point, one of the three, after establishing its credibility with appearances at the prestigious Pebble Beach, Santa Barbara and Newport Beach concours, rolled across the stage at the Barrett-Jackson auction in Scottsdale in 1990, and sold for just under a half-million dollars.

Lesson learned? These cars, in their original era, fell into the pig-in-a-poke class where it was difficult to establish a known value. They were unknown, an odd hybrid shunned by the stringback-racing-glove wearing Ferrari-Maserati crowd and viewed with suspicion by the Corvette folk because it was bodied by a guy whose name you could hardly pronounce.

But in time the audience became more sophisticated. The other parties involved (besides Carroll Shelby) became better known. So the angle to be played in selling it at auction was: are the famous people associated with it famous enough to make the car desirable? You can buy a famous car owned by a famous person and usually make out in the re-sale because there is a contingent of car buffs who like a car tied in with a famous owner (Elvis, Diana Dors, Liberace, yadda yadda). Or you can buy an obscure car created by a famous person and hope, during the time you own it, that person becomes more famous. That was the angle the Gooding Co. counted on in 2009 when they put it in an auction. They hyped Scaglietti's name more than they did Shelby but ended up promoting all the famous personalities who had been tied in with the cars. They wrote in their catalog, "The first Scaglietti Corvette is an utterly unique and irreplaceable piece of history that has always had direct connections to some of the most significant international personalities." It took many decades for the trio of Scaglietti Corvettes to become known so going the route of buying an obscure castoff connected to a famous person is a risky one. But in this case the cars ultimately proved to have collector value. This author likes the Scaglietti Corvettes for one reason—they represent Shelby's first good poke in the nose at ol' Enzo…the very same same man who, back in the Fifties, had refused to hire Shelby as a race driver for what Shelby thought he was worth.

Chapter 11
THE LAMBORGHINI WALLFLOWER
(1963 LAMBORGHINI 350GTV)
When I say the first, I really do mean "The First."

Y'know how guys on forums on the net brag they got the "first" of this car or the "last" of that one? Well, this is about the rediscovery and subsequent resurrection of the first Lamborghini. Not the first production car, nor the first road car, but the first Lamborghini of them all. Numero uno.

And where was it found? At the factory, covered with dust, in almost the same place it sat for 20 years (though other reports say it was parked outside exposed to the elements for years). This is a case where semantics can get you all tripped up. Some Lambo enthusiasts in Italy will say, "It was never lost; we knew where it was all the time." Well, that may be true. But it was lost to the Lamborghini community in that it was not a running driving car that could have made a promotional appearance at many an event.

First a little background on the firm...When Italian tractor manufacturer Ferruccio Lamborghini decided to take on Ferrari with a Grand Touring car of his own, he commissioned the brilliant but mercurial designer Franco Scaglione to design a car that would upstage Ferrari.

He succeeded in making a daring car that was as sophisticated and even more polished looking than the production Ferraris. But it wasn't exactly a running driving car in its first incarnation.

Now, it comes out in subsequent decades that the car shown at the Turin Auto Salon in 1963 with the engine on a stand next to it was actually a "pushmobile," the phrase used internally by designers in the auto industry to mean a concept car that is not a running and driving car.

The engine was parked next to it on its own stand, so you could marvel at its technical features.

Not that Ferrucio didn't have an actual running engine. It just wasn't mounted in the car when the car made its world premiere. The brand new engine was a V12 designed by ex-Ferrari engineer Giotto Bizzarrini. Bizzarrini had been part of the famous "walk out" of several Ferrari engineers who had bolted from the plant in 1961 over the matter of Enzo's wife meddling too much in the company business, even the race team's business. Several of the engineers started an auto company meant to rival Ferrari, called ATS, but that venture failed. The call from Lamborghini gave Bizzarrini a legitimate, well-funded company to consult with.

The engine Bizzarrini had designed was a real *tour de force*. Ing. Bizzarrini's assignment had been to design a 4-cam 6-carburetor dry sump V12 that would beat the Ferrari 250GT horsepower right out of the box. The power output of that first engine on the first tests was 360 hp at 8000 rpm; but as much as he liked the power, Ferrucio had Giotto dial back the power to a more modest 270 bhp at 6500 rpm for the first production car to add a little longevity. Torque was 241 lb-ft at 4500 rpm.

The square steel tube chassis on the prototype—carrying chassis number 1016—was cobbled together by a small shop called Neri and Bonacini of Modena, who actually made two slightly different chassis. The suspension was fully independent, a big step up from Ferrari who was still running live rear axles at the time. The gearbox was bought from ZF in Germany but Lamborghini planned to make their own later. The differential is from Salisbury, actually an English-made part. The interior of the car was credited to Sargiotto Bodyworks of Turin while the coachbuilder was Carrozzeria Sargiotto of Turin.

The GTV was much better conceived than the ATS because it looked right from the outset like a car that could be built and sold. It actually looked more luxurious than a Ferrari because it had hidden headlights, a feature that had only been tried on Ferrari's experimental (SN2207) Superfast II show car but not put into production. The GTV is appreciated as an object d'art because it was a no compromise design, a strong statement. Inevitably, though, when you go to a production car you have to pull back on what looked so good on the prototype. The truth is you can't have such crisp edges on a car or, when it is machine polished, the polisher will "burn through" the paint. So Touring of Milan was hired to make the production design, and certain things were changed, and the lines softened.

Not that many would miss the original design. Ken Gross writing in a *Road & Track* special magazine on Lamborghini said of that first car: "Its Franco Scaglione-designed coachwork was, in a word, awkward. The car's pop-up headlamps were interesting but there were far too many vents and slots peppering the bodywork."

The biggest change mechanically when they redesigned it for production was a switch to horizontal sidedraft carbs for the production car, to permit a lower hoodline. The biggest change styling wise for the production car was a switch to exposed headlights. Sadly, among the items dropped from the prototype was the chrome copy of Ferrucio's signature (not that unique, it turns out, as a couple of early Ferrari's also had a chrome-plated facsimile of Ferrari's signature).

It is seldom mentioned that Ferrucio considered other coachbuilders and that two shortened chassis of the first production 350GT cars were sent to Zagato, renowned for their lightweight construction, to create alternative creations to the Touring design. Ercole Spada of Zagato was the designer. The Zagato version was shown at the 1965 London Motor Show under the name Lamborghini 3500 GTZ. Only two examples were made, one kept by the factory while the other was sold to a private customer.

In retrospect, nearly 50 years later, some aspects of the original 350GTV look a little "dated." But less dated ironically than the 350GT production car that followed it!

THE RE-DISCOVERY

There are, as usual with car histories stretching over many decades, slightly different accounts of how the GTV was unearthed. One is that some supplier to Lamborghini noticed the car in the corner of the plant and asked to buy it. Lamborghini had been through many ups and downs in those first twenty years and the last thing they wanted to spend money on was making it a running car. After all, it had served the company well as a concept car and then they had gone into production. It wasn't really needed by the plant, though they thought, if they ever get their museum going, it could be the star exhibit. Most accounts agree that the 350 GTV remained in storage until the mid-1980s, when car dealer Romano Bernandoni and his cousin, Lamborghini expert Stefano Pasini (author of at least one book on Lamborghini) convinced the management to allow them to find a restoration shop to get it into running condition. Some accounts say they actually purchased the car at this point, but at any rate they got the restoration started.

A firm called Emilianauto of Bologna took on the task of making it a running car. Bolstering the story that it was not really a running car when first shown, apparently quite a few modifications had to be made to the chassis to fit the engine inside it (others argue the engine dropped right in—but then the restoration took some time and accounts differ).

One of the ironies of the restoration was that some retired Lamborghini employees were called back in to recount what they remembered of the car and even they disagreed on how the car had looked when originally first shown!

THE FIRST COLLECTOR

Originally the goal was to put the car in pride of place at the official Lamborghini museum, but cash talks and you-know-what walks so next thing you know a collector in Japan owned the car, a Mr. Isao Noritake, who more recently has sponsored a Lamborghini racing team and was President of the Japanese Lamborghini Club. Inevitably again, in the restoration you can find raging discussions in the forum section of some websites like FerrariChat.com (which has a Lamborghini section) over whether the car should have been restored as it looked when it was shown in Turin, or as it looks today. For instance, the steering wheel and gauges in the car at Turin were missing so others had to be sourced. This writer won't step into that minefield except to say that, after seeing other prototypes made into running cars, some compromises inevitably have to be made in the conversion from pushmobile to running car. One site even says the incomplete show car also lacked brake calipers and foot pedals. Hey, lighten up, guys, in its first incarnation, it was only a pushmobile!

The car eventually reached a Swiss enthusiast who also owns another first-ever model of Lamborghini and he is fulfilling Lamborghini's original intention in allowing it to be sold—now someone else is showing it and Lamborghini gets the rub-off glamor. On occasion it even graces the factory museum at Sant'Agata Bolognese.

Lesson to be learned here? That, while there is the romantic myth that great collector cars are best found in dusty barns out in Nebraska or hidden in gold mines in California, or in caves in Tuscany, the truth is that some can be found right there at the very same factory that made them, "hidden in plain sight" as it were, just as this car was.

So if you desire a specific brand and model of car, your very first stop in your quest should be the factory where it was conceived. Look in the warehouse, the fabrication shops that supplied the firm in their beginning days, and then, and only then, should you widen your search area.

Chapter 12
THE CHRYSLER-POWERED FERRARI
(1951 FERRARI 340 AMERICA)

With a Le Mans history, it was a bargain
even without the right engine.

When I first used to hang around the Ferrari Owner's Club in 1970, one of the most splendid entrances at each event was always made by Lincoln Cabraloff, a tall, tanned silver haired gent sporting a big cigar. He also wore a Ferrari prancing horse on a gold chain, a badge that looked suspiciously like it had been pried from right off the grille of a Ferrari and gold-plated. In fact he might have been the prototype for the moniker laid on Ferrari owners of being "the gold chain crowd." He was driving a red Rosso Corsa Ferrari 340 America, SN0118A, right hand drive no less, with flip-down glass racing windscreens, possibly from a Jaguar. These required goggles, you know, the kind with separate panes of glass set into metal frames; and he wore a cloth "poor boy" hat set on top of that.

First, a little background on the 340 America is in order…The Ferrari 340 America came about in the early 1950s when Enzo Ferrari asked Aurelio Lampredi, a brilliant engineer with a background in the aeronautic field, to develop a more powerful engine.

Lampredi came up with an engine called the 'long-block' V-12, that nickname because the distance between adjacent cylinders was some 20mm greater than in the previous Colombo-designed V-12. The long-block engine had its debut in the single-seater grand prix cars in 1950 as a 340-hp, 4.5-liter powering Ferrari's 375 F. To tame it down somewhat for use in Ferrari's road cars, the 375's V12's bore and stroke was reduced to 4.1 liters, and its compression ratio lowered. The resulting engine was specified for the Ferrari 340 America, a car that was "dual purpose," good for use on both road and track. The "America" name was a deliberate choice as Enzo knew achieving success in America was key to keeping his factory going. Bodywork for the 340 Americas was by a variety of outside suppliers, including Ghia, Touring, or Vignale. Only 24 examples were built.

Turns out Linc's Touring-bodied car, SN 0118A, was really a storied one. It had been driven in Le Mans in 1951 with American Bill Spear co-driving. It went out with clutch trouble. Spear and Briggs Cunningham also ran it at Sebring in '52 but it broke. It was also driven by American racing great (and WWII pilot and POW John Fitch) and then went to Charles Brown who ran a lot of races with it all over the U.S. In' 53 Brown offered it for $7,000 which was a lot of money back then. I dare say that, at the time, you could buy a two-bedroom house in Florida with that kind of money.

WAKING FROM THE LONG SLEEP

Then it went for what I like to call "The Long Sleep." Like from '53 to 1971 it was off the map, unknown to Los Angeles car enthusiasts until Los Angeles-based Lincoln Cabraloff, a wholesale grocery buyer, popped up with it at club meetings. It looked stock except for the Jag fold-down racing windscreens and you couldn't tell that there was a slant six Chrysler engine under the hood. It was called the "slant six" because, in Chrysler products, the engine was leaned over in the car so you could have lower hood clearance.

According to correspondence found on a Ferrari website, Cabraloff had bought the car from Whittier, California, car collector Ron Kellogg who in turn got the car back in the Fifties from a "guy in Downey" who was an *LA Times* pressman who used that job to his advantage by spotting cars as early as Friday for ads that weren't supposed to come out in the *Collector Car* classifieds until

Sunday! At the time Cabraloff bought it, a wooden dash had been added by Kellogg and there were a few other incorrect details, such as a two-piece flip-up windscreen from a racing Jaguar.

Cabraloff drove it to all sorts of Ferrari events where it was always the oldest car there. He owned it for 17 years until 1987 when it was sold to a Ferrari restoration shop. At some point in 1970, according to the website www.barchetta.cc, it was fitted with a Ferrari 365GT V12 engine, no. 11187, which at least made it all Ferrari again. But meanwhile there was a search on for the original engine. This author remembers Cabraloff telling him that the original engine had been located with a collector back East and he had to employ a lawyer experienced in the old Ferrari world to wrest the engine from the owner, whereupon it immensely improved the value of the car. Around 1989 the correct engine was installed and the car went on to other owners and to a vintage racing career, some of it by bottled water plant owner Fabrizio Violatti in Italy. It ran in at least five of the Mille Miglia re-creations.

It is easily one of the oldest Ferrari barchetta body styles available and one of the most authentic looking. This author has lost track of where it is today, but the lesson to be learned here for barn finders is clear: where a given car has the correct chassis, the correct body, a (mostly) correct interior, and is a rare car that competed in the most famous race in sports car history, it's okay to buy it with the wrong engine in it. Especially if it is a Ferrari! In this case the installation of a Ferrari V12 engine—albeit one made many years later than the original—was step one in improving its value, and when it finally got the original matching numbered engine put under the bonnet, it became pure gold. This author hasn't found Cabraloff to ask him what he sold it for, but you can bet that during the 17 years he owned it, the car went up in value hundreds of times from what he paid for it…and think of all the fun he had driving it!

Chapter 13
HARLEY'S HONEY
(1953 CADILLAC LE MANS)
A million-dollar showcar vanishes from Oklahoma.

The crime, if it was a crime, happened over 60 years ago. The car was a Cadillac Le Mans, a two-seat concept, one of four made. They were built at the behest of 6-foot-plus Harley Earl, the towering showman who was General Motors' first VP in charge of design.

Raised in Los Angeles, Earl had come from a tradition of custom car building. In fact, he grew up working in his father's business, which customized cars for show biz folk like Roscoe "Fatty" Arbuckle. The GM management noticed his efforts and hired him to come to Detroit in 1927 and spice up their cars. This really hurt Ford Motor Co. because Henry was still espousing his "any color as long as it's black" philosophy while Harley laid on the bright colors and chrome. His unit was originally called the "Art and Colour Section."

Earl was a showman through and through. It was Earl who started the Motorama shows, Broadway-type unveilings of concept cars—then called "dream cars"—accompanied by beautiful show girls. These shows kicked off at the Waldorf Astoria hotel in New York then went on tour across the country.

Special one-off cars, called "dream cars" by the public, were conceived for these shows, the idea being something like "we'll run this one up the flagpole and see who salutes." Some concept cars did make it to production. The '53 Corvette, for instance, went from being a Motorama show car to a production vehicle that same year with the first 300 hand-built in Flint, Michigan.

But the missing show car last spotted in Oklahoma was not a prototype Corvette (though it also made its appearance in 1953 and also wore a fiberglass body). It was a Cadillac Le Mans concept car, one of just four made. It had a longer wheelbase than a Corvette—115 inches compared to the Corvette's 102 inches, and had the oddity of three-across seating. The engine was a 350-hp, 332-cubic-inch Cadillac V8 with dual quads.

In choosing the name, Earl wasn't just borrowing the name of a famous automobile race—the 24 Hours of Le Mans—and sticking it on a marque that had no connection whatsoever to motorsport. Sportsman millionaire Briggs Cunningham had, in fact, run Cadillacs at Le Mans in 1950. So, GM had every right to crow that fact in a concept car's name (unlike the Le Mans name GM would shamelessly tack on to a production Pontiac Tempest a decade or so later).

The Cadillac Le Mans was a success as a styling study, with cues appearing across the Cadillac lineup throughout the 1950s. One of the four made even received a refresh, re-emerging from GM's styling division sporting quad headlamps and sleeker fins. But the Le Mans prototypes never led directly to two-seat Cadillac production vehicles, so they were of little use to GM once their time as Motorama dream cars came to an end.

Now Earl knew all these movie stars, and there weren't any emissions or safety equipment laws back then, so he could, and did, give or sell the ex-Motorama show cars to celebrities after their show biz days were over. One of the Cadillac Le Mans cars went to Harry Karl, a shoe magnate who gifted it to his wife, a statuesque blonde named Marie "The Body" MacDonald. Another was sold to a big Cadillac dealer in Beverly Hills who could have been customer from the Earl family days of customizing cars in California.

Now, about that Oklahoma connection. One of the Cadillac Le Mans show cars was one of the stars of the Oil Progress Exhibition at the Oklahoma City airport in 1953, along with two other Motorama show cars: the Wildcat I and the Starfire. Then the Cadillac went on exhibit at Greenhouse-Moore Cadillac Chevrolet for two days during the first week of November. After Nov. 8 the car flat disappeared.

Some say it went to Tulsa but the trail, if you want to pick up on it, is cold—real cold. One report says that Floyd Akers, a Cadillac dealer in the Washington, D.C. area bought it, raising the hopes of Cadillac history fans. But that report was scotched later on when it was discovered that he had bought one of the other Le Mans show cars.

As an incentive to set you on the trail, this author calculates that the missing Le Mans is today worth between $400,000 and $2 million—never mind that it might have to be completely restored when and if it is found. One of the four Le Mans show cars was reportedly destroyed in a fire in 1985—that one belonging to Ms. McDonald—and then there's one missing so that makes the missing one more rare than it was in the Fifties when there were still four.

And it has since become recognized that privately-owned GM prototypes are very special cars. Once the Harley Earl era ended, GM tightened up considerably when it came to selling concept cars and prototypes—especially after the passage of emissions and safety regulations laws which made it illegal to sell cars that did not meet the standards of that model year.

Despite those prohibitions, in the collector car world, owning a prototype is somewhat of a special honor. Every year half a dozen or so seem to slip out of the grasp of automakers and into private hands. At auction, they sometimes go for several million—like the 1954 Oldsmobile F-88 (another ex-Motorama show car). In that case, the founder of a cable channel wanted to make it the star of his own car museum, and he paid over $3 million for the privilege (that car profiled in *Incredible Barn Finds*).

But back to the missing Le Mans...Innumerable questions remain: did GM ever report the car stolen? Did another statuesque blonde end up with the car? Is it still on the roads of Oklahoma, hiding under a nondescript car body? Maybe it remains a barn find waiting to happen.

Chapter 14

THE GOLDEN FERRARI
(1967 FERRARI 330GT)

One body, three chassis, and only two right times to buy it!

Remember that old shell game that you used to see at carnivals or on street corners—where there's one pea and three walnut shells and the carny moves around the shells at dizzying speed until you can no longer tell with certainty which one the pea is under? Well, this is almost the same story, except with a car body. A very sexy racecar body that became known as "the Golden Ferrari." It started out as a racing Ferrari body that was on a factory racecar, then that body was removed and put on a second factory racecar, which had its body removed. Then in its second guise the car, painted gold, became the "star" of a Fellini movie no less, only to have the chassis and body then go their separate ways, the body the third time laid onto a purely road car Ferrari with zilch racing history. Somewhere in there is a collectible. Or maybe all three were, at one point, collectible!

First, chronologically, the Ferrari that this body was first seen on was of the highest order of Ferrari, a full fledged works racecar—SN0808, 330 TR LM #0808TR—which won its class at Le Mans in 1962. You would think that, having distinguished itself in combat, the body would stay with the car, but no, the body was taken off that car and put on a 330LMB, chassis 4381SA, a car which looked like a Lusso road car that was customized with a 250GTO-style nose.

A little history on the 330LMB is in order: four 330LMBs were developed for Ferrari by Michael Parkes, a British development engineer in their employ who also doubled as a factory race driver. It was rightfully called the "SA" because it used a modified powertrain out of Ferrari's "luxury car," the 400 Superamerica, the model built for CEOs and Captains of industry (not to mention some royalty). The race tuners threw out the three Webers, replacing them with six to help jump the horsepower from 340 to 390. It was still stuck with a four-speed gearbox, inexplicable when its predecessor, the 250GTO, had a 5-speed.

Both the 400SA and the Ferrari 330 LMB had double wishbones and coil springs up front, and a rigid axle and semielliptic leafs at the rear. Pininfarina did the coachwork for both models, and while the 400SA was its own design the 330LMB looked like a pastiche of existing Ferrari models. From the windshield forward it looked like a Ferrari 250 GTO. From the windshield back it strongly resembled a 250 Lusso, though the rear fenders had a sort of rectangular horizontal scoop funneling air to the brakes.

Although it was mix-and-match with the design cues, the 330LMB was a pretty fast son of a gun, clocking almost 190-mph on the Le Mans Mulsanne straight. And at that time front-engined racecars were thought to be almost obsolete, so Ferrari was worried that it would be faster than their state-of-the-art mid-engine V-12 prototype, the Ferrari 250 P. After all, what was the point of sinking all that development money into the new mid-engine cars if an old front-engine car could still outrun it?

Four Ferrari 330 LMBs were run by the factory in the '63 24 Hours of Le Mans; but only one survived to the end, finishing fifth overall. That turned out to be the 330LMB's high point. From that race on, the factory lost interest and put all their racing money on their mid-engined cars. Front-engined Ferrari racecars were history.

A SHORT-LIVED MOVIE CAREER

Now, back to the Golden Ferrari. Are you still with me? Because there's more curves in the road ahead. Who wanted that racecar open body on the formerly coupe bodied 330LMB? A Milan film company Crossograph SpA in Italy, who were making a film directed by Federico Fellini called *Toby Dammit* (some say the title was *Histoires Extraordinaires*) and the actor driving the car was Terrance Stamp. Actually the now gold-painted Ferrari was only in one third the movie because that movie had three different directors, each telling a separate story.

THE BODY GOES ONE WAY, THE CHASSIS ANOTHER
Meanwhile, Ferrari Chassis #0808TR—the Le Mans class winner in '62—received a new coupe body by Fantuzzi and had its own life for a time. Sometime after the film was made, the golden hued body of the movie car was lifted off. And, happily for Ferrari purists, LMB chassis #4381SA was reunited with its original LM Berlinetta-body, making it a complete original racecar again and no doubt greatly improving its value for collectors when Ferraris began to rise in value in the '80s.

So did the "Golden Ferrari" bodywork get scrapped? Not on your life. It was really too much of a work of art to throw into a dumpster. Surely there must be another sporting gent who wants a racy looking Ferrari but doesn't want to pay for a full all-on racecar with a history? That customer came along around 1973 and a 330 GT 2+2, SN 8733, a car of 1966-vintage, was selected for the body transplant. Unfortunately though, it now has the racy body, and the almost obligatory Ferrari racecar color of "Rosso Corsa." It had a taller windscreen put on it probably to comply with the laws of the State in which it was registered, so it's not nearly as dramatic looking a car as it was when that body was on a racecar where it had a cut-down wraparound plexiglass windscreen—the same configuration it was run in during its role as a "movie star."

Ed Niles, the attorney in California who has owned over 100 Ferraris, wrote a Ferrari forum: "I'm sure that this open body, in gold, was on 0808 in early 1965....But here's the story: That gold car was offered to me back in the day, with a spare berlinetta body (I could have either or both bodies), and the chassis was definitely 0808, the 330 TR Le Mans winner. The car ended up in N.Y. with the coupe body, so I suppose that the gold body could have then been put on a 330LMB. But that seems like such a stretch that I wonder if somewhere along the line '330TR' got translated as '330LMB?'"

So in the end, when all is said and done, someone in New York is driving around a Ferrari that looks kinda like a racecar, and if anyone asks, "Is that a racecar?" the owner can say "kinda/sorta" because, well, the truth is that the body was in a race. And, it was, after all, a star of the silver screen as well. Too bad for the present owner of the body that it wasn't still on the LMB chassis when he bought it because an LMB today is worth many times what a 330GT is worth, though the one carrying this storied body is no doubt worth more than the standard Pininfarina-bodied 330GT. That LMB that once had the golden Ferrari body by the way, went on to fame and fortune with its correct body, selling for over $2 million way back in 1994. It has appeared at many events in Europe, one time even being piloted by Indy great Bobby Rahal, who is a great supporter of vintage racing, i.e. racing for the fun of it.

Lesson to be learned here? Again, timing is everything. If you would have seen the Fellini movie and paid careful attention to the credits at the end, you would have seen the studio name. And if you would've then got on the horn and called that production company in Italy and said you have money in hand and you want to buy that car, you might have been able to intercept the car's evolution at the point where there was still a racecar chassis with racing history underneath that curvaceous body. You would have had to do all this before 1973.

But the question is: Did anyone really want a 330LMB back then? It was a short-lived car, with only a one-season racing history. It had already been shuffled off racing's stage in one hell of a hurry and it was not considered that collectible compared to say, a 250GTO. So you would have had to be far-seeing to realize this so many decades ago.

Lesson to be learned here? When you hear of a purebred car (chassis and engine by the same manufacturer) with an unusual body, it's worth checking out. You never know when you'll find treasure underneath.

Chapter 15
MELLOW YELLOW
(1968 MASERATI GHIBLI)
Go where no car buyer has gone before.

Now this here is a story about the importance of "thinking on your feet" which I interpret to mean "able to function under rapidly-changing circumstances."

In that sense buying an old collector car is not at all like going to a dealership and buying a car, where everything is cut-and-dried. In the old car world, you have to be able to roll with the punches, and be ready to come back with a knock-out punch.

Unfortunately, I don't do it that often but here's the story of one time when I did and, for a day or two, I was the owner of a fly yellow Maserati, though with no small amount of peril.

This was back in the '80s when I lived in Los Angeles and was doing some writing plus barn finding. My New York City customer (a man who owned commercial real estate and dabbled in car collecting, buying and selling weekly) called and said he wanted a Maserati Ghibli, preferably a manual shift rather than their lame automatic.

Now it so happened that the Ghibli was always one of my favorite cars, style-wise, being a product of the fertile mind of Giorgetto

Giugiaro while he was at Carrozzeria Ghia. That was the second phase of his design career, following the many successful designs he had created at Carrozzeria Bertone. For Ghia's client Maserati, he designed both a coupe and Spyder versions of the Ghibli.

Here's a little background on the model. Production of the Ghibli began with the fastback coupe first in April 1967, joined by the Spyder in 1969. The engine was a race-bred, aluminum block 4,719 cc V8 engine with dry-sump lubrication and two chain-driven overhead-camshafts per cylinder bank. The engine was rated at 330 bhp.

The one I was assigned to buy had a 5-speed manual gearbox but they were available with a Borg-Warner three-speed automatic transmission. All of them had an independent front suspension with unequal-length wishbones, coil springs and anti-roll bar up front and a live rear axle with radius arms and semi-elliptic leaf springs in the rear. Brakes were hydraulic disc brakes all the way around.

The Ghibli was a true gentleman's sports car, something you tooled along the highway in at 100 mph like you are standing still. Top speed was reported to be near 170 mph (though other accounts say it couldn't top 155 mph). It was predictable, balanced and had forgiving handling, thanks to its almost 50/50 weight distribution and a low center of gravity. On the downside, though I bought two or three of them over a couple years, I couldn't ever get them to run evenly for even two days in a row, which made me disgusted with them compared to Ferraris.

Ghiblis are fairly rare cars, with 1,274 Ghiblis made between 1967 and 1972 (another source says 1,170; still another says 1,150 coupes and 125 Spyders, including 25 Spyder SS), numbers that were amazingly close to Ferrari's later production of the 365GTB/4 (Daytona). Record keeping in the Maserati world isn't quite up to the fanatic record keeping in the Ferrari community.

There were two engine sizes. Ghiblis came with either 4.7- or 4.9-liter engines. Those with the 4.9-liter engines were usually called Ghibli SS. The performance difference of two/tenths of a liter between the two engines is negligible and a 4.7 can easily outrun a 4.9 if it is well tuned. In the USA, cars came with power-robbing overly restrictive exhaust manifolds intended at reducing emissions, but you can change back to European manifolds.

Personally, I would have liked to have looked for a Spyder (the odd spelled nickname for a convertible in Italy that had no padding on the top). While the Spyders are more desirable I was glad I didn't have to look for one of those because I wasn't sure I could tell a "cut one" (cut from a coupe) from an original factory Spyder so it was best not to send me to do that task.

Now my assignment was to go up North to the address of someone who was going to sell my patron a Ghibli. My job was to hand over the check and take delivery. I flew up there and rented a car in the San Francisco area, but something happened between the cup and the lip. This was at least 30 years ago so my memory fogs as to what spoiled the original deal. Maybe they didn't like the amount on my cashier's check (or weren't telling me that they had a higher offer) and I was not empowered to write another check on top of what my client was offering (that was a definite flaw in our buying arrangement but no matter now...decades later). Despairing that I had wasted my time, I fired off the question that turned defeat into triumph. I asked: "Well, before I leave town, tell me, who the hell else has one?"

IMPROBABLE BUT TRUE

That's when someone said "Well, there's a hospital up the road where there's a surgeon that's got a yellow one for sale. I saw a picture of it on the bulletin board."

I got the directions to the hospital and dutifully drove up there. I asked for the Doctor (someone must have given me the name) but they said "he's in surgery."

Well, I'm here to tell you that, in the barn-finding trade, fate throws all kinds of obstructions in your path but, if you want to earn your stripes as a barn finder, you have to treat these obstacles as mere temporary obstructions to be tossed aside as you move in for the kill.

You can't see a clear field to throw a pass? You lateral. So I asked, "What floor?"

They tell me and I go up there. I ask for the Doctor and they say, "Down the hall, room B." I go down the hall and I see it's an operating theatre. I duck into the wash-up room. There's a bunch of doctors in there in green scrubs dutifully washing their hands. I see the Ghibli picture on the wall and snatch it off. I ask, "Where's Doctor So-and-so?"

One of the docs looks up and says, "That's me."

"I'm here to buy your car," I said, waving the picture.

"Well, you'll have to wait. I've got an operation to do," he said.

"Okay, fine," I said, "I'll be in the waiting room."

So I went down the cafeteria and ate and came back. Just about that time he came out, drying his hands. Now, here's where my memory fogs. I think a day might have gone by when I had to wait for a new cashier's check as of course I wasn't sent to San Francisco with a check in his name. At any rate, we made the deal and I picked up the car—a super clean fly yellow coupe—at his house and set off late in the evening for the drive home to Los Angeles. The car was running smooth. I had previously found with Ghiblis that either they ran smooth as glass or misfired all over the place. This was a smooth one.

BUSTED

At any rate, I thought it was going to be a non-eventful trip until, as I was going South on route 5, I decided to take a coffee break before I fell asleep. I pulled off the freeway and, at the point the exit road joined the local highway, I encountered a stop sign. I made the mistake of effecting what the authorities call "a rolling stop."

She nailed me.

A woman cop. I think she was local but she may have been Highway Patrol. Blonde. Late Twenties. Snugly-fitted and freshly starched uniform. But with an attitude. That could have been due to the fact I had no registration, no title to the car and no bill of sale though I said I had just bought it.

Not having any of that was the result of my client's insistence I always Fed Ex all that to him the moment I bought a car because if I crashed or fell asleep or was way-laid in some way (that happened, but that's for another book), whoever found the car, the keys and the signed off title could sign their name on the pink slip and thereby own the car. I should have copied all that at a copy shop before Fed Exing the originals to New York.

But what really grinded her was the serial number—some tiny number with just a few digits. And that stamped into a plate no bigger than a business card affixed by a couple of ten-cent rivets, not like on Detroit cars where the serial number is over a dozen numbers and letters. She was sure I was lying, that a car couldn't possibly have a SN that short! I assured her that this here car was a hand-built Italian car and Maserati had been lucky to make 500 a year back then. I think, to tell the truth, she was busting my balls because it was 2 o'clock in the morning and you don't find many yellow Maseratis blasting through your nameless burg. Or maybe she wanted to show the male cops who she was in touch with by radio how tough she was, taking down a big ol' exotic car driver lacking in any paperwork.

Well, after an hour and a half of this cat-and-mouse stuff, she let me go after getting tired of her little game. I must have sounded so clueless—not smart enough to be a major league criminal/exotic car thief.

I got back to L.A., called the shipper, and the car went out of my life. I collected my buyer's commission.

Lesson learned? Several here. One is always take a few extra checks or money orders in case the price turns out not to be what you agreed to on the phone. Two: be ready, if you are buying a car for someone else, to have a Plan B where you can get a new cashier's check issued and sent out immediately. Three: copy the paperwork even if you intend to send it off as soon as you buy the car. It is still a good idea, though, to separate the originals from the car as car-plus-signed-off-title is tempting to a thief.

Oh, and be sure to ask the seller if there are any other cars just like it in the neighborhood for sale. Before the deal, they won't tell you because they are worried knowledge of a competitive car would screw up their sale. But after you buy their car, they might, because at that point they have nothing to lose. So when the first deal was cancelled, I asked the question and, as a result, I still drove a Ghibli home.

Chapter 16
THE CASE OF THE TOPLESS GOOSE
(1966 DETOMASO MANGUSTA SPYDER)
An early Giugiaro, sold much too soon.

This is a love story—unrequited love, in a way. Two guys come across a famous concept car. They fall in love with it. They import their Italian beauty to America, spend beaucoup money on restoring her to her former glory, and hope the world will reward them for their vision when they take the car to a famous auction. There the car fetches only $87,000, which in the world of one-off prototypes, is today considered chump change.

The finder was Steve Wilkinson, a businessman in Paramount, California, near Long Beach, who became the importer of DeTomaso parts to America back in 1986. He specializes in restoring Panteras and Mangustas, two of DeTomaso's V8-powered mid-engine cars that are only now, after four decades, coming to be recognized as collector's specials on a par with Iso Grifos and other Italian GT cars.

The Mangusta, designed by Giorgetto Giugiaro of Ghia carrozzeria back in 1966, is an incomparably bold design statement, one that went from prototype to finished car with hardly any changes (well, they did make the wheels less deep dished for fear of overloading the wheel bearings). The car had back bumpers but very skimpy ones, called bumperettes. The original prototype had a side-to-side sunroof that didn't open (must have made it miserable in hot weather). The coupes were in production from '67 to '71, the last ones coming off the line at Ghia when its successor, the Panteras, were coming off the DeTomaso assembly lines at Vignale.

Italians like open air as much as Americans so a one-off Spyder was made in 1966 to exhibit at major auto shows to see if there would be any demand for it as they readied the Mangusta coupe for production. Over in Europe they call cars with skimpy tops with no padding "Spyders," as opposed to cabriolets which have padded tops and more weather protection. The lines of the Spyder suffer somewhat compared to the coupe as there is no longer a fastback rear window like the Mangusta coupe, but it was pretty daring to have the side window frames fixed. And making the car two-tone, that was a bold move, too.

Californian Steve Wilkinson tells the story of his barn find, which came in the late '80s: "I was over in Italy at the factory in Modena buying parts one day and I walk around the corner and see the Mangusta Spyder. I had seen the car in pictures but of course that was when it was new and now, after a sojourn in Greece, it was a little run down by this time. It had been sold to a man who had customized it in tasteless ways like attaching a hood scoop—though the engine was in the rear—and added a sort of temporary canvas top for when it rained." Wilkinson found that the Greek was trying to sell it back to DeTomaso and Wilkinson thought he had a customer. He contacted Steve Nanny, a DeTomaso enthusiast back in the U.S., and together they went partners on the car.

The car was shipped by sea to nearby Long Beach harbor and picked up. "It took nine months to restore it," says Wilkinson. The DeTomaso family furnished many pictures of the car during its show career so they had a good idea of where to aim in the restoration. "The steel body wasn't too rusty but there was some fabrication involved, like making a new one-piece steel bumper whereas the production Mangustas had two separate rear bumpers. In fact not a single part of the car could be interchanged with the production cars."

The color chosen for the exterior was the same as it had been in its show career, a sort of ivory white and a orange-red color two tone. The interior was done in the stock tan leather. The car, SN 8MA512, came with the better engine—the 289 rated at 300 hp, which bolts right in, where the American-market cars imported by British Motor Car Distributors got the less powerful 302 Ford which was reportedly an industrial engine (one used in industry to drive a generator). It had torque but no rev ability. Anatoly Arutonoff, a famous American car collector of the more obscure Italian brands said, " The 5,100 rev limit, I think, was due to a points spring so weak that you could open the points easily with the nail on your little finger."

Wilkinson said the engine came from Carroll Shelby himself, who was partnered with DeTomaso in 1965 on a Can Am car later introduced as the 70P Ghia show car.

Why DeTomaso would make the world's sexiest coupe and then offer a mundane engine as standard fitment is inexplicable but then Alejandro de Tomaso, the firm's proprietor, a native Argentinian working in Italy, was a quirky individual who did things his own way. And, though he was a struggling automaker, he had one ace up his sleeve: a rich wife, from New Jersey high society no less. So, if anyone criticized him he could tell them to go pound sand. Which he did, often, in a variety of languages.

Steve Wilkinson had this comment on the Spyder's handling: "The Spyder handled much better than the coupes and was easier to work on because of the gullwing engine hatches." Of course, being an open car he had no headroom problems.

It is difficult to gauge the cost of such a restoration because Wilkinson put in so much of his own time as he was financially tied into the car. Suffice to say that a comparable restoration today would be over $200,000. The only saving grace would be that the engine problems would be minor compared to what a Ferrari or Maserati V8 would cost.

The restored car was first shown at Pebble Beach where it won the second in its class award at Pebble Beach in 1991. Mark Sassak's Bizzarrini Spyder (see *Incredible Barn Finds*) took first place, and fittingly, Wilkinson and restored that car with Bill DeCarr.

Then co-owner Steve Nanny had a situation where he needed money and the partners decided to put it into a car auction. At the time the big auction was the Barrett-Jackson auction in Scottsdale. This was in 2001 and hopes were high but in the end when the gavel fell, it only fetched $86,400, bought by a Canadian who treasured it as the queen of his collection.

Now with the benefit of hindsight, all parties involved would all look at it differently. Giugiaro is now a superstar in the design world. Ghia is no more, so there's some nostalgia there. Mangustas have soared way past Panteras in value, in one way inexplicable because Panteras are arguably better built cars for daily driving. Maybe it is because they are more beautiful or because Giugiaro is more known than Tjaarda, the designer of the Pantera.

Wilkinson feels part of the reason for Mangustas going up in value is because, from the beginning, Mangusta owners took pains to keep their cars original and didn't go in for the customizing Pantera owners did. Then there's the rarity factor—with only 402 Mangustas made compared to over 6,000 Panteras imported to America—they are extremely rare, over twice as rare as, for instance, Ferrari Daytonas. So rarity counts.

The auctions have evolved too, with more specialized audiences for each auction and the auction to put a class act like the one-off Mangusta Spyder in today would be Gooding or RM, not the B-J which is still more musclecar oriented. Taking a purebred (well, hybrid if the chassis was Italian and engine American) car to the B-J back in 1991 was like taking a gourmet meal to a hamburger joint. The audience didn't appreciate it. Wilkinson also feels in retrospect that it was the wrong time of year to sell it, January, compared to the summer auctions in August at the Monterey peninsula when the whole peninsula is packed cheek-by-jowl with monied buyers.

Lesson learned? First, you can fall in love with your dream but please, don't spend too much on her unless it's for your own long-term enjoyment. Because the world may not share your enthusiasm. Another lesson would be to take the car as found, unrestored, and tuck it away on blocks in a relative's barn until such time as the values go up (of course you have to balance that with the thought that restoration costs will be going up commensurately in the meantime). Ironically, though, a fresh new breeze has come into in the collector car auction world since 1991. One which allows you, the barn finder, to sell your four-wheeled treasure "AS FOUND," cobwebs and all. Sometimes unrestored cars go up for sale and still fetch good amounts even with flattened-out paint and torn upholstery because they have great potential. That is because there is a new "original" contingent of the car world that want their cars with scars of their original history still evident, not something repainted (often the wrong color) or reupholstered (often the wrong material), yadda-yadda. They don't want to pay a high price to un-do an incorrect restoration. Today, that same Spyder, totally unrestored, would fetch $200,000. Wilkinson also estimates that, today, at the proper auction, one where the educated audience appreciates it, and restored as it was, period correct in color inside and out, this would be be more like a million-dollar car. Lesson learned? Some cars are like vintage wine. They have to age to reach their full potential.

Chapter 17
THE RUBBER COBRA
(1965 XD A.C. COBRA)

Hiding in plain sight.

You're looking at a rubber Cobra, built by Ford back in the day... Truth be told, back in the day, Ford was never that crazy about the A.C. Cobra's eggshell-thin aluminum body. It would dent if you even so much as breathed on it. So from the very beginning, they were trying to develop an alternative body that was durable, easier to make and could be made in the USA instead of far-off England where no less an authority than Shelby himself said that Cobra bodies were "whacked out by winos under bridges."

Ford's styling department built two concept cars on Cobra chassis in the mid-1960s. Both were designed by the head of Ford Styling at that time, Eugene Bordinat. One was a roadster which came to be called the XD Cobra, presumably for "Experimental Design." But its in-house nickname was the "Bordinat Cobra" because everyone knew that Bordinat wanted a toy built for himself to tool around in. After all, his counterpart at GM, William L. Mitchell, had half a dozen such toys built and nobody made a squeak about it. It was about time, Bordinat thought, that some other Detroit styling director showed he had clout too.

The coupe prototype, based on the leaf-sprung Cobra, was called the "Cougar II" (profiled in *Incredible Barn Finds*). Despite the nominal publicity when they were first introduced, the two American-bodied Cobras fell into obscurity for decades and their existence was almost forgotten. The Bordinat Cobra was reportedly built on the first coil sprung chassis developed for the 427 Cobra. Though the chassis was developed for the big block, for some reason in this particular show car, Ford chose to work with the coil sprung chassis but instead of a big block chose to install the smaller 289 cu. in. High-Performance V8 mated to a C4 automatic transmission. That could have been to achieve a lower hood line than the big block would have required. Or maybe because Bordinat himself, who was planning to drive it around town, didn't want to cope with the beastly 427. (Even Shelby was quoted as saying ominously: "The 427 will kill you in a second.")

The Cobra XD had not only its own special modernized interior (the production Cobras used a dashboard layout not much different from the A.C. "Ace" that preceded the Cobra) but also boasted a lift-off hardtop covered with vinyl as was the fashion in Detroit back then. The body of the Bordinat Cobra was vacuum-formed out of a new plastic material called "Royalex," developed by U.S. Royal, known as a tire company but they also made other products. Rumor had it that three bodies had been molded—one used for this car and the other two have disappeared into the sands of time.

U.S. Rubber co-operated in the experiment. They had seen how fiberglass suppliers like Owens-Corning had made out supplying the material for Corvette bodies since 1953 so they thought, hey, we got a product that could be even better. In SAE paper 660434 published in 1966, there's a whole presentation on a replica called the Cord Sportsman Model 810 that did in fact make it to production with a "Thermoformed Royalex" body. So it was not just an executive's toy that was being created but a genuine legitimate experiment that, if adopted on a larger scale, would have had advantages in lower weight, longer durability, corrosion resistance and low cost tooling. Alas, only the Cord replicar benefitted from the XD Cobra's first plunge into the pool.

Ironically, the coupe show car, the Cougar II, had a fiberglass body, but then you had the problem of only one company in America ready to do fiberglass bodies en masse and they were busy doing the Corvette (though one could argue the 300 or so Cobra bodies Ford would need in a model year was a small enough number that MFG, Molded Fiber Glass, maker of Corvette bodywork, could have handled it as a side job, though doing something with Ford at the same time they were contracted to Chevy might have ticked off Chevy).

Both prototypes disappeared from public view after their original show careers. Ford had a falling out with Shelby in 1969, and, much to Shelby's consternation, Ford continued to use the name "Cobra" on all sorts of cars, which Shelby could do nothing about (in a moment of weakness he had sold Ford the rights to the name "Cobra" for one dollar!). It turned out the two Cobra "one-offs" weren't really "lost" per se, just not in the public eye. You have to remember that an automaker like Ford is similar to a movie company. They are always concerned about the next product (or movie) coming out and the old ones are of little concern, unless they can be brought back to promote the new product.

The man credited with finding them is former Ford employee Jeff Burgy, a stalwart of a national Shelby club. He was looking for some cars to display at a local motel that would be the headquarters for the Club when they had their annual convention in Detroit (the convention is held on alternate coasts every other year). After discussing the cars with another retired Ford employee, Burgy determined they had been donated to a Detroit museum. He contacted the Detroit Historical Museum and yes, indeed, there they were, somewhat forlorn and dusty, in a storage building.

The sad part was that the Museum had neither the funds to restore them or room to display them. Of the two, the Cougar II was in better shape cosmetically, having been shown at Pebble Beach on the "dream car" lawn in recent times. This, by the way, shows the Detroit Museum was fulfilling its museum function, rotating its wares to other venues, much as art museums temporarily "trade" art. So that car just took a good cleaning up to go to the Shelby club show.

But the Bordinat Cobra was in worse shape, so Burgy, having volunteered to put the display together, spent his own time trying to spruce it up. A few trim parts, such as the hood and steering wheel emblems, were missing, par for the course when cars go unguarded while being moved or stored. Burgy contacted Tony Branda, who sells Cobra parts, who came up with a new wood-rimmed steering wheel plus a Cobra nose badge. He even had to scrounge around junkyards to find some of the small trim pieces before the cars went on display. The cars made the Shelby group's convention and have been shown more recently at the Amelia

Island concours, an annual event fast growing in stature to be the "Pebble Beach of the South."

Being a historian by nature, besides being an artist, Burgy also tried to nail down the serial numbers of the two cars. But, as easy as it is to find a CSX2000 or CSX3000 series Cobra SN number on the standard-bodied cars, the way the bodywork had been laid on these two chassis defied him finding the stampings in the usual place, such as on the frame's front X-member upright. In both cases, the designers had covered it up with the new bodywork. He contacted a man who had compiled a registry of Cobra serial numbers and it was unearthed that the Corporation had scheduled a chassis called 3001 for a styling study (which in retrospect makes CSX3002 among the most valuable big block Cobras in that it went out to the public as the first coil spring big block Cobra).

The two prototype Cobras have since gone back into seclusion, not forgotten but definitely out of sight. Now barn finders want to know: are they for sale? Ask the Museum. Any automaker who donates a car usually finds their control ends from the moment they are granted a tax deduction for donating the car. Most car museums reserve the right to sell cars that are surplus to their needs. If this is indeed an early 427 Cobra chassis, the question facing a collector who approaches the Museum checkbook in hand would be: Is this car worth more as a stock-bodied A.C. Cobra than it is as the XD Cobra? As a one-off I'd peg its value as the XD Cobra at $2 million. Stock 427 Cobras (at least one with no racing history) haven't reached that yet, but then again, that might depend on the chassis number (and someone will have to cut into the one-off bodywork of the XD Cobra to find that number). If it turns out it is the first big block Cobra made, well, any car hobbyist knows it's the first and last of any series that is worth the most (though of course with Cobras, racing history counts mightily).

Lesson learned? It pays for an industrious barn-finder to go back to the automaker's barn with his or her inquiry as to the whereabouts of a long-lost prototype. The fact is, some cars—especially those used for promotional purposes—never left the nest. Some do leave, eventually, but only go down the road a few miles to the nearest museum. These two one-off Cobras were there all the time in Detroit—only ten miles from Dearborn, in the hands of the same institution Ford gave them to—but the plain and simple fact is that, for decades, no one cared.

Chapter 18

THE LAST REAL BUGATTI
(1956/'65 GHIA EXNER BUGATTI T-101)

*Found as a chassis only, but it became
more significant once it was bodied.*

In a way, for the car collector, an automaker's failing is a "zero-sum" game. One party loses. The other party wins. So when automakers go under, while it's tragic for the employees (and sometimes stockholders) it can be a boon for car collectors who get to buy the last cars that come off the line. Such is the case with this postwar Bugatti.

First we introduce onstage the snow-haired and urbane Virgil Exner Sr., who was one of the most tasteful designers in Detroit in the Fifties. It is he who is credited with bringing the tailfin to Detroit, where his "Forward Look" tailfinned cars at Chrysler rivaled GM's Cadillacs.

Now this story involves another legend, that of Bugatti—a storied name in the car collecting world. Started by Ettore Bugatti in the 1920s, Bugatti built racing cars that were state of the art in the 1920s and eventually built luxury cars, the Royale being the grandest one of all (only six built).

According to the website www.madle.org, "Ettore's death in 1947 split what could be recovered of the Bugatti enterprise into two camps along the lines of the families of his two marriages. Yet, out of this disorder, the allure of the Bugatti automobile emerged, not only from its honoured tradition, but also from, it seems, a sense of duty felt by the family, the workers, and the designers who had laboured under Le Patron's influence."

Four years after Ettore's death, the family patched up its differences and rebuilt the factory. Historians credit general manager Pierre Marco, working with Roland Bugatti, the son of Bugatti from his first marriage, with getting the new design rolling down the assembly line.

The first one to come along was at the 1947 Paris Salon, the Type 73 (a car that could be used for racing and for the road). Some feel the project was a bit too ambitious, and it never got beyond the prototype stage. But it still showed Bugatti had survived the war. Meanwhile, Bugatti put food on the table by taking orders for parts and service for the Bugatti-powered rail cars, production of weaving looms and machining work for Citroen.

Slightly more successful, coming along in 1951, was the Type 101. This new model was based on the pre-War Type 57 and powered by a 3.3-liter dual overhead-cam inline eight mated to a Cotal electrically-controlled gearbox. In fact the first car built was an actual prewar Type 57 rebuilt to be the new model. Several modifications were made to update the engine from its prewar design, including replacing of the Stromberg carburetor with a down-draught Weber unit. One model, the T191C, had a supercharger.

The suspension was still a semi-independent front setup with a live rear axle. The bodies had a full-width streamlined envelope design—no longer separate fenders like before the war—still with the traditional "horseshoe" radiator grille. Three bodybuilders this author has found represented on these '50s Type 101s (besides the feature car here) were Guilloré, Gangloff and Antem. Their cars were interesting but had nothing like the grandeur of the prewar Type 57s.

They only made it to 1956 with this model, only a handful made. The postwar Bugattis of the Fifties failed, not because of their styling or performance, but because of a horrendous tax on engine displacement imposed by the French government, enough to make the annual taxes imposed on owners too onerous.

So the sad story is that only six chassis/engine combinations (another source says 7, still another 8) were built of the 101 before the revived Bugatti company closed its doors. Yet there was one chassis that hadn't been bodied, one sent to Italy to a coachbuilder and never bodied. Its SN was #101506, which leads one to suspect there were only six type 57 chassis laid down in the Fifties, not seven and not eight. The engine number of this car was 101506-C which you can see on the data plate on the car.

AN AMERICAN DESIGN

That car became a unique car, one created by two of Detroit's most independent designers—the Exners, father and son, both of whom had worked for Detroit automakers and now were on their own in a studio right off Woodward Ave. (where your author used to peek through the windows, hoping to see a new design).

It was almost serendipity that they got the chassis. Chassis #101506 had been built in France, shipped to Italy and was sitting at Ghia. And Ghia owed the Exners money—a mere $2,500. In lieu of a cash payment, the chassis was given by Ghia to the Exners (Sr. and Jr.) in 1961 as payment for their design work on the Due-senberg "revival" cars—an ill-fated venture in the U.S. involving a relative of the famed Duesenberg family, where an all-new proto-type was built bearing the name Duesenberg.

The Exners, now independent of Detroit automakers, were look-ing for a chassis on which to base an all-new design. Since they could get this one for free, and it already carried a storied name, they chose it to build an actual car that fulfilled in part Virgil Exner's "classic" prewar revival designs which had been featured in an article in *Esquire* magazine.

The Exners were hoping the Bugatti-based prototype would result in orders which, if the Bugatti chassis was no longer avail-able, presumably could go on some other chassis.

When the Exners sent Ghia a scale model of their design for the car, Ghia shortened it by 46cm. The press releases at the time said the body was designed by Virgil Exner Sr. while Virgil Exner Jr. designed the interior. It took Ghia half a year to build the steel-bodied one-off which made its debut at the Turin Salon in 1965. The design did much to fulfill Virgil Exner's dream of creating a whole line of modern cars that reflected the design themes of the prewar era where some "grand routier" cars had long hoods and short tails and small passenger compartments; but at that point in time the world wasn't ready for such grand conceptions and no one ordered a copy. It was probably good that they didn't— Bugatti couldn't make any more chassis anyway.

The fact that the Bugatti factory stopped making cars around 1956 and this car wasn't presented until nine years later is looked at askance by some purists who figure that, it might have a Bugatti chassis but it was made "out of sequence." Their thought would be that it can't be considered in the same ball park—in terms of historical significance—as those type 101s bodied while Bugatti was still making cars. In a way you can understand their objections. If a P-51 Mustang is assembled after V-J day in 1945 it is technically no longer a WWII plane but a WWII-era plane. Still this car has significance more as a "personality-connected" car in this case the personalities being Virgil Exner, Sr. and Jr. If you like some of their other designs and want in your own way to pay tribute to their talents, owning something they designed is one way to do it. The car went from the Exners to auction magnate Thomas Barrett III who then sold it to Irving Tushinsky who sold it to someone who sold it to the Blackhawk Behring Museum in 1984 who sold it in 1988 to Gen. William Lyon, a California property developer who later sold it.

In this author's opinion, the car is a never-to-be-repeated homage to the beauty of naturally finished metal, there being several types of brass and copper on the car, finished different in different areas of the car. And it's a fitting rendition in metal of the drawing for such a car depicted by Exner in *Esquire*. Lesson to be learned? Well, you would have been watching the Bugatti family's fortunes to know they had failed in '56, but the point is that this last chassis was available for several more years could have been found out. Presumably it could have been bought from Ghia, who still needed money to pay back the Exners. So, the lesson is—if you want a handbuilt European car—go to those coachbuilders, or any automaker's outside suppliers to see if they have unfinished cars they would very much like to clear from the books. When auto companies die, there's always leftovers, and in this case the Exners knew where to go.

Now I can hear you, the reader, saying: "Sure, I'll just fire up the ol' time machine, and go back to the failure of X and Y company and do that," but the point is that automakers fail all the time. Just recently Oldsmobile and Pontiac, to name two. And they always have unfinished cars sitting on the line the day the axe falls. Need I mention Fisker or the failed attempt at a revived Cunningham? And there's many more—dozens of automakers have failed since WWII. Of course it's a crap shoot for the barn finder to be able to guess which modern era car from a failed automaker will be worth more in the future, but suffice to say one glance at Bugatti's more than 1,000 racing victories should have been a hint in 1961 that, even though a great name was going down, anything built by them would be a keeper. And even a revived one-off would be a collector's item with its coachwork designed by Detroit's only father-son design team, and then built by a legendary Italian coachbuilder. So this was a "double barnfind"—first of all the Exners scoring the chassis from Ghia and secondly for those who owned it subsequently, a car with three pedigrees so to speak.

Chapter 19
A CAR FIT FOR A KING?
(1954 DeSoto Adventurer II)
Well, apparently not.

When the soldiers and sailors and airmen came back from World War II, they were ready for new cars. When World War II ended, automobile makers were not quite ready to offer new designs. Chrysler got their all-new designs out by 1949. The problem was that company president K.T. Keller was a champion of good engineering but didn't have a handle on what was good styling. Ford and GM were running circles around him in that regard.

Especially that damn Harley Earl at GM who would have million dollar show cars built and drive them around, getting people excited about GM styling. Chrysler got the idea when Keller left the presidency of Chrysler Corp. in late 1950 and Lester "Tex" Colbert arrived to take up the cause. There had already been one Chrysler prototype done at Ghia in Italy so when he met Virgil Exner, who had already been with the firm a year, it was a marriage made in heaven.

Under Colbert, Exner was "green lighted" on many more show cars which would be bodied in Italy including the Chrysler K-310, Chrysler C-200, Chrysler Special, Dodge Firearrow, DeSoto Adventurer I, etc. Ironically Chrysler never produced a car that had the complete bodywork done in Italy (other than the run of

55 turbine cars, which were still experimental—see Whoosh chapter) but you can see Ghia influences in many Fifties Chrysler cars.

Colbert was also an engineering guy and it was he who helped make the Chrysler Hemi V8 one of the firm's most appealing sales points. The Hemi had been under development since 1935 but was finally produced in 1951, offered in Chryslers and Imperials first. Chrysler's "Fire Power" V8 displaced 331 cubic inches while Dodge, DeSoto, and Plymouth Divisions got smaller, less powerful versions in following model years. DeSoto's Hemi displaced 276.1 cubic inches and provided 160 hp for 1953 and 170 hp for 1954. The beauty of the hemi-head was that it offered more power from a given displacement without the need for high octane fuel. The key was the hemispherical combustion chamber shape (thus the name). The design minimized the chance for pre-ignition, allowing higher volumetric efficiency, and making for a cooler running engine.

THE ADVENTURER II

This was a one-off "dream car," one of a whole series of almost 40 show cars bodied in Italy, the styling of which was usually directed by Virgil Exner, Sr. The car was built on the S-19 Series chassis, which had a wheelbase of 125.5 inches, but was a two seater coupe, almost sinfully wasteful to have just two seats considering how long it was. It was powered by a DeSoto "Red Ram" V8 rated at 170 hp, and used a two-speed Powerflite automatic transmission.

Though it was named the Adventurer II, it didn't share a single line with the preceding first Adventurer, a four-passenger car. That one was all Exner though, built by Ghia in Italy. The Adventurer II came about because Exner had fallen in love with pictures of a Fiat 8V that Detroiter Paul Farago, a man with a shop doing imports, had imported, the first one carrying the "Supersonic" body designed by Giovanni Savonuzzi, a man with aircraft design experience. That car had been built at Ghia on a tube-framed Alfa Romeo racecar chassis conceived by famed tuner Virgilio Conrero for the 1953 Mille Miglia. There were approximately 50 8V cars made in all (the odd name resulted from Fiat mistakingly thinking Ford owned the name "V8") but only a few had this body. When Exner saw the design in person, he wanted it for the Chrysler show cars and decided to upscale the design for a follow-up car to the Adventurer.

In one way his decision was to haunt him, as by adopting an off-the-shelf pre-existing body that was already out on the market, the resulting Chrysler car looked like some of the other cars that had already received the Supersonic body, including an Alfa 1900, a Jaguar XK-140 and a 1956 Aston Martin DB2/4 Mk. II.

The DeSoto Adventurer II was rolled out to show the press on June 16, 1954, at the new Chrysler proving grounds near Chelsea, Michigan. It went to its European debut at the Turin Auto Show that same year. Surprisingly, for a magazine that slavishly praised Detroit cars (in hopes of selling ads to automakers), in its August 1954 issue *Motor Trend* trash-talked the styling of the Adventurer II, saying the car's "slab sides and illusion of excessive width" violated Exner's philosophy of "emphasis on the mechanical beauty and function of an automobile." Their criticism had some merit as the Chrysler chassis was huge compared to the smaller European chassis the same body was used on (it didn't upscale well). But Virgil Exner Jr. quoted in *Road & Track's Exotic Cars Quarterly* that his father approved of the car's styling and "realized that Savonuzzi was not only a great engineer but had a terrific styling eye." That comment shows that Exner was not a mere copyist of Italian design because when the Italians came up with something he liked more than a Chrysler design, he liked to let them run with it.

The car had a couple of unique features. The rear window was retractable into the body, and it had fitted luggage, meaning it was a two seater just right for a weekend trip. It was necessary to put the luggage inside the cockpit because the spare tire and wheel took most of the luggage space in the trunk.

ENTER THE KING

After the Turin Auto Show in the summer of '54, the history of the Adventurer II is a bit unclear. The Chrysler dealer in Casablanca purchased the show car at an auction following the auto show in Brussels. This was Chrysler's way of getting some of the development cost back, and besides, there might have been the problem of having to pay duty on the bodywork if they kept it in the U.S. According to *Exotic Cars Quarterly*, the dealer had bought the car thinking it would be something that would appeal to Morocco's King Mohammed V, who had triumphantly resumed his Kingship duties after being exiled for a while to the island

Corsica by the French, whose meddling in Moroccan affairs he heartily opposed. The dealer got the car to the King for a sample drive all right but the car must have not infatuated him because His Royal Highness returned it a week later. The dealer then displayed the Adventurer II in his showroom while hoping someone would be willing to pay the $25,000 asking price. This is where an American working in Morocco, Art Spanjian, saw an opportunity. He kept working on the car dealer for three years trying to get it for less. He finally won over the dealer but *Exotic Cars Quarterly* says only that the price was between $2,500 and $10,000, still a lot of money in those days when a two bedroom home in the San Fernando Valley was maybe $25,000. He took it back to the U.S. where he was going to be the chief of Maintenance Planning in Dayton, Ohio.

By around 1960, the Adventurer II was once again in a showroom—this time at a Chrysler-Plymouth dealership in Dayton, Ohio. It was sold on December 26, 1960, to a Florida enthusiast, Fort Lauderdale resident Armand Archer, Sr., a developer from Fort Lauderdale who saw it during a Christmas visit, bought it and drove it home. Another account, on conceptcarz.com says Armand Archer bought it, making no mention of Art Spanjian whatsoever. (Hey, don't you think he gets credit for finding the car in Morocco?) But whatever the timeline of owners, Archer no sooner got it home before he began worrying about the downsides of owning a one-off car—a car where no body panels were available, or glass. One accident and he would have to look for someone who could hand-make those parts. So he locks it in the garage. *Hemmings*, in an article on their blog website reprinted from *Special Interest Autos* by a great barn-finding zealot, Michael Lamm, stated Archer went to work in Europe for ten years while the car sat at a friend's house in Florida…for 25 years.

It was rescued by his son, Armand Archer Jr., a commercial airline pilot, who finally got the car out of storage in 1986. It was still a low-mileage car, at 15,000 miles, and still shod with its original Dayton General tires. In 1988, Ken Behring, the collector who started the Blackhawk Museum in Northern California, bought it to be a star of his collection. He had it restored in time to make the 1989 Pebble Beach Concours. Another story of how it got to the Museum, one confirmed by Michael Lamm in his extensive article in *Special Interest Autos*, is that an anonymous West Coast collector bought the car, had it restored, and then kindly donated it to the Behring Auto Museum.

Several websites report the car, SN 1493862, sold in 2012 at the Barrett-Jackson auction in Scottsdale for $1,430,000. When I last heard of the Adventurer II, it is part of the collection of San Diego resident Chuck Swimmer.

Lesson to be learned here? First, the American in Morocco recognized that, if the King wasn't interested, there wasn't much chance the dealer could sell it to anyone local so kudos to him for keeping the pressure on until he got the car. Secondly, anybody who had seen the car in Ohio should have kept the Armand family on their periodic re-contact list, because it turned out they had it moldering away in the garage for a quarter century. In the old car world a 25-year shot at buying a car ought to be enough opportunity.

Odds are a copy of a cashier's check sent to them out of nowhere would have carried some weight. I have found cashier's checks carry a great deal of weight (see final chapter for strategies). Of course once the car was restored, it vaulted up into the million-dollar class but the main lesson here is that some cars are still where they were 10, 20 or 25 years ago so, no matter how cold you think that trail is, old leads are worth pursuing.

Chapter 20

THE PRINCES PLEASURE
(1964 ROLLS ROYCE CONVERTIBLE)

When you are a monied Prince, it's like having a time machine.

This is one of those "Once upon a time" stories. In *Vanity Fair* back in 2010 Mark Seal wrote a story about the Sultan of a country called Brunei that sits on the large island of Borneo, in Southeast Asia. The place was hardly noticed by the rest of the world, Seal explains, until 1926 when oil was discovered. The country was subservient to England. The jackpot came in '84 when the country became independent. Only three years later the Sultan of Brunei was the richest man in the world with a fortune estimated at $40 billion.

As Seal says: "As word spread of the sultan's gaping wallet, merchants from all corners of the globe swarmed into Brunei, selling him practically everything they had to offer—17 private jets, thousands of luxury cars, what one diamond dealer called "a Smithsonian" of major jewels, and a trove of art masterpieces, including a Renoir for a record $70 million."

Now it turns out that the Prince's younger brother, Prince Jefri, was a major car guy. Oh, he liked other things, such as his yachts (naming one of his "Tits," and its tenders "Nipple 1" and "Nipple 2"), polo ponies, five-star hotels (the Dorchester, in London, the

Hôtel Plaza Athénée, in Paris, the New York Palace, and Hotel Bel-Air and the Beverly Hills Hotel, in Los Angeles. These aren't hotels he stayed at, he bought each of those hotels! I won't even mention the women. Boy, were there women! And cars, boy oh boy did Jefri like cars.

So here's the story in brief on how Prince Jefri went back in his time machine and created a Rolls Royce Silver Cloud III convertible. First a little history on the model is in order…The Rolls-Royce Silver Cloud was the basic offering of Rolls Royce from April 1955 until March 1966. It replaced the smaller Silver Dawn, and in turn was replaced by the more modern Silver Shadow. J. P. Blatchley is credited with the Cloud's design (except for the Mulliner Park Ward variant designed by a Norwegian named Koran).

The Silver Cloud III was the last of the Silver Clouds. It came along in in 1963. It had a slightly more powerful engine. The transmission was a GM Hydramatic which Rolls-Royce used under license, oddly a 3-speed compared to the previous 4-speed automatic. Though shocking at the time, the Cloud III had quad headlamps. The drop-head coupe was the way Brits described the convertible version, the soft top being the "head." Rolls made Rolls-Royce produced 2,044 SCIIIs, but only a few were convertibles.

Now it happened that one day in the 1990s, Prince decided he wanted a Silver Cloud convertible. Maybe he had owned one before or seen one in his worldly hop-scotching. He called up Rolls to relay his request. They replied something to the effect of: "But we haven't made that car for decades." Clearly they were appalled by the request. Many of the people who had built the originals had retired or died, including the original designer Batchley. And the Cloud had its flaws, to note a few: the brakes, the handling, the ride—all inadequate compared to modern Rolls Royces. But even Rolls would admit you couldn't knock its elegance, its sheer presence. It made a statement, no doubt about that.

And the Prince was too important a person to turn down. A book written on Rolls after the year 2000 asserts it was the special orders for special cars from Brunei that kept the firm afloat until it could be bought by a larger automaker (in this case BMW). It turns out that RR was not the only beneficiary of their munificence—they were also ordering special models from Ferrari and Aston Martin, cars not on the books so to speak.

Now back to the Prince's pleasure. He wanted what he wanted.

And isn't the customer always right? So Rolls sent word out and a regular four-door steel saloon, chassis #SFU197, was found and bought, a car with very low mileage. It had been built for Sir C.J. Graham of N. Ireland and delivered new to him in early 1964.

The car was first cut down into a two-door drophead coupe (the reason it looks different than merely making a four-door into a two-door is that the front door in the dropheads and two-door coupes are longer than the sedan doors), and then various improvements made to the driveline, including modern braking. It took Rolls two years to build it. The only modifications to spec, according to the dealers who have handled it since, were the fitting of an alternator, full air-conditioning and boot-mounted CD player. The exterior color choice was bright red, you might say "fire engine red."

The hides are Magnolia with red piping. Now the choice of red for the exterior and red piping for the interior might be quibbled with by a purist but we're talking assuaging the whims of royalty here. When the Prince took delivery of it, as far as this writer can recall from reading an article in a British magazine long ago, he didn't like it as much as he thought he would. Either Rolls had updated it mechanically too much and it wasn't feeling like the ones he'd driven before or maybe he had been exposed to too many more modern exotic luxury cars and it was too "old hat." Whatever, the car was ordered sold.

When offered in the late 1990s by Lawrence Millett, the car had only 2,000 miles on it and was priced at $250,000. When last heard of the car was at a collection in Las Vegas, still for sale but you have to apply to get a price quote. Now I can hear you asking: "But how could you possibly consider a cut-car, i.e. a convertible cut from a sedan, even collectible?" I hear ya. Here's the answer: true, this is a "cut car," but it was cut by none other than Rolls Royce, the very same people who engineered, designed, and built the originals, so in a sense it's still a factory-built drophead coupe just like all the other Silver Cloud drophead coupes.

Now the next problem, one more insurmountable, is that it was built out-of-sequence, way, way out of sequence, like decades later. That is only a problem for the historians, the ones who wrote books up to the '80s with what they thought were the correct numbers of SCIIIs made. Well, get over it. Rich people do things like that. There's a guy in Michigan that wanted a P51 Mustang fighter plane. So he builds one, from scratch. Others have brand new yachts built that, from the outside, resemble classic yachts of the 1930s. Old is in. Or I should say, looking old is in. I could go on, but you get the point. If you have the money, you can buy whatever you want whenever you want (though there was some financial scandal later about the Prince's expenditures, which we won't go into here).

Your next quibble, I suspect, is going to be the price. Well, I'll catch flak for this but I think back when it was priced at $250,000 it was a bargain. Why? Because other dead stock SCIII dropheads are getting there already, and this one has Royalty attached (albeit briefly). Lesson to be learned here? There's oddball cars out there, cars like this that don't meet the rules. But who, I ask, makes the rules? Ordinary men, not princes. I agree there are rules, but if you are an automaker, and there's a prince waiting in the lobby ordering a car, and he's a billionaire, you break the damn rules—enough said.

Chapter 21

THE LOST LIGHTWEIGHT
(1963 JAGUAR E-TYPE)
*Hey, after you've flown an airplane nearly 1,900 mph,
any racecar is slow.*

There are heroes that walk the earth. Heroes in my book any-how—guys like Howard Gidovlenko who was an all-American hero, a decorated fighter pilot and World War II ace for the RAF. After the war, he continued to go fast, having his own tuned up, clipped-wing P51 Mustang. But flying for fun wasn't enough, so he volunteered to be a test pilot on the X2 rocket plane and thus was a friend and compadre to legendary American flying hero Chuck Yeager.

Sometime after his flying career was winding down, Howard got in his head that he was a race driver. After all, what was the big deal about toddling along at 150 mph when you've piloted a plane at nearly 2,000 mph?

In pursuit of this goal, Gidovlenko bought a slightly used Jaguar XKE roadster from British Motors of San Francisco, Jaguar distributors and retailers with an eye toward going racing.

NOT YOUR ORDINARY E-TYPE

According to the website Coventry-Classics.com, "Unlike the D Type, the E Type was never designed as a racing car but that did not stop the factory backing certain well known privateers. Graham Hill for Equipe Endeavour in ECD400 and Roy Salvadori for John Coombs in BUY1 had some success during 1961 against the all-conquering Ferrari 250 GT racers but it was clearly a contest between a road car (the E type) and a purpose-built racecar (the Ferrari) which was 6 cwt lighter. No Jaguars appeared at Le Mans in 1961. But during 1961 John Coombs' car was effectively a works' development car. It was rebuilt with a thinner gauge steel monocoque reappearing at the start of 1962 with a wet sump D Type engine, uprated brakes and suspension and an aluminum hardtop. This car was written off (British racing slang for 'smashed beyond repair') at the Goodwood Easter meeting (Salvadori) and rebuilt by the factory to what would become the specs for all the lightweight roadsters. Subsequently 11 more full lightweight E type roadsters were built plus another two semi-lightweight fastback coupes. All survive."

The specs included a full aluminum monocoque, an all alloy 3.8-liter dry sump engine, a D-type wide angle cylinder head, Lucas mechanical fuel injection, a 5-speed ZF gearbox, MK IX disc brakes, a bolted and vented aluminum roadster hardtop, aluminum bonnet, doors and vented bootlid, a wider rear track using modified MK X wishbones, altered front suspension with anti-dive geometry, a lowered steering rack, competition seats and special Dunlop slotted alloy wheels similar to those used on D types. This removed 600 pounds in weight compared to the stock E-type roadster. On paper, with over 340 hp, the lightweight E Type seemed to be a match for the Ferrari 250 GTO. But because of reliability problems many of the all-alloy engines and ZF gearboxes were soon replaced with standard D-Type cast iron engines and Moss gearboxes.

All this alloy content gave them the name "Lightweights" and made up for the engine not being up to snuff compared to the Ferraris, even though mighty efforts were made to pump up the horsepower.

Now, considering the Federation d'Internationale d'Automobile (FIA) race sanctioning organization required that 100 identical cars be made at that time for a car to be considered "production," you kind of wonder how Jaguar got the lightweight approved when they only made twelve. Paul Skilleter, the British Jaguar historian, explains in his book *Jaguar Sports Cars* that Jaguar claimed the steel-bodied one was the racecar and the aluminum-chassied one was the production car, hence if it was classified as a production car, the FIA would assume its numbers would be vastly more than the racecar. It was a mightier trick than Ferrari had played with the 250GTO, having it homologated as "an evolution of type," basically a swb250GT with a different body though it was almost a completely different car.

MILLIONAIRE'S TOY VANISHES

Jaguar managed to crank out twelve Lightweights (and two spare bodies) in 1963. The American multimillionaire sportsman Briggs Cunningham pressed Button A and ordered four of them when he got the word on availability, all to be painted the American colors of white and blue (back in those days each country had a designated color, Britain British Racing Green and so forth).

Now normally when a multi-millionaire, a man who is spending his own money to promote your brand of car, orders several special cars, you as an automaker bend over backwards and say, "Yessir, yessir, three bags full."

But somehow there was many a slip between the cup and the lip with that one car and wouldn't cha' know, one of Cunningham's lightweights, chassis S850659, was sold instead to West Coast Jaguar distributor British Motor Cars, an outfit run by Norwegian immigrant Kjell Qvale (pronounced SHELL CUE-VOLLEY).

Hey, all's fair in love and war. Qvale was not just some multi-millionaire out for a lark like Cunningham. He was a businessman and had a business to promote. And damn it, having a car you sponsor win races was part of the promotion (take that, Briggs!) Qvale didn't waste any time getting it to a significant race. The car was such an important find (or should we say "steal"?) for Qvale, that he had it air-freighted directly to Miami, where he picked it up himself. Then in the Grand Olde British tradition it was driven on the regular highway right to Sebring where it was wheeled into the pits for the 12 Hours of Sebring and further prepared for the upcoming race.

This all no doubt annoyed Cunningham mightily as the car he "lost" to Qvale arrived at Sebring painted in Cunningham's white and blue livery, which would of course have caused consternation in the Cunningham pits when they saw one of "their" cars ignoring their pit signals. So some red paint was found in the pits and stripes added to the Qvale car to distinguish the car from the immaculate Cunningham Equipe's entries. The future Gidovleno car also began to take on a more home-built look with holes being cut here and there and strengthening parts welded on.

But damned if the car wasn't a purebred thoroughbred which came through in the stretch (sorry for all these horsy terms…it's one of my hobbies).

With drivers Ed Leslie and Frank Morrill it finished first in class and seventh overall—trouncing not only Cunningham's lightweight Jag E-type piloted by Walt Hansgen and Bruce McLaren, but all the other Jaguars entered. It had the best finish for the Jaguar marque of any of the Lightweights run in the Sixties in major international races. Qvale continued to sponsor the car for the rest of the season, and at the end of the year, it was an old, used racecar (and believe you me a brand new car can be reduced to being an old used car in just one season of racing).

Okay, maybe I was using a little used-car lot lingo when I said "slightly used." The truth was it was thrashed, rode hard and put away wet. Even that half-day run at the 12 Hours of Sebring in '63 had resulted in cracks which some dimwit thought could be prevented from spreading by drilling holes in the end of the cracks. It was sold for the reported sum of $5,230 to Gidovlenko.

Howard was not deterred by the fact he had no racing experience to speak of. He had, after all, piloted a rocket plane, so what was the big deal about 150 mph? Piece of cake.

Gidovlenko wrote the factory in '64 as part of his plan to run the car at the famous Daytona 24 Hours in 1964. He had taken delivery of a long range oil tank, and asked them how he could have larger section wheel rims to fit wider rubber. There was also correspondence back and forth to Coventry regarding the 5-speed ZF gearbox from Germany and Lucas fuel injection. But after all these letters were answered and some parts sent, the car never appeared at Daytona. Jaguar didn't hear from the owner for some time. The semi-official word was that his racing ambitions were conflicting with his booming marine-racing-engine business. It could have been maybe Gidovlenko was realizing that Shelby's damn Cobras—with their crude cast-iron lumpkin proletariat pushrod Ford V8—were now masters of the game.

Another reason the factory helping Howard realize his ambitions wasn't happening might be that the factory realized by 1964 it was all over. The sad truth was that the lightweight was two years too late in being fielded and was never sufficiently developed enough to beat the 250GT0s.

So what happened to the lightweight Jag? It became a recluse. No races. No Sunday jaunts to the beach. It became a garage queen, seen by none.

THE BIG SLEEP

It sat in Mission Viejo, a suburb in Orange County, California, for the next 35 years, sleeping in the confidence that it had scored well for Jaguar in its one and only race. One magazine explained why the car was not prettied up, or driven. They scurrilously reported that "a costly divorce was looming" and, as any car enthusiast who has been this route knows, it wouldn't do to have a four-wheeled asset look too spiffy or the wife's divorce lawyer might not just see it as a scuzzy old car (been there myself, actually). So the report further alleged that the owner himself took a machine tool to the car to scar up the outside so anybody looking at the car would conclude it was a candidate not for a racetrack but a junkyard (shame on you, Howard!).

Howard died in early 1998. According to a Forbes magazine article published in 2003 by Michael Frank, after 35 years of zero happening with the car, things happened fast. "(The) family was clearing out his personal effects and discovered an old sports car hidden under a number of boxes. Not realizing how significant the car was, the family put out a message on the Internet appealing for any information."

Terry McGrath, an Australian Jaguar expert and author, recalled to the author how the car was discovered by the Jaguar crowd: "Basically Paul Skilleter received an e-mail on the 19th Feb 1998 that he read (initially) as a bit of a scam. (It said something to the effect of: We have an all-aluminum XKE for sale there are only 2 one in the U.K. one in my dad's. He has recently passed away. If you are interested....)."

"Paul forwarded me the e-mail by fax (I wasn't on e-mail at that point) about 3 weeks later and I got it after midnight but the inference from Paul was that it was a joke or someone who didn't know the difference between steel and aluminum."

"Anyway I got the fax around 1 am in the morning, and having nothing better to do, rang the number provided (in California) and someone answered."

"The person at the other end of the line couldn't quote a car number as it was buried but quoted an engine number which was an alloy E type engine number but I wasn't sure if they weren't just quoting a number they had read as these numbers have all been written up in books. He noted the engine and gearbox were on a stand and asking the number of gearbox he said ZF70 and that's when (I got excited because) I knew this was the real thing."

"I rang Paul Skilleter (another Jaguar historian—Ed.) back and asked if he wanted to fly out to take pics as he was sort of closer from U.K. to L.A. than Western Australia to L.A....then there was the cost. We decided to call Terry Larson (a Jaguar expert in Arizona) who flew out the next morning insisting (beforehand that the car owners) on the people not to touch a thing, leave it as it was. This was all written up in Paul Skilleter's *Jaguar World* magazine who got the story."

Jaguar expert Terry Larson did some minor repairs and reinstalled the motor and gearbox but this was one of the great barn-find cars so effort was made to keep its genuine patina (a restorer's word for dust) on the car and it went that way to auction.

It generated a lot of interest.

The entire Jaguar world was now aware that the "lost Lightweight"—believed destroyed in 1963—had been found in a private garage in Mission Viejo, California, completely untouched and with less than 3,400 miles on the odometer!"

Somehow an auction company had gotten in touch with them, and it was a good choice as RM is one of the best auction companies (having their own restoration shop) and RM Auctions picked their Monterey event in August 1998 to roll the Lightweight across the stage during what has now become one week of heaven; known as the Monterey Car Week.

There the 40-year old factory racecar, still with its factory-installed piston rings and valve springs, and with a tad less than 3,350 miles showing on the odometer, sold for $1,375,000.

The buyer was an Englishman, who, not wanting to dent an already-dented car, air-freighted it back to Blighty where a restoration was planned in the words of *Forbes* magazine: "to preserve all of the car's many original aspects," i.e. leave the car looking like it had when found. The Sussex-based Jaguar experts Lynx Motors International did the race prep and it ran in the March 1999 Sebring Historic Racing Endurance Challenge where it showed its mettle by winning its class in the two races it ran.

The True Brit's attitude was a big change in vintage racing. Whereas before old cars dragged from the barn were treated to from-the-ground-up restorations, the philosophy for this car was: "Nothing on the car will be modified or altered. Only work required for safe recommissioning will be undertaken." No doubt owners of restoration shops were seen weeping in both the U.K. and in America. Attitudes like that could start a trend. Who needs painters?

Lesson to be learned here?

Shame on all the wanna-be barn finders who, before 1998 (the year the car came to light) claimed they loved Jags. After all, we are not dealing with a "nobody" here. Howard had an outsize persona—he should not have been that hard to find. Look at who he was—a prominent war veteran, well-known in aircraft and powerboat fields, resident of Orange County for over 35 years, homeowner, a very unusual name, and grown children that probably could have been found. Even a brand new cub detective with peach fuzz on his face could have found Howard and the car in one day. (How cheap are we? Compare the cost of a detective for one day to what the car sold for unrestored). Now, this is not to say that, Howard, if broached on the subject, would have entertained thoughts of selling it, but the key thing here (and, please, read the last chapter for more strategies) is that, as a barn finder, your first task is finding a significant car. Once you've found it and ascertained it is both rare and has great appreciation potential, then you plan your approach. Much like, say, a fighter pilot. Howard would say, first you put the target in your sights, then you poise your finger on the trigger, and then you move in for the kill.

Chapter 22
HERE BE DRAGONS
(1954 MERCEDES 300SL GULLWING)
In the '50s, nothing said exotic more than gullwings.

In the old maps of the 16th century, cartographers would draw the continents (as much as they knew of anyway) and then, in the areas which they weren't sure of, where there was just open ocean, they would explain the failure of explorers to go there by drawing foreboding creatures and write the legend: "Here be dragons." Well, that's a warning for those investing in old cars. Like that hapless Washington politician used to say: "You don't know what you don't know." Here's another one of my personal stories to show you I've been in the trenches; and, I warn you, for me it's not a story with a happy ending. (Not that I am trying to discourage you.)

The car involved is the fabulous Mercedes 300SL gullwing. I barn-found and owned two of them. First a little background in the model...Mercedes emerged from WWII much battered, even building some cars in buildings without roofs. One of their first entries into the luxury car field after the war was the 300 sedan, followed by a two-seater 300S available as a coupe and convertible; but then they decided to get back into racing. Some engineers working on their own developed a sports car using a tubular bar space frame (that weighed only 181 pounds), with their 300 luxury car engine re-tuned to be a sports car engine. Management bought it, even if only for a racecar. In order to have a low hoodline, they tilted the straight six over. The first racing ones had carburetors but eventually they went to fuel injection in the production version. The "gullwing" got its unique doors because at first the frame was so high on the sides you couldn't have doors deep enough for normal doors so they cut a door into the roof and then had it go down to where the side frame tubes ended. They were successful in racing, especially in the Carrera Panamericana in Mexico.

I was a young advertising copywriter in Detroit at the time I bought my first one. I was intrigued whenever I saw one. The first time I saw one was in Switzerland in '56 when I saw one stopped on the Brenner Pass as the occupants took pictures of the winding mountain road below. At one point after I graduated from college, a GM designer named Dan Hosler from Birmingham, Michigan, showed me his gullwing, which was apart at his house. He had bought it from GM who had studied the frame before building the Corvette SS racecar in '57. He didn't want to sell it so I asked him if he knew anyone else who had one and he said, "Well, I had a room-mate in college, a guy who bought two gullwings the same day—one for him and one for his father."

I asked for the fellow's name and even though it was a 10-to-12 year old lead he was throwing me, the guy's name was in the phone book, up in Toronto. I called and he still had the car. Well, I offered something like $4,000 (memory fades now) but there was one more hitch in my get along—there was a war going in South East Asia and I had joined the Army Reserve. I was scheduled for active duty in the U.S. Army. There I would get what, $50 a month? So I told him I would pay him $50 a month and collect the car when I got out. So when I finished my 4 1/2 months active duty at Ft. Bragg and other forts (never did go overseas) I called him up, borrowed a trailer and headed for Toronto. The car was a bit tacky, being stored in a basement and of course hadn't been run in years, but I loaded it on the trailer and headed for the Ambassador Bridge leading from Canada to Detroit.

Now there I admit I fibbed a bit on what I bought it for but some cognoscenti of a customs guy decided he knew what gullwings were really worth. He took my name as a person to be investigated; but it was Christmas Day or some such so there were so many Americans smuggling Johnny Walker whiskey across from Canada that they plumb forgot to call me. Plus there was another glitch: they compared the title with the number on the car and saw it was one number off! I realized the problem—the guy I had bought the car from had bought two gullwings the same day and, now decades later, had given me the wrong pink slip (title)! It was too late to get in touch with him in the middle of a bridge with traffic backed up for miles in each direction.

Once I got back to Berkley, Michigan, I went to the Department of Motor Vehicles to register it. They also considered the non-matching title vis-a-vis the VIN of the car to be a minor problem and registered it. No doubt five decades later two gullwing collectors are trying to figure out how there's two cars with the same serial number! I got the car home and trailered it to a Mercedes dealer where they got it running. The mechanic was suspicious when I said it had been running the other day when he saw all the spider webs on the engine. But he took it into the dealership and got it running.

THE RACE

I really didn't drive the car that much. It didn't start easily, always polluting the huge separate oil reservoir with raw gas as it tried to start up so that at some point you had to decide to change the many quarts of oil because when you took the reservoir cap off, it reeked of gasoline. The brakes were dodgey. I remember at speed, if I hit them hard the car would dart left or right. I was always wary of the rear wheels tucking under in cornering. It was something other gullwing owners didn't talk about, maybe because those who experienced it were dead and dead men tell no tales. Suffice to say, when Mercedes got to the roadster model in '57, they redesigned a rear axle with a low pivot that kept the rear wheels more upright in high speed cornering.

The car was also hot as hell with no A/C in Michigan's summer heat, and you couldn't roll down the windows; though you could take them out and keep them protected in little bags. Sometimes I'd drive down my street with the gullwing doors opened. One time one door opened by itself at speed (scary). I remember one laugh I had the first time I tried to fill the 32-gallon tank. I went to a station on nearby Woodward Ave. (the famous Vinsetta garage when they were still selling gas, not a restaurant) and at that time the pumps only went to $10 so when I got 7 or 8 gallons in and the pump reached $10 it went to zero and the gas jockey (back then you had gas station attendants to pump gas for you) looked under the car to see where it was leaking. I never did completely fill the tank until the day I sold it.

I had one race with it on fabled Woodward Ave against my room-mate's Suzuki X6 Hustler. He experienced wheelstand on acceleration which spooked him but I smoked him. I lived with my father at the time, in a 3 bedroom house but it only had a one-car garage. So I enjoyed the car for a few months but eventually winter was coming and pop wanted the garage for his car, a Pontiac Catalina. I was heartbroken. I couldn't envision parking the gullwing outside, where ice and snow would encase it for months at a time. I was too dumb to think of a place to store it (even though in retrospect we knew a farmer who had a barn and there was also the family farm out in Mendocino, California—imagine driving that car 2,500 miles in that time when many Western states still had no speed limit).

So I drove it to Chicago and sold it to Harry Woodnorth, an exotic car dealer who advertised cars in *Road & Track* classifieds. I think I got all of $2,500 for it. Lesson Learned? Ah...no.

LIGHTNING STRIKES TWICE

Living out in California in the '80s I went to an auction and was sitting on a deck chair next to a 300SL gullwing when a guy came up and said, "I got one of those." I said, "Is it for sale?" and wouldn't you know, it was. A few days later I went and looked at it. Like Hosler's car it was running but mostly apart. He was an airline pilot who had lost his job after sneaking a buddy aboard so they could go party after the flight. He got caught and lost his job. He wanted $7,000. Again, I was wary of buying a car that was apart. (Big mistake as you will see later.)

Then wouldn't you know there was a second guy who had come along at the same auction a few minutes later who also said, "I have one of those." I dutifully wrote down his number as well. After the first car didn't pan out, I call the second guy. His car is running. It's white. It's also a 1954 car (despite press releases that say gullwings are '55-57 models). He is also an architect. He is willing to sell it for $7,000 or $8,000 (the memory dims). I buy it. At the time I am living near the UCLA campus. My live-in girl-friend loans me $3,000 of the money for this investment.

I decided to get it painted. I took it to one hobbyist who restored

Jaguars at the time and he gives me a $300 figure but I yank the car away when I see him doing what I think is too much sanding, which to me will dull the subtle shape of the car (making it all soft and blobby like a 356 Porsche). Then I find a young man whose father is backing him in a new body shop and he does it right, making it metallic silver for I think $700. Again, I experience the problems in starting and braking. Again, I hardly ever drive it; compounded by the fact my apartment had only parking space for only one car.

I decide to sell it. I take it to the Kruse auction in Oakland, California, with my girlfriend following me in my Karmann Ghia. She keeps falling asleep on the way and drifting to the shoulder and I have to go back and wake her up. I go into the auction with a $17,000 reserve. The auctioneers press around me as the bids are coming in all too slowly and chant: "drop the reserve—sell the car, sell the car." All I can think of is: I have to sell it in order to pay my girlfriend back her $3,000. I sell it and they take their commission out of that $11,000 plus take a month to pay me; but in one way I was glad to sell it. Why? Because when it was sitting in the auction I heard a guy walk by and turn to his friend saying, "Look at the gullwing with the 190SL nose."

It was then I remembered that, when I had taken a piece of chrome to be rechromed for that second car, and told the chromer that I had bought a gullwing and who I bought it from, he said, "Yeah, I remember that car, hit all the way to the windshield." Then I realized, I'd been suckered—the car had been hit and repaired with a lower cost 190SL grille and front grille cavity pieces. I began to live in fear the new owner who had bought the car at auction would call and bitch, unwinding the deal (which happens). He did call, but only to report he was happy with the car, and only wanted to buy the bumper guards I hadn't put on the car.

I missed that car, especially as prices went higher, higher until today they are about $500,000 even for a steel one. You talk the 29 all-aluminum ones; they could go to a million, especially if it belonged to some legend like '50s playboy (and creator of the Scarab racecar) Count Lance Reventlow. Years after I sold it, I had a dream that, instead of lowering my reserve at that Oakland auction I had gotten into the car, put it in gear and driven it out onto Highway 101, pointed her North and three hours later pulled into the grounds of my uncle's farm in Mendocino. He had lots of chicken coops, each one big enough for a dozen cars, and no longer any chickens. In the dream I am climbing into the gullwing door, pulling out the choke and laboriously starting it. It roars into life and I smile, eagerly anticipating the drive to that little village of Mendocino for a cuppa java.

Then I woke up. It took me all of 15 minutes to realize it was only a dream, that I had indeed sold the car decades before. It was so realistic a dream that I could count the Phillips head screws on the dash, and feel the plaid cloth upholstery. I was furious at myself. Again. Looking back, I see another error. Legally I hadn't put my girlfriend's name on the car, I could have told her "tough luck, babe, I'm going to store the car up at the Ranch in Mendocino and I'll pay you back when I get around to it." But oh no, I was noble (Please don't say, "sucker"). So that ended my gullwing era.

Now, lessons learned: first, if you want to find a car, take a folding chair and food and drink container to an auction and plunk that chair down outside next to your favorite car and it's guaranteed some owners of that same car are going to come along and say they have one. Be ready to take notes. Secondly, I should have inspected that second car better and realized something was funny about the nose. Lesson No. 3? Buying a running car with the floor panels and interior out is no big deal. A running car is about 75-percent of where you want to be. The rest of the stuff on that cashiered pilot's car could have been installed in a day. In my case, the partly disassembled car would've been the one to buy, not the running driving one that had a duff body. Lesson No. 4 (the biggest lesson of them all): have a place to dead store the car if you run out of money to restore it or aren't ready to sell it. If you pick the right car in the first place, it could appreciate better than the Dow Jones Industrial average. Lesson No. 5: no partners, even wives (especially wives, as too many have insisted their husband sell a car at a loss so they can re-do the kitchen). If you own it by yourself, you alone can decide its fate.

Chapter 23
THE BEATLES-INSPIRED COBRA
(1966 COBRA MK. III)

Ars longa, vita brevis.

O kay, it's the Sixties. One bloke once said of the Sixties, "If you were there you don't remember it."

Let's just say there were a lot of social upheavals at the time, the psychedelic drug LSD was being touted by Dr. Timothy Leary (and still not illegal), cocaine was raining down everywhere and marijuana, well, that was just the beginning.

And in art, the new trend of pop art, a la Andy Warhol and Peter Max, was flourishing.

Over in the car world, failed chicken farmer Carroll Shelby was creating his immortal Cobras.

So it was that all these forces, for one brief shining moment, came together in the creation of an "art Cobra" that was only on stage in this livery for a nanosecond.

THE CHICKEN FARMER'S EXPRESS

First, allow me to indulge in a little mini-history of the Cobra... Fundamentally it was a Texan, one Carroll Hall Shelby, a failed chicken farmer, who became a sports car success. After a short career as a driver, he saw an opportunity by taking advantage of an English sports car that was reaching the end of its life. That car was the A.C. Ace, a solid little aluminum-bodied two-seater sports car that had done well with its Bristol six-cylinder engine until Bristol decided to stop making the engine. A.C. Cars Ltd. then turned to the 2.6-liter Ford Zephyr engine, but that engine moved the car into a racing class where it was no longer competitive. Then Carroll Shelby, a failed chicken farmer who had made a name for himself as a racing driver, saved the day with his bright idea of fitting a Ford V8 engine into it.

Ford had started making a lightweight V8 even though it was still cast iron, in 4.2-liter (260-cubic-inch) displacement.

A.C. partnered with Shelby on the Cobra and something close to 1,000 original Cobras were made (one figure you hear most is 998) to the year 1968, and today they are worth almost a half-million dollars each.

Now back to our subject car. It is one of the made-for-Britain Cobras that never saw Shelby's west coast Los Angeles plant. That deal was made because Shelby saw no sense in shipping chassis and bodywork all the way from England to California just to have the transmissions and engines installed, so there were separate series for England and for the Continent. The ones made for England had COB (Cobra of Britain) SN prefixes, the California built ones carried CSX (Carroll Shelby Experimental) numbers. The object of our affection here is COB6107, a coil spring 289, that left A.C.'s Thames Ditton factory on November 11, 1965. Now I know you Cobra guys are hopping up and down now saying, "if it's coil spring it must be big block," but this car was part of a special run for Europe. The Hurlock Brothers, who ran A.C., figured early on that the public in England wanted the 427 Cobra body style and coil springs but that, owing to much higher fuel costs, wouldn't be able to live with the hairy chested 427 or even its tamer 428 derivative (not advertised much but fitted to many a 427 Cobra by Shelby-American) so they offered the 271-hp small block 289 (4.7 liters) in the big block body style. They called it the "289 Sports" instead of the name Cobra, maybe some hint that they were tired of Shelby, who from their standpoint was a mere customer, taking all the credit for the Cobra. It had the advantage of the updated chassis design made for the big block including twin wishbone and coil spring suspension, and the more muscular looking body of the big block Cobra (though the narrow tires of 185-15 on 6.5x15-inch wheels looked lost in the huge wheel wells).

INTRODUCING THE RIGHT HONOURABLE TARA BROWNE

COB6107 was delivered new to the Right Honourable Tara Browne. Yes, that is how you introduce an aristocrat. (God am I glad we don't have aristocrats in the U.S.) He was what is called "a member of the gentry," fully entitled to the "Honourable" appellation. He was in fact also an heir to the vast Guinness brewery fortune.

Now it so happens that Browne wasn't only a car guy, he was in fact a young mop-topped lad tuned in to all that was new in the arts and pop music of the period. Those with long memories might know that this was the time of the Beatles' greatest flowering. He hung out with both the Beatles and the Stones, and various and sundry actors that were making the scene. There is even a photo of him spinning records with Paul McCartney! And it is a rumor that he was involved with the graphics on the *Sgt. Pepper's Lonely Hearts Club* production.

But I digress. Young master Browne picked up his Cobra once it was delivered to the dealer, Len Street Engineering Company Ltd. in Bayswater, and blasted over to the art studio of Dudley Edwards, who was at the time fast emerging as one of the most important artists of the pop-art scene, being in a group called Binder, Edwards and Vaughn ("BEV" for short)—Douglas Binder being one artist, Dudley Edwards another and Vaughn being the manager. They were doing psychedelic-themed murals for trendy boutiques on King's Road and Lord John on Carnaby Street. According to the website RockPopFashion.com, BEV also decorated interiors for Lord Snowdon, Paul McCartney and Ringo Starr, along with a stunning array of furniture and cars. "In fact," says the website, "it was Edwards who painted McCartney's piano; he lived with the Beatle for six months."

The website even quotes McCartney: "I wrote Getting Better on my magic Binder, Edwards & Vaughan piano. Of course the way in which it was painted added to the fun of it all."

Seeking greater exposure BEV thought the next logical thing to do to would be an "art" car.

Their first "art car" was a Buick convertible but, alas, when their manager got them a gig to show the Buick in Robert Fraser's gallery at 69 Duke Street, Mayfair, they found it wouldn't fit through the front window because of its gargantuan size, so a smaller car was sought.

Browne saved the day. Being a true patron of the arts, and adventuresome to boot, he commissioned Binder and Edwards to repaint his brand new Cobra as they saw fit. It came out similar to the Buick but the psychedelic paint scheme reflected more the curves of the Cobra. In a story by Steve Wakefield on the website ClassicCar.com, Wakefield quotes Edwards as saying: "I feel the effect of our dissonant colour combinations was somewhat akin to the chords played by Thelonious Monk."

For those who seek to emulate their work, the process was: a few coats of gesso sanded down to a "glass-like finish," then the color (household gloss paint mixed with Flamboyant Enamel) applied by hand.

And so it was that this psychedelic Cobra was created and became an "art car" well before Andy Warhol set his brushes onto a BMW M1. One report, which this writer hasn't authenticated, is that the plan was for Browne and a friend to later take the car to the U.S. and drive it across the country, no doubt blowing minds with not only the speed of the Cobra but the wild paint scheme. This was mentioned when the car, in all its psychedelic glory, was pictured in *LOOK* magazine. That trip must have been planned for the following spring, as the car was installed in the art gallery to be on display not so much as a car but as an "object d'art."

But then tragedy struck—on December 18, 1966, Browne, whilst enroute in a Lotus to see a new mural put on by BEV onto Dandie Fashions, a store he owned, blew through a red light near Earl's Court in London. He slammed into a truck (at a reported 100 mph!) and died of his injuries the following day. His girlfriend survived.

It is thought that Paul McCartney and John Lennon missed their friend so much that they incorporated the following lyrics into the anthem "A Day in the Life" from *Sergeant Pepper's Lonely Hearts Club* album, to whit:

"He blew his mind out in a car
He didn't notice that the lights had changed
A crowd of people stood and stared

They'd seen his face before
Nobody was really sure
If he was from the House of Lords"

The confusion was understandable. Browne's father Dominick Browne, actually was a member of the House of Lords (for 72 years)!

The Cobra wasn't involved, as it was already on display at the gallery on Duke Street in St James. After word of the accident arrived, the owners of the gallery were desolate. The car was removed forthwith from the display and, on the instructions of Lord Sligo, painted black and quickly sold.

Then the car vanished from the British scene.

REDISCOVERED IN AMERICA

At some point, the car was brought to America where it was owned for a time by John Tupasi of San Francisco, who painted in a light purple metalflake. Later, it went back to England where, for almost forty years, it was part of a private collection in Southern England.

Then Coys, a British car dealer, advertised it in 2013 and finally put it in an auction where it was estimated it would sell for between £300,000 to £350,000. In the pictures it still appeared to be a light metalflake purple. They were right on the money. A Bromley, England-based buyer bought it for £360,000 including buyer's premium which would be roughly $535,000 U.S. dollars.

Now we come to the ultimate question, which is more one for art historians (or whoever makes the rules in the highfalutin fine art world). Should this Cobra be re-painted in the exact same livery as the two artists painted it when they transformed into an "object d'art?" I don't know the rules of the art world (though I have in fact painted some of the illustrations in this book). Is anyone allowed to replicate an artist's art without the artist's permission? Or would in fact the artists themselves be interested? Your author opines it would be difficult to replicate the exact contours of the original paint scheme unless pictures could be unearthed showing the car from all angles, and even then, artists hate to paint the same picture exactly the same twice.

Art cars have become, in the years since Mr. Browne's untimely death, more prominent in collector's circles, most notably the BMW M1 racecar (painted by Andy Warhol in less than an hour I might add). In that car's case, the paint job is almost more important than the car itself!

Let's hope the new owner of COB6106 reads this suggestion… and forgives it being posed by someone who remains hopelessly nostalgic about England in the '60s. (And, yes, I do remember England in the '60s, even the first time my sister April mentioned a new band called "The Beatles." I had her spell out the name whereupon I said, "They spelled it wrong.")

Meanwhile, lesson learned? A car can have an identity not only as the model it is, and be prized for its styling, its rarity or its performance, but in some cases it can be very strongly identified with its owner, if the owner was, by chance, someone very celebrated or of renown. That was the case of this car, a car that, I contend, were it brought back to its BEV paint scheme, would be a tribute to its original owner and his exciting times (and might be worth double what it is now).

Chapter 24

WHEN PARTS LED TO A PORSCHE
(1955 PORSCHE SPEEDSTER)

Proving there's more than one way to skin a cat.

Now some guys happen across a car when they know nothing about that brand. Such is not the case with Matt Wright, who with his brother Adam, are among New York State's most rabid Porsche 356 aficionados. Adam describes it: "We are Porsche drivers and fanatics who escaped the business world 10 years ago to become full time peddlers of vintage Porsches through our company, Unobtanium Inc. When we're not enjoying back road cruising in either my 1960 Roadster or Matt's 1987 911 Carrera (nicknamed The Baboon) we can be found wandering the aisles of Porsche events and swap meets passing out Unobtanium's signature goodie bags, or ankle deep in mouse poop while scouring barns for forgotten Porsches."

The barn find here (and yes, this one was in a real barn, which has its attendant perils as you will soon find out) is a 1955 Porsche 356 Speedster.

First a little about the 356 in general and the Speedster in particular…The 356s were first built in Austria but Porsche moved production to Germany in 1950. The Speedster was introduced in late 1954 after Max Hoffman, the sole U.S. importer of Porsches, advised the company that what was really needed was a lower-cost, somewhat spartan open-top version instead of the padded top version with full windows. The Speedster was sex on wheels with its low, raked semi-wraparound windscreen (which could be removed for weekend racing), removal side curtains, and bucket seats.

Production of the Speedster peaked at 1,171 cars in 1957 and then it started to decline. It was replaced in late 1958 by the "Convertible D" model which had a taller windscreen and real roll-up glass windows and lost a lot of mystery and glamor in the process. There are several engines that were offered in Speedsters—the base engine, the Super and the ultimate, the 4-cam Carrera (practically worth its weight in gold).

THE QUESTION

Now we get back to our heroes, Matt and Adam Wright of rural New York state. Their technique is to talk to everyone they meet about Porsches in hope a lead will come up on parts or whole cars. This story is about when a lead came up a few years ago in the picturesquely named town of Trout Run, Pennsylvania, in the mountains near the Maryland border.

It was Matt who first got the nibble on his hook. "My brother was going to Pennsylvania to see a Porsche 911 for sale," recalls Adam.

That car unfortunately, turned out to be a downer, the car in person didn't look as good as it had in the pictures. But Matt Wright is no dummy, so, before he left, he turned to the shop owner and asked what I like to call The Question (which I define as the all important question that leads to untold fortune if it's asked right)…

THE QUESTION

"Are there any other old Porsches around I should look at before I leave the area?"

And damned if Matt Wright, intrepid barn finder, didn't get The Answer: one fraught with possibilities of real treasure.

The shop owner volunteered, "Yeah, an old guy was in here last week with a list of old 356 stuff." He dutifully wrote out the contact number and handed it to Matt.

Matt Wright immediately called the man and got an invitation to come out to the shop, way up in the mountains. He called his brother and they made an appointment with the seller in Trout Run. They drove a 4WD truck there which was a good idea, because in Pennsylvania in the dead of winter, there's snow and you need 4WD just to get there.

Now we come to what separates the men from the boys, barn finder-wise. The not-so-dedicated would say: "Hey, it's snowing. It's cold. Let's go there in Spring when the weather breaks." But these were 356 Porsche parts, which meant they were rare and fitting the title of something to be sold by their business called Unobtanium Inc. We're talking 50- to 60-year old cars here. They continued the mission. When the brothers arrived at the seller's shop, they liked the Porsche parts they saw but when they said they wanted to buy them, according to Adam's telling of the tale: "the guy gets weird, says he has another guy who wants to come out and he isn't sure how to price everything. Here we had just driven through a snowstorm to be told, 'maybe next trip.' Yes, this is what you deal with. But the guy also mentions he has a 55 Speedster that he bought in 1969 for $500, that he is having the local shop restore for him, the hot rod shop. Oh, the horror!" (Not that a hot rodder couldn't do a good job but the Wrights believe Porsche 356s are a breed that needs someone so expert in Porsches that they know exactly which screws to use when re-assembling an engine.)

Adam continues: "Now that there is a Speedster in play we are in it for the long haul, parts or no parts. Fast forward a few months, we're traveling picking up another car and we call the guy again, he says come on by, he is ready to sell the parts, and he wants to show us the Speedster, great! We stop off, I get to look at the parts, which we buy and he takes us down the road to see Mr. Sick (yes, the hot rod restorer was indeed named Mr. Sick), who is working on the car."

COMPLICATIONS

Now, dear reader, thank you for your patience. You've hung in thus far, and begging your indulgence, I'm telling the tale just as Adam told it to me in verbatim quotes because this gives some idea of the twists and turns you can expect to find out there on the trail. (Hell, if you can't stand all this fooling around, and following duff leads, then go to a car dealer, point out the car you want and take out your checkbook. But what's the fun in that?)

Adam continues: "Sure enough, it's a '55 Speedster in paint (techno car term meaning "painted but all the trim hasn't been put back on), but it's not for sale because he has promised it to his grandson when he turns 16. As he says this, his grandson comes flying up the driveway on his dirt bike, popping wheelies, and I suddenly have a vision of him wrapping the Speedster around a tree. So when the whole family is within earshot I say real loud, 'How about we all go over to the Acura dealer and I will buy him (the grandson) any car on the lot, for cash, if you give me the Speedster.'"

"This gets everyone real excited, but still it isn't enough to pry the Speedster loose. This is the first year of trying to buy that car. Over the next four years, we make multiple trips to nowhere Pennsylvania to talk once again about making a deal. At one point he wanted to trade it for a safer Porsche for his grandson, so I come up with everything possible to trade, no dice again. Another time we had a very nice 356 coupe that he said he might want to trade, so we swing by with that, but he couldn't make a decision. Another time he calls me up and tells me how much *Excellence Magazine* says Speedsters are worth, and says his is probably worth $90,000, my current offer at this point was $60,000, up from $50,000 the year before. Over the next few years we run into the guy at Porsche events, he says he is almost ready to sell, his wife at this point is very ready, once she realizes that the $500 car is now worth more than the log cabin they live in. But every time I call him he isn't quite ready. Finally after five years of back and forth he says his wife has broken her hip and with her new hip won't be able to get in and out of the Speedster, so he is ready to sell."

DON'T DO THIS EVEN IF IT WORKED FOR THE WRIGHTS

For some insane reason, the Wright brothers stuck to their guns and still kept calling the guy. Adam wrote: "Mind you, he has had the car since 1969 and has never even driven it, but now and only now will he sell. He wants $80,000, I am still at $60,000. We arrive at $70,000, all cash. Getting that much money in today's banking environment is tough, I have to go to nine banks, and they freeze my account half-way through because they think something is wrong. So after two days of driving to banks I load $70,000 in a brown paper bag and go to the guy with the Speedster. It is on his farm at this point, a working farm I might add, because my feet are squishing in what I think is mud, turns out it is field fertilizer time, so it is cow poop I am squishing in, but whatever, I am there to pick up a Speedster. So after five years of frustration, failed deals, circles within circles, numerous gifts and dashed hopes, the Speedster is finally on my trailer."

VICTORY

(Dear reader: At this point you have my permission to stop reading momentarily and do a victory dance, irish jig, hokey-pokey, whatever floats your boat.)

The prize was a 1955 Porsche 356 Pre-A Speedster, without a motor, but sporting some very period racing wheels. On the downside, it used up a lot of the Wright Bros. time and money plus they emerged covered in cow poop (and there are people that complain that not all the cars in this book are found in barns, well, let me tell ya, I've worked as a cowboy on a ranch in Montana and cows poop continuously).

On the plus side, the Wright Bros. were able to vend the car fast. They already had cars of their own and wanted to turn it around rather than restore it. Says Adam: "Word got out fast that there was a Speedster in play, so the car was quickly sold back to the Fatherland for $125,000, and once restored will probably command $250,000-300,000. My buyer was able to secure a period correct motor, a Super, the car was originally a Super, so pretty rare, on top of being a Speedster."

Note to readers: Speedsters are among the most celebrated Porsches in movies, such as Harper with Paul Newman but it doesn't hurt that James Dean owned and raced one. It is a car with a certain amount of image, despite the fact it was marketed as a low-price Porsche back in the day.

Lessons to be learned here? First, Matt Wright was smart enough to be diplomatic when the first car offered–the 911—was not worth the money being asked. He turned it down like a young lady who thinks the guy asking her out is not quite up to snuff but, hey, with a little polish, maybe he could get there someday. That paved the way toward the asking of The Question. If Matt would have been snippy on seeing the 911 (like "thanks for wasting my time," etc.) he wouldn't have gotten the answer to The Question. And The Question, properly asked, led to The Answer which led to the car. Oh happy day.

Chapter 25
THE BANK ROBBER'S PORSCHE
(1956 PORSCHE CARRERA)
The question was: go back to dead stock or keep it custom?

Okay, imagine this. It is 1971. You are 19 years old. You come across a vintage Porsche, purely by accident, spying it in a driveway while visiting a friend. You don't know that much about Porsches, you just know it's old and you know old cars, if they are the right ones, could be worth more than new ones eventually. The car even has a nickname, since it was customized way back in 1956 by Dean Jeffries, a pinstriper who ended up being one of Tinsel Town's most famous customizers. It was called the "Outlaw," and after being built in 1957, was featured in at least a dozen magazines and books, most memorably on the cover of *Rod & Custom*. The teenage barn finder was Jack Walter. Walter dug deep down in his jeans and bought it for not very much money. It hadn't run for years but still had the original engine.

First a little more on the background of Dean Jeffries…It was his personal car, not one he did for a customer, and he saw it as his way to break into the ranks of customizers after first being a known painter or pinstriper.

The car was his calling card and through it he succeeded in becoming known as a customizer. His most famous cars, many the stars of films, were Mantaray, the Kyote dune buggy, the Mon-keemobile, The Green Hornet car, the Landmaster in *Damnation Alley* and a bunch of other movie cars. He painted James Dean's 550 Spyder before he built this Porsche and was friends with Von Dutch, James Dean, Steve McQueen, and racers Lance Revent-low, Carroll Shelby and A.J. Foyt.

With ambitions of customizing being his future, Jeffries didn't worry about offending purists. In fact he told interviewers decades later he couldn't stand the front of the Porsche as it was stock so he extended the front fenders and frenched in the headlights and driving lights to accentuate the curves of the 356 body. In the rear he installed a set of functional roof vents (like those on the 300SL Gullwing), then added a custom scoop and grill for the rear deck-lid and some custom tail lights. He kept the car's 1500cc 4-cam Carrera engine and fully customized the interior. Back at the time pearlescents (made with real fish scales!) were the hot setup in custom cars so he mixed his own silver pearlescent paint and still later sprayed it metalflake gold. Says Walter, the man who bought it while still a teenager: "He isn't as well known as some of his con-temporaries but he's got a great talent. I used to build models of some of his cars when I was a kid—with this kind of background it wasn't hard for me to hold on to the car for all these years."

At the time Walter bought it, it had been through a collision with a pickup truck about a year before. The lady who owned it had some vague idea of restoring it, but the trouble with a custom car is, you can't easily "restore" it with bolt-on parts ordered at the dealer, because no patterns exist. That might have been one reason it was not repaired. Walter kept it all those years and only in 1973 began to restore it. The question then was: should he keep it as a customized car or bring it back to dead stock where it would be worth a bunch as an early 356 Carrera? "I can't take much credit for the taste," says Walter, "although I've always felt it was the perfect combination of California lead sled/hot rod/sports car all wrapped into one. I've had to defend it at many Porsche club out-ings back in the seventies (radical custom Porsches were just not done, especially Carreras) but the wheel has turned and its being appreciated for its history." He drove it for a few years but was never satisfied with the quality of the original restoration.

In 2010, he found a bodyman from Croatia—a resident of Geor-gia in the U.S.A., and had confidence the man could "bring it back" to how the car was in its prime. So he began to restore it all over again, this time a full restoration involving a rotisserie (armature that rotates the car so you can work on the bottom). Now a word about the origin of the rare four-cam engine offered in the 356. When the Porsche 356 engine first came out, it was not a four-cam. The four-cam engine was designed from the start in a very different manner than the normal pushrod engine. While they both had the same opposed four-cylinder layout, the normal engine relied on old-fashioned pushrods to open the valves, while the four-cam used bevel gears and shafts. The plugs were fired from twin ignition coils, and a distributor was placed on the end of each intake camshaft to distribute the ignition spark. A dry sump lubrication system drew oil from a storage tank into the oil pump, returning it to the engine by means of steel braided lines. Lubrication was critical in the four-cam, as a roller bearing crankshaft manufactured by Hirth was used. The Hirth crank moved a high-domed piston inside aluminum cylinders with chrome-plated walls. Air cooling was, of course, used to help dissipate heat created in the engine; a large, rounded fan tower that was characteristic of the four-cam's appearance housed a fan capable of moving over 1,000 liters of air per second at high rpm. But Ernst Fuhrmann, a Porsche designer, designed this one for racing. Given the anonymous designation 547 instead of something obvious like "competition engine," this engine-transmission unit was noted for the vertical drive of its camshafts, its dual-plug ignition, roller bearings, and double-sided cooling fan. Those in the know also call it the "Schubladenmotor,"or "drawer engine." The young engineer Ernst Fuhrmann received his doctorate with this design. But not everybody was supposed to know about the unit while it was under construction and the legend is that some of the parts were made under the work bench, so to speak, hidden in a drawer when unauthorized personnel walked by. Trimmed for racing, the 547 generated 110 hp at 6200 rpm. It was installed in the new Porsche racing car, the 550 Spyder. With this car and engine, Hans Herrmann took third place in the over-all rankings for the 1954 Carrera Panamericana (thereby getting its name). Since then, the name Carrera has played a prominent part in the history of Porsche models. In 1955, Porsche decided to make it available in the standard 356 as well. The first Carrera had 100 hp. By 1956, the Fuhrmann engine was up to 130 hp in the 550 A. In one of these cars at the 1956 Targa Florio, Umberto Maglioli celebrated the first overall victory for Porsche in a world championship race. Two years later, the engine was producing 164 hp. In the Porsche RS 60 of 1960, the capacity grew to 1,604 cubic centimeters, and by 1961 to two liters. Porsche was trying on the one hand to reserve the Carrera engines for cars intended for racing but conversely knew it was a great sales point and offered them all the way to 1959 when the 356B was introduced without a 4-cam in the catalogue.

But Porsche soon realized their mistake and built a series of some 40 lightweight B coupes for 1960, using 1600 GS GT engines. The next step was the 2000 GS, that began as a 356B too, the fastest road 356 ever built although its quoted top speed remained the same, 125 mph.

Walter had bought the car with a pushrod engine that had replaced the original some years before. Once he decided to seriously begin restoration of his coupe in '73, he was able to buy a period correct type 547 4-cam engine. But once he realized that the engine he had bought originally had been in a pure racing car, a 550, and since he knew that owner of that specific car, he contacted him and the owner was very happy indeed to be afforded the opportunity to buy the exact engine his car had come with (which greatly improved the value of his car). In turn, Walter was able to buy another 4-cam engine (adding the money from his engine sale plus a little money on top) for his coupe.

To rebuild the engine, Walter found a famous 4-cam wizard, Dieter Wurster, who had been repairing the complicated engine since 1960. He came to Porsche in 1956 when the engines were still in production.

Wurstur told one magazine editor: "The engine is a delight to behold. Every little screw is highly polished. All the screws used to be galvanized as white as these ones." Wurstur reminisces, "But this type of screw isn't made anymore. Nowadays they're only chrome-plated yellow." So for the restoration work, each screw is sand-blasted individually and its surface is treated. Many other parts, large and small, received the same treatment when he restored them because Dieter Wurster restorations have to be original down to the nut and bolt.

The engines rebuilt by Wurster routinely exchange hands for as much as 150,000 marks.

RESTORATION THE SECOND TIME AROUND

When restoring the car the second time, Walter had some pictures of the car that were taken in 1962 when Dean Jeffries had it parked outside of his shop in Hollywood. "Someone was kind enough to send me copies of these pictures after reading the article about the car in the 356 Registry a few years ago. Dean had repainted the car gold shortly before he sold it to Albert Nussbaum."

Now it turns out Nussbaum had an interesting occupation. He was a bank robber, even on the FBI's ten most wanted list. Forgive your author for adding a bit of a bio on Nussbaum. Nussbaum and "One Eye" Wilcoxson allegedly robbed at least eight banks from 1960 to 1962, hauling in at least $250,000—the rough equivalent of $2.8 million in 2008. They were heavily armed. Back in those days you could buy DEWAT Thompson submachine guns legally and then order a few parts by mail to make them fully automatic. They didn't stop at that—they also used hand grenades, and military-style armor-piercing anti-tank guns to blast the doors off bank vaults. They were nabbed on November 4, 1962, when Nussbaum's mother-in-law ratted him out, telling the FBI that Nussbaum was in Buffalo to secretly visit his wife and infant daughter. Nussbaum found out they were coming, and led a parade of FBI agents on a 100-mph chase through the cold, wet streets of Buffalo before being rammed by some city worker who heard of the chase.

This writer hasn't ascertained if his getaway car was the Porsche. But I digress. Walter, in the second restoration, installed new brakes, tie rods, a Koni steering damper, a dual master brake cylinder, and trunk insulation. He reinstalled the Koni shocks, the headlights and horns and rewired the lights. His big impetus to getting the car done was the Amelia Island concours. "Once they said they would accept it, I was working on the car 24 hours a day to get it ready," he recalls. He was a little worried how Porsche purists would take it, it being a "Kustom" from Out West. But happily, the car was well received and Walter feels he did the right thing, honoring Jeffries, who by the way, flew out for the car's unveiling at the concours. It was actually unveiled at the concours HQ hotel where there was a panel discussion featuring some hot rod illuminaries as Pete Chapouris, Dean Jeffries, drag racer Tommy Ivo, drag racer Don Prudhomme, and collector Bruce Meyer.

Walter recalls, "As I stood in the ballroom on Friday afternoon, bleary eyed from being up for the past 36 hours, I was very glad that we were able to pull this off. Frankly, most of my friends are as amazed as I am that we actually drove the car onto the field on Sunday morning."

Lesson to be learned here? Custom cars (or "Kustom" as some west coast customizers called them) are not to be passed by, not when they are a purebred underneath. I would venture to say though, that the decision to stay true to the customizer's vision rather than go back to stock would be a tough one if the customizer was an unknown. Jeffries had become world famous so hence the honoring of his initial intention. If the same car was customized by Joe Blow from Idaho, perhaps that wouldn't stop me from buying the car, but would likely stop me from honoring Joe Blow's vision. Where Jack Walter really deserves congratulations is keeping the car through thick and thin. There must have been times when a wife would ask, "Can't we sell that so we can re-do the kitchen?" And he stood firm and is now reaping the reward for keeping true to his vision. The best part of the story is that he invited Jeffries to bask in the glory of the finished car.

Lesson to be learned? A purebred car is a purebred car, despite changes wrought in the bodywork by a private owner. I can't imagine that Jeffries knew how rare a Carrera was when he bought it, but then with friends like McQueen to clue him in, maybe he knew, and it wasn't just blind luck. So to all those who passed it by earlier in its life because it was customized, read this and weap. Jeffries started his customizing career with this car and never looked back. So the car is famous on two counts, first for being a Carrera, and second for launching a famous customizer's career.

Chapter 26
THE MINI-ATLANTIC
(1931 BUGATTI TYPE 31)
If you can't have an Atlantic, just build one.

Okay, picture Paris, "The City of Light" in the early '30s. The Nazis haven't marched in yet so it's still all fun and games and hot American jazz and art deco and surrealistic painting and free flowing champagne if you are a rich playboy and also a man with consummate taste in both women and cars. Oh, and you happen to own a Grand Prix Bugatti. But you are not as interested in racing it as much as you are in having a car capable of winning a Concours d'Elegance. Yes, that event is like it sounds—a contest of which car is the most elegant. That's the story of this particular Bugatti, a story that spans over half a century with a separation at some point of custom body and chassis only to be reunited roughly half a century later by one very determined collector.

The car started out in 1931 as a Grand Prix car, SN 51133, an open two seater intended as a works racer. The engine was a DOHC 2.3-liter straight-eight rated at 185 hp. With driver Louis Chiron behind the wheel, this same car won the 1931 Monaco, French and possibly the Czech Grand Prix (he won, but it has not been certain that it was in this same car). Ettore Bugatti, a lot more generous than Enzo Ferrari later on, gave his driver the car at season's end. Though, that might have also been because he owned Chiron money. Another report says it was invoiced to him, but no matter, he owned the car.

Chiron and Rene Dreyfus raced it in non-factory entered events between '32 and '34. It changed hands, at one point being owned by a racer that died in another car. Andre Bith, an heir to a pharmaceutical fortune, and only 26 years old in 1936, bought the Bugatti racecar from the race driver's widow in either '35 or '36. He actually rallied and raced the car in its Grand Prix form but kept adding road-like accoutrements, things like a spare tire at the rear, fenders and headlamps, each change making it less of a racecar and more of a tourer. He even upholstered it in white leather! At some point in 1936 he decided he wanted a really distinctive grand touring car and decided to commission a local body shop, Louis Dubos Carrosserie, to make a coupe body for the car.

JEAN'S RIDE LIGHTS THE FLAME

Legend has it that it was only after Bith had lunch with Ettore Bugatti's son, Jean, who had arrived for their appointment in a Bugatti Atlantic coupe, that Bith got the idea of not only making it a coupe but a sort of mini-Atlantic. So Bith and his friend, race driver André Rolland, began planning a coupe body. They were inspired by Jean Bugatti's design for the Atlantic, a fixedhead coupe whose sweeping lines started with a sweptback windscreen and ended with a sloping fastback. But of course it could never look exactly like an Atlantic because the racecar had a shorter wheelbase. And then you had the problem of Bith being a bit stocky so the coupe had to fit both him and his girlfriend! Although coachbuilder Louis Dubos usually toiled on makes of lesser prestige, he did a magnificent job on the car and completed it in only 14 weeks. The body was of light steel with magnesium (they called it "Duralumin") fenders and bonnet. Alas, the new body made the car a bit too heavy to race but it made a fine road car. Bith's color choice was bright Bugatti blue, with a tan pigskin and sycamore interior; but his girlfriend, Mademoiselle Jacqueline Janet, had other ideas so he repainted it in her choice, called "South Seas Blue," a dark violet color.

The car was exhibited in a toney concours, entered by Mme.

Janet who by that time was a.k.a. Miss France of 1937. The event was the Bagatelle Concours d'Elegance in Paris, the car taking first in class and second overall. The Bagatelle is the site of the annual concours, even today. Of note, the chateau on the property was built on the orders of Marie Antoinette, another lady with very strong ideas of design.

Skip Marketti, of the Nethercutt Museum who have the car now, says that Bith proudly showed the car to Jean Bugatti and the Bugatti family had no objection to him having copied one of their designs, as Bith was a friend of the family.

Bith still wanted to race it occasionally and even entered it in the Paris-to-Nice rally, where it at least proved reliable. Bith sold the car in September, 1938, through the same dealer he had bought it from, a man named Schaeffer. The buyer was Andre Berson who kept it until 1940 when he sold it to an aviator in Dijon (some say an American aviator, but what an American aviator was doing in France at that point in time, is unknown, as the Wehrmacht rolled into France on May 10, 1940).

The car next appeared in the South of France where it was owned by famed race driver Maurice Trintignant who did nothing with the car, using it only as a parts car for his own racing Type 51. He took the parts he needed, including the supercharger, and soon sold it off, whereupon its distinctive paint job was changed a couple of more times. After the war, the next owner was a mining engineer in Clamant, near Paris. The car was then black with no supercharger. The last known owner in Europe was a Mr. Revolle who painted it white

ITS AMERICAN LIFE

Then the car came to America. The car was imported to the USA in 1955 from Bugatti dealer Jean de Dobbeleer of Belgium by Gene Cesari of Pennsylvania who, perhaps wanting to go back to a racecar, sold off the body. From that point, the owner chain gets murky. Cesari sold the body to Major Eric Richardson, a Bugatti collector from Washington State described by one auction house as "the leading American Bugatti authority of his day." But a conflicting report says that it was Richardson himself who bought the car in France in 1950 and shipped it back to America. He was known to be searching for a Bugatti soon after the war in France.

THE BODY GOES ASTRAY

According to Skip Marketti of the Nethercutt Museum, who have the car in their collection now, Richardson restored the chassis for Cesari in exchange for the body, which was traded and bartered several times to Bugatti enthusiasts.

Then came J.B. Nethercutt, founder of a very successful cosmetics firm in the Northwest end of the San Fernando valley above Los Angeles. He bought the partially restored chassis of SN 51133 from Cesari in 1959, and commissioned famous Bugatti mechanic, one Overton Axton "Bunny" Phillips, of Pasadena, California, to construct a replica Grand Prix-style body for it, and that racecar became a cornerstone for over 40 years.

BACK TO THE FUTURE

But what of the distinctive Dubos body? Ah, turns out that it had been following its own destiny, bouncing around from one owner to another and from one chassis to another when it finally reached a man who knew Bugattis, Robert D. Sutherland, who put it on a high-quality replica chassis in the 1980s, one which the auction company that sold it said was done by Ray Jones, who was at one time a Detroit resident.

Side note here: The author once visited Ray Jones' home in the northern suburbs of Detroit. It looked like an ordinary one story home from the front but if you drove around back there was a vast underground garage which had, at the time I visited, boasted at least ten Bugattis, some stacked on top of the others. I talked to him years later, when he was in Florida and he said he was out of Bugattis but was now into WWII airplanes. (Always ahead of the game, that Jones fellow.)

Sutherland showed it, rallied it and most notably ran it in the Colorado Grand, a touring event he founded. Then Sutherland died in 1999, and in 2000 the Dubos mini-Atlantic body appeared on the block at the Christies auction in Monterey on the replica chassis. Nethercutt, alerted to the availability, bought the car and began having his shop re-unite the Dubos body with the GP chassis it had been built for.

In a nostalgic touch, he contacted Bith, who was still alive in France, though in his early '90s, to see if there were any clues to the original build—documents, photographs and the like. Bith was eager to help—it turned out he still had several reminders of those glory days with the car before the war. All this proves that some things in the old car world go around and come around and end up damn close to the way they started.

Lesson to be learned here? Some very distinctive cars get separated (the gearhead phrase is "parted out") and the major pieces scattered hither and yon but this story shows that you can, if you are really determined, get the parts back eventually. Of course he who holds the chassis is king and if given a choice, I would always choose chassis over engine or body because you can always replace the engine or body and still have an "original" car, whereas if the chassis is fabricated out-of-time-sequence or long after the original makers of the chassis have closed their doors, it could be termed a "replica." One has to congratulate the late Mr. J.B. Nethercutt for the way he never stopped looking for a chance to buy that body back to make his car whole once again. And I would congratulate him again for making the effort to reach out to the man who commissioned the body, Andre Bith, and personally consulting with him to make sure the restored car matched the car so firmly imbedded in his memory. In my mind's eye, I can envision what would have happened had Bith been re-united with the car, and had the opportunity to sit behind the wheel. I can envision him starting it up after more than a half century being away from it, hearing that supercharger spool up. At that point I think I would forgive him for quoting the line Rick Blaine, the American night club owner from the film *Casablanca* (1942), lays on his girlfriend played by Ingrid Bergman, "And we'll always have Paris. Vive la France!"

Chapter 27
WHOOSH!
(1963 CHRYSLER TURBINE CAR)
*You can own one, it's keeping it running that's
the challenge.*

Yes, that is indeed a jet engine powering that car ahead of you
(and, oh by the way, melting your car's plastic grille), and no,
it's not the year 2020—but this could have happened way back in
'63, when the Beatles were still no. 1 on the charts. For those of
you who weren't around back then, a quick review. Chrysler was
a progressive company engineering-wise back in the Sixties. (Ask
any drag racer about the vaunted 426 "Hemi" engine.)

They had been experimenting with small jet engines, called turbines, for decades. Among the claims they made for them: reduced
maintenance, longer engine-life expectancy, development potential,
80-percent parts reduction, virtual elimination of tune-ups, and no
low-temperature starting problems. Plus, no warm-up necessary, no
antifreeze, instant interior heat in the winter, no stalling because of
sudden overloading, negligible oil consumption, low engine weight,
no engine vibration, and "cool and clean" exhaust gases.

Their experimental turbine cars ran on a variety of liquids:
unleaded gas, diesel fuel, kerosene, JP-4, and other fuels. The basic
principle was simple. You compress and pre-heat intake air, then
burn it in an open chamber, out of which the rapidly expanding

gases flow onto and turn two turbines—one is running the compressor and accessories, and the other one driving the car.

THE EYE-TALIAN CONNECTION

Chrysler made a few one-off prototypes with American bodywork, so by the time they got to the one bodied in Italy, it was their fourth generation turbine design.

Chrysler's first turbine car appeared back in 1954, in a Plymouth.

Subsequent turbine cars and engines included a 1955, '56, '59, and '60 Plymouth, a '62 Dodge, even a 1960 Dodge two-and-a-half-ton truck. Then, Chrysler went oh-so-Continental and called upon the same famous Italian coachbuilder who had built most of the one-off prototypes for them in the Fifties—Ghia.

For Chrysler Ghia built a fleet of 55 identical turbine cars and Chrysler loaned them to 203 American families on a rotating basis. Originally over 30,000 people applied but only a few were chosen. Chrysler also took the turbines to shopping malls and on a 47,000-mile world tour of 21 countries. They were selling the engine of the future!

Except for the engine, the car was not outstanding mechanically (although the futuristic styling and fit and finish went far beyond the average Chrysler). It was a regular Chrysler chassis, a four-seater, with front coil springs, leafs in the back and a solid axle, and drum brakes (though discs had been invented, they weren't on Detroit cars yet).

Chrysler's fourth-generation turbine was rated 130 hp and 425 pound-feet. Transmission was under the hood, connected to a three-speed TorqueFlite. The usual torque converter wasn't needed (the secondary turbine fan can stop with the engine running).

The styling was credited to Elwood Engel, a tasteful designer lured away from Ford Motor Company where he was famous for doing the slab-sided four-door '61 Continental. Engel replaced Virgil Exner, the man who had led Chrysler on many an adventure in Italy, but who had fallen out of grace with management when, based on a rumor he heard at a party, he thought that GM was making everything smaller and urged Chrysler to do likewise, when in fact, GM was making a new mid-size generation. That mistake showed management that he didn't have a handle on the pulse of what was happening.

Mark E. Olson, who runs the website TurbineCar.com, says Charles Mashigan and the designer Giovanni Savonuzzi from Ghia have also come to light as being very influential in the design of the turbine car. Savonuzzi worked in the background during the Exner and Engel eras. Mashigan is also credited with the Typhoon show car on which the Turbine was based and later, after moving to AMC, became celebrated for his work on the AMX/3.

Olson terms Engel "a student of Exner" in a way—he had some themes on the car worthy of Exner, turbine "tokens" you might say, like a rounded transmission tunnel splitting the buckets front and back. The taillamps had what looked like rocket exhausts. Many of the controls were airplane-like, including headlamp switches and the heater/outside air fan control, all located on the center hump, near the gearshift.

Reduction gears lowered the output speed to 5,360 rpm, but the max speed of the second-stage turbine is 45,700 rpm. When you start it up it sounds like the world's biggest vacuum cleaner, idling at a cool 15,000 rpm. Acceleration is progressive and oh-so-smooth, but the downside is that the car is so heavy, 4,000 pounds, that the car is not feeling jet-powered—a Chrysler with a 318 could pass it in a quarter mile and a Hemi would flat blow its doors off.

Why did it weigh so much? Well, they were steel-bodied, had a separate steel frame and to make the smooth body surface the Italians laid on the lead by the bucketful to smooth out dimples in the metal.

Typical of the Sixties luxury cars, it was softly sprung and wallowed around the turns like a drunk elephant. What killed the turbine off (specifically Chrysler's plan to make 500 1966 Dodge Chargers powered by it) was impending smog regulations that would have required the engine to meet new standards on nitrogen oxide emissions. Even after canceling the project Chrysler got three more generations built, under contract with the Department of Energy and NASA.

Alas, that program ended with the conclusion that, emission and fuel economy-wise, the engines didn't cut it when you consider how precisely turbine engines have to be made and the major changes that would have had to be made at service departments.

Sometimes lucky Chrysler employees got to drive them. On one website, run by the Chrysler 300 Club, Burt Bouwkamp reported:

"I drove turbine cars overnight/weekends several times. It was fun. I always cruised Woodward Avenue in the evening because the turbine car drove the performance car driver's nuts. After idling through Ted's Drive-In (Square Lake and Woodward) I usually had a caravan of cars following me – and challenging me to a drag race on Woodward Ave. I resisted because I knew that I would lose because most of these cars were modified and tuned for 1/4 mile drag racing."

"I also awarded two turbine cars in the 90 day consumer research program. One in Indianapolis (I think?) and one in Jackson, Mississippi. They were mostly publicity events with local TV and newspaper reporters present. All Chrysler learned from the 200 respondents was that people loved the turbine car—especially because it was unique looking and free. And, the respondents became celebrities in their community."

He got that right. Coming of age in the Sixties, your author drove one for a few minutes of glory. My neighbor in Berkley, Michigan, Lou Bettega, used one when he went on recruiting expeditions to hire engineers for Chrysler Engineering. You can imagine the pulling power of the car when he drove up to a college like, say, Michigan Tech in Houghton, where the snow was six feet deep in winter. When he drove up in that turbine car the snow melted around the car. The young engineers would choose Chrysler to work for, thinking they would be working on such wonderful cars but alas, were assigned work on Polaras and other drek.

It was slower than I expected but couldn't get over the orange leather upholstery and fit and finish of the car—and the sound. It was cooler than the Batmobile (ironically the first Batmobile was built atop a Lincoln concept car bodied by Ghia, the same firm that later bodied the Chrysler turbines).

Years later I saw a movie with James Darren (*The Lively Set*) where the turbine cars were being raced (remarkably still with the turbine engines). I thought it was sad that the promising turbine cars were reduced to being but a footnote in automotive history. One was even crashed in the movie. How did they get in the movies? That happens a lot with Detroit dream cars. Automakers think, "Hell, if we have to crush 'em, we might as well let Hollywood put them in a film." Chrysler engineers actually did much of the stunt driving.

THE TAX MAN COMETH

To avoid import duties on the Italian-built bodies, 46 of the 55 Chrysler Corporation Turbine Cars were summarily destroyed. Another reason was that they didn't want to have to support 50 vehicles in customer hands for years making small runs of parts and providing service, which would mean training a whole cadre of mechanics to service fifty cars.

A few went to museums, as Chrysler could donate them and not have to pay the customs duty they had already posted in advance on each car in the form of a bond. But Mark Olson, who runs the website www.Turbinecar.com, a clearinghouse for information on all turbine cars, says it was not so much customs duties that scared Chrysler, it was the hot rodders. "The whole tax reason for destroying the cars has been pretty much laid to rest. Yes there was a duty on each car and they were in the country on a six year visa—Chrysler would have paid the duty to keep them in museums but very few museums wanted them. They were far more concerned about the cars getting into hot rodder hands and making trouble for the image and corporation. Standard policy was to destroy them. The car that was destroyed at the proving grounds was crushed and shipped to a scrap yard in Ohio along with a bunch of other cars that were piling up at the proving grounds."

Chrysler kept only two cars while they sold the last one to a late-night TV comedian for an undisclosed (but huge) sum.

How one turbine car was bought, though, is a basic lesson in barn finding. Thomas Monahgan, the pizza magnate from Ann Arbor, Michigan, bought one from Harrah's Auto Museum when they had a big sale after the death of William Harrah, who had made no provisions in his will for the continuation of the 1,000-car museum after his death.

According to Mark Olson: "Tom bought it and found out it would cost a small fortune to make running and decided to sell it at the huge Hershey (Pennsylvania) auto meet. Frank Kleptz, of Terre Haute, Indiana, was staying at the same hotel as Tom and saw the car on Tom's trailer. Frank slipped a note under the windshield and the sale was consummated before the car was offered to the public. Once Frank had the car, he was faced with the problem of how to make it run. Jay Leno had heard that Frank had the car and because they both felt all cars should be driven, Jay worked with Frank to get one of the last running engines from

Chrysler's archives. Frank has since passed away (November 2010) and his son David now owns the car. In the summer of 2012, the engine quit, it was taken apart and inspected by Bill Carry, former Chrysler engineer in charge of the distribution of the cars in 1963-1966. That engine was ruled completely destroyed and there are no spares left at Chrysler."

During their test by volunteer drivers, the cars had problems, and Chrysler changed quite a few engines so that all the volunteers selected could drive one. The electrical system was susceptible to heat damage. But many of the cars were driven by the volunteer testers as much as 10,000 miles in three months. Olson feels that the cars are more reliable than piston engine cars because they have 1/5th the number of parts. "That's on paper, but in real life, when you had trouble, you would have had to replace the entire engine," he says.

Says Olson, "If you want to run a one-of-a-kind auto, you really need to have unlimited financial resources and a lot of luck." Ironically, all of Chrysler's work on a turbine engine was not for naught. If you lift the hood on an M1 Abrams tank, you find what? A turbine. But the Army can afford to replace engines willy nilly.

Where are they now? Go to Olson's website for confirmation but there's one owned by the Detroit Historical Museum, one owned by the Petersen Museum in Los Angeles, another by the Smithsonian, one by Chrysler, and so forth. The good news is that museums do sell cars, as their missions change.

Lesson to be learned? First, sometimes the simplest ideas work. As basic a technique as the ol' time-honored note-on-the-windshield trick worked for the Indiana buyer. He got one of the world's rarest cars as a result.

But on the realistic side, the Chrysler turbines are probably the most expensive cars to keep running (unless you want to count racing Ferraris or low production cars like the ATS/Serenissimas).

You can't maintain one unless you have unlimited funds, and this writer is unaware if anybody has retrofitted an ol' Chrysler V8 (which should fit) so they can at least enjoy the styling, and craftsmanship. But then it would qualify for the lyric line, "It Don't Mean a Thing If It Ain't Got That Swing" (the title of a 1931 composition by Duke Ellington, with lyrics by Irving Mills). In this scribe's humble opinion, a Chrysler Turbine without a turbine wouldn't mean nothing without that WOOSH!

Chapter 28
SAVONUZZI'S DREAM
(1955 GHIA GILDA)
Wherein one man's dream car becomes
another man's reality.

Back in the Fifties the world was full of wonderful possibilities. Those of us who read *Popular Science* and *Popular Mechanics* thought that in a few short years we'll have flying cars, wrist watch telephones, atomic power for everything (maybe even cars), and robots would cook our food.

And some things were still ahead of us, like short-shorts and thong bikinis.

One of the things that Detroit and even European automakers would always hold out as "just down the road" was the gas turbine engine.

This is the story of a man who bought one that originally was not a running car and spent a fortune on making it a running driving turbine car.

The man was Scott Grundfor, of central California, who has spent a lifetime working on Mercedes 300SLs, restoring them.

German cars are well built, sturdy but not necessarily seductive. Which explains why Scott Grundfor ended up buying an Italian prototype that was one of one—a car designed with a jet-age engine.

What made the car unique was that it was designed around a turbine powerplant—not actually installed, but the car was designed (by an engineer named Savonuzzi) as if the powerplant were available. Much use was made of the wind tunnel, then something fairly new in auto design, which up until then had been most "by guess and by gosh" on the theory that "what looks good goes good."

The Gilda's sleek shape shows Savonuzzi's design sensitivity and wind-tunnel testing. What makes cars like this art are details such as the arrow-shaped door handle and a superb use of colors.

One reason the Ghia Gilda existed is that the young people, after the war, wanted fresh new ideas. And the assignment was given to create the car more or less as a technical exercise.

The Italians were interested in selling Italian cars in America, so they wanted to do a car that would capture the imagination of America, a country which, owing to not being bombed during the war (except Pearl Harbor) was growing at a fantastic rate with jet planes, TV and many other new inventions pouring out. They felt they needed a radical design to show that, they too, were on the forefront of technology.

Italians already understood aerodynamics. One of the first really aerodynamic postwar cars was the Cisitalia 202 Berlinetta, a fastback design that set the pace for other Italian designs. Other daring designs that followed were Carlo Felice Bianchi Anderloni and Carrozzeria Touring's one-off Pegaso Thrill and the Alfa Romeo based Disco Volantes (Italian for "flying saucers"). Over at Carrozzeria Bertone, Nuccio Bertone and the mercurial designer Franco Scaglione came out with the radical Alfa Romeo B.A.T. series, the, 5, 7, and 9 where the tailfins were so tall they almost wrapped around the roof!

Giovanni Savonuzzi was celebrated for his avant-garde Cisitalia CMMs of 1947. He was still in his thirties when those were built, and he was one of the few car designers who was also in the aircraft field as he worked for Fiat's Aero engine testing division where he kept abreast of the latest airplane developments. So when he became Cisitalia's technical director in August 1945 he began to apply what he had learned about airplanes to cars. That little Cisitalia had an engine displacing just over a liter, a 1100cc four-cylinder powerplant cranking out just 61 hp, but could top 125 mph because of its superb aerodynamics. It placed third overall at 1947's Mille Miglia.

The model later became known as the Savonuzzi Streamliner in honor of its creator. He left Cisitalia in 1948 to form his own design and engineering consulting firm and then went into the world of academia, as a lecturer at a technical school.

In the 1950s, one of his clients was Carrozzeria Ghia, which in 1953 had constructed the body for a one-off car he had designed for the silver-haired Virgilio Conrero, a legendary Alfa Romeo tuner. That opened the door to what came next.

THE GHIA CONNECTION

Ghia was an old-line well-established carrozzeria, coachbuilder, but there was drama going on at Ghia. The key Ghia officials were design director Mario Boano and commercial director Luigi Segre, but Boano had such a falling out with Segre that Boano and his son, Gian Paolo, left Ghia to form their own carrozzeria, so Segre called Savonuzzi and appointed him to be the new design and technical director.

One of the "hits" that Ghia had at the time was the "Supersonic" that Savonuzzi had designed, built in small quantities and put on various chassis, including nine Fiat 8Vs, a one-off Aston and a Jaguar.

Ghia was also getting a lot of work from Chrysler in the U.S. to do concept cars (then called "dream cars"). Ghia eventually did near 40 prototypes for Chrysler, most of them supervised by head Chrysler designer Virgil Exner Sr.

At one point, Segre saw an interesting sculptural model on the desk of Virgil Exner at Chrysler in Detroit. He asked permission to photograph it and took the pictures back to Ghia. According to Scott Grundfor, the barn finder who bought and restored the Gilda, when Exner saw that Savonuzzi was enthusiastic, he gave Ghia the job of building it as an experimental project that provided Exner with solid data regarding the legitimacy of tailfins (form following function) in providing directional stability. He presented this information in a paper at SAE Annual Convention at the Greenbrier Resort in 1957.

The Gilda was the genesis of Chrysler's "Forward Look." Savonuzzi's goal was to design a jet fighter-styled car, a trend at the time as Ford and GM both had dream cars with wings, fighter-plane tails, and transparent bubble canopies such as Ford's FX-Atmos (1954), Lincoln's Futura (1955, constructed at Ghia), and the turbine-powered

GM XP-21 Firebird (1954). GM, with the excess of zeal shown by Harley Earl, their VP in charge of styling, had gone over the top with their Firebird I, which looked much more like a jet fighter plane that had lost its wings in some frightful accident than a car. The Savonuzzi design still looked like a sports car.

Much of the design was inspired by his ten-year-old Cisitalia Streamliner, which was tested on a scale model in the Turin Politechnic wind tunnel, one of the first car designs to be scientifically tested as to its aerodynamics, a step past "if it looks right, it is right."

The Gilda was created in 1955, and made its debut painted silver. It was billed as the "Streamline X Gilda." The name came from the movie *Gilda*, starring Hollywood's bombshell Rita Hayworth in the title role. *Gilda*, for you film buffs, was a 1946 American black-and-white film noir directed by Charles Vidor starring Glenn Ford opposite a slinkily-dressed Rita Hayworth working it as a femme fatale. (Hayworth herself had a Ghia connection, having been gifted a Cadillac by her Royal husband, the car made by Ghia, whose story is told in this book.)

The non-running, fully trimmed Gilda debuted at 1955's Turin auto show, where it was the superstar. *Motor Trend* put it on their September 1955 cover with the headline, "The Engine-less Ghia X" ('X' for Chrysler's Gas Turbine).

GILDA IN AMERICA

The car was sent to Dearborn for the Henry Ford Museum's Sports Cars In Review Exhibit in 1956. It also appeared at the New York auto show, and greatly influenced other dream cars to come, including the Chrysler Dart and Ferrari 410 Super Gilda (1956), the Chrysler Diablo (1957), and the Guzzi-powered speed-record-setting Nibbio II, done for Count Giovanni Lurani.

After New York, the Gilda went to the Henry Ford Museum, where it stayed until 1969. Then it became part of the 1,000-car collection of Reno casino owner William F. Harrah's collection. Automakers in America who had cars bodied in Europe liked to donate them to Museums because then they didn't get charged the customs fees ordinarily applying to something you import from another country.

An interesting side note is that the Gilda was a good calling card for Savonuzzi. In 1957 he was hired by Chrysler Corporation as Chief Engineer in charge of Turbine Research and developed the Turbine car—both the motor and the body. But his wife missed LaDolceVita in Italy and talked him into moving back, so in 1969, Ing. Savonuzzi returned to FIAT to be Director of Research at the Orbassano Research Center, a job he held until his retirement in 1977.

Meanwhile, in America, the Gilda continued to change owners. In 1985, the Gilda became part of the Blackhawk Collection's group of Ghia show cars, which included the De Soto Adventurer II.

SOMETIMES THE BARNFIND COMES TO YOU

Two decades passed with the car almost forgotten when Scott Grundfor, a Mercedes restorer on the Central California coast, got a phone call asking if he wanted to buy the car. He knew the car. He said "Yes" and bought it sight unseen for $125,000. The Gilda, it turned out, was in excellent cosmetic condition but had no drivetrain, though some reports say that at some point it had a 1491cc OSCA four-cylinder that could get it up to 145 mph.

But Grundfor wanted to follow Savonuzzi's lead as Savonuzzi had gone to work for Chrysler in developing their turbine car. Grundfor wanted a running driving turbine car. Grundfor located a period-correct AiResearch single-stage turbine, and had it, a power transfer case and Hydrostatic automatic gearbox installed in so that the styling wasn't compromised in any way.

The result is a car that has a sound like a jet engine (which it is), a sound you can only hear on the highway if you are near the only other running gas turbine car in America, the Chrysler turbine car owned by a car-collecting TV personality.

Grundfor later put it in an auction but it failed to meet his reserve.

Lesson learned? First, museums do, in fact, sell cars. As a hand-built one-off car, the Gilda was as *Sports Car Market* magazine is wont to say "well bought." But it cost Grundfor a lot to find, install and make drivable the jet powerplant. So when it comes to cars with unusual powerplants, you have to figure that restoring the drivetrain alone is going to cost you maybe several times what the rest of the restoration will cost. Nonetheless, Grundfor achieved Savonuzzi's dream of owning a turbine-powered car, a goal that Giovanni could never quite achieve in his own lifetime. But Grundfor spent almost a million dollars achieving that goal. You might say both men, Savonuzzi and Grundfor, were seduced by Gilda.

Chapter 29
EVERY HIGH SCHOOL NEEDS ONE
(1963 FERRARI 250GTO)

You think I'm kidding?

The first time I was offered a Ferrari 250GTO was in December, 1969. I was reporting for my first day of work at 1499 Monrovia, Newport Beach, California, where I was to be an associate editor of a magazine published there called *Car Life*, sister magazine to *Road & Track*, and run by the same couple, John and Elaine Bond. When I was about a block from the office, which overlooked the Newport coastline, a dark blue sports car roared by me, belching smoke. When I got to the company parking lot, the mustachoied driver of that same car accosted me and said I could have it for $18,000. As it happened I had $10,000 in my briefcase (having just moved from Michigan) but didn't think of offering it because I didn't know what kind of car it was, and I thought "who the hell wants an older car that belches smoke?" I would live to regret that decision.

I found out later it was a Ferrari 250GTO, now the most desired car in the world. Some 40-odd years later, while doing research for this book, I find the car R&T contributor Henry Manney III was driving was 5111GT, a 250GTO which had been sold new to a French racer who had raced it twice in the Tour de France, winning in '63 and coming in second overall in '64. Manney had bought it in 1965 along with another Ferrari and brought them both back to California. He couldn't afford to own both so he offered the GTO for sale, which was when he accosted me. Sadly I left that magazine in 1970 for *Motor Trend* and didn't know that he later sold it for a mere $8,500 (an amount I had in hand when he first talked to me) to Chris Cord, a relative of the man who started the Cord automobile empire. Cord vintage raced it in the first Monterey Historics and then switched to racing a modern Dekon Chevy Monza.

Cord sold it only a year later to Don Fong who sold it to dealer Paul Pappalardo. The trail ends (as far as my research went) in 2008 with a collection called the Torrota Collection in Switzerland. But I digress. Indulge me, dear reader, for enough time to paint a picture of first, what makes this one particular model of Ferrari currently the most sought after car in the world.

THE DNA

If there is a mythological sports car, and a mythological Barn Find all in one it is this particular 250GTO. First a few words about the marque…The Ferrari marque was started in Italy in 1949 by Enzo Ferrari, formerly a driver and team manager with Alfa Romeo before the war. He decided to strike out on his own after the war, distinguishing his cars by having 12-cylinder engines. By the early '60s, he had a fast, reliable car in the short wheelbase 250GT but was scared by the announcement from Jaguar of the E-type Jag which looked considerably more slippery than his stubby-looking swb (short wheelbase) 250GT. So he assigned his ace engineer, Giotto Bizzarrini, to build a faster swb 250GT even if it meant changing the body. The swb was descended from the 1954 250 GT Europa which started a whole line of dual purpose Ferrari sports cars that you could drive to the track, race and drive home. The powerplant in these 3-liter 250GTs was the Gioacchino Colombo-designed short-block V12. This engine was so versatile that it could power road cars, with usually three carburetors, or full racecars like the Testa Rossa if you went to six carburetors. The chassis was a strong steel tubular ladder-frame suspended by wishbones at the front and a live axle at the rear. You couldn't call them terribly sophisticated but they were reliable. After the first series of cars were built in 1955, the Europa name was dropped and for awhile it was called the 250 GT. It was only after gaining a victory in the Tour de France in 1956, that the name Tour de France (TdF) was unofficially adopted for all the long wheelbase (LWB) cars built after the Europa GT. It was a good name particularly because that model went on to win that particular French event for eight more years in a row. Then came the short wheelbase which had a number of improvements. Ing. Bizzarrini had improved that as well, with the so-called SEFAC "hot-rod" version.

THE ANTEATER

Enzo Ferrari decided that they would use the hot-rodded swb 250GT as the basis for a more aerodynamic car to beat the Jaguars. Ing. Bizzarrini was of the opinion that, as far as the body shape, he didn't need a designer (take that, you designers). He first engineered the chassis, moving the V12 engine lower and more rearward, and attaching that to a 5-speed transaxle and then designed his own body in a sort of by-guess-and-by-gosh technique which involved heaping on loads of bondo on a Ferrari equipped with his proposed drivetrain. He would reshape the bondo each night, eventually making a needlenose car (nicknamed the "Anteater") and test each new shape night after night by a run on the autostrada between two set points. When he got his average speed up to around 175 mph, faster than the E-type, he felt that body was the right shape and turned it over to Sergio Scaglietti, Ferrari's in-house coachbuilder for racecars, for final bodywork. Now ordinarily when you make a new model car, if you want to run it in the production class you have to make a minimum number to qualify. In this case the FIA wanted to see 100 cars. Ferrari had no intention of building that many—only as many as he needed. So he filed FIA papers for it, claiming it to be but a mere "evolution of body type" on the already existing swb250GT. The FIA approved it and Enzo went to battle with the GTO, without having to build another 44 cars. The GTOs were successful. They made short work of the E-type Jaguars (which Enzo had vastly overestimated as a threat) and gave the Cobras a run for their money. Only 36 were made from 1962 to 1964, and remarkably all 36 cars survive.

Ferrari's temporary save in the GT category paid off, with victory in the world championship for three years in a row. Finally Shelby's Daytona coupe, of which only six were made, began to crack the Ferrari wall and in '65 Shelby took the World Championship away from Ferrari.

MY RIDE

I had a ride in one courtesy of Chuck Queener, the associate art director of *Motor Trend*, a magazine I had moved to shortly before *Car Life* folded. Queener had borrowed it from Steve Earle, the founder of the Monterey Historics, when it was fully restored but still just an old car of indeterminate value (maybe $70,000 or so in 1970).

Now bearing in mind this ride took place 40 years ago, it's amazing that I can still recall details like the blue cloth upholstery, the gated shifter, the ease at which it tooled along Sunset Strip until he floored it and it got past 3,500 rpm wherein it transformed into an animal uncaged, yowling and screaming like some caged jungle cat.

Some cars, like some women, you just don't forget.

OBSOLETE IN RACING

Up until the early 1970s, the GTO, as a used racecar, wasn't particularly valuable—it was a front-engined car when Ferrari prototypes had gone mid-engined. Its pedigree finally began to be appreciated as vintage racing turned to postwar cars with events like the Monterey Historic and they became more valuable year by year until now they are the world's most desired car. I even helped to sell one when they were still under $100,000 when a Japanese friend asked me if I knew of any for sale. I told him "Call Steve Earle." I should have asked him for a sales commission (but he did buy me a nice dinner in Tokyo).

One price I do have from the early '70s is a now quite famous one belonging to Nick Mason, the drummer from the band Pink Floyd. He supposedly dipped into his share of the money his band made from their eighth studio album, *Dark Side of the Moon*, to get 37,000 British pounds (about $64,000 then) to buy the old racecar his dad—a former racing mechanic—recommended, a 1962 250GTO. He continues to vintage race it, saying, "It's almost an act of faith to keep it on the track."

I WASN'T KIDDING ABOUT THE HIGH SCHOOL

Okay, so I blew it. But turns out, there were other great bargains in 250GTOs at the time that I was unaware of. One of the most amazing is the one donated to a high school shop class in Texas, only to be rescued and then put in peril by being parked in an open field in Ohio, in the center of the dreaded Rust Belt. That 250GTO was SN 3589. First, a brief mention of that car's illustrious racing career...It was bought new by Tommy Sopwith for his Equipe Endeavour team in England. If the name sounds familiar, Sopwith was indeed a relative of the bloke that designed the Sopwith Camel, a WWI fighter plane. Michael Parkes, the British race driver/development engineer who later helped Ferrari develop the 330LMB, piloted 3589 to several first-place victories in England. In '62 it went over to the States to Tom O'Connor's Rosebud Racing Team in Victoria, Texas, where it taken to events at Nassau and at Daytona by Innes Ireland, a Scotsman who was a former paratrooper, who won the '61 U.S. Grand Prix for Lotus only to be dismissed a few weeks later by Colin Chapman who saw Jim Clark as a brighter prospect. At Sebring it finished 6th overall and 3rd in GT with Richie Ginther and Innes Ireland sharing driving tasks. They would have done better but a burst water hose kept them in the pits for too long. So much for the glory.

Now comes the genuinely so-crazy-that-you-can't-make-this-stuff-up part. Tom Conner, a reported oil man who dabbled in racing enough to build his own private racetrack at his Texas ranch, up and donates this pure-blooded racecar, a high strung 175-mph car, plus a few misc. Ferrari engines, to Victoria High School to be used for auto mechanics practice. (Ireland reported that the Ferrari was even used in parades!) It somehow survived that—you can see one of those Victoria High mechanics today saying, "Yeh, in high school, I learned to change spark plugs on a Ferrari 250GTO." Now that was laudable, if not laughable, but from there, starting in 1982, the car entered an odd sort of purgatory, being parked out in an open farm field outside of Royalton, Ohio, for years, through all the seasons: winter, spring, fall, summer for a reported fourteen years from 1972 to 1986. Innes Ireland reported in *Road & Track* that the farmer told him he had paid $6,500. That lucky farmer was a cantankerous old coot named Joe Kortan, who not only left that car to rot out in a field but several others of note, including a DeTomaso Mangusta, a Mercedes 300SL gullwing, a Maserati 3500, a Ferrari 275GTB and assorted English sports cars. As the word spread among the cognoscenti, Ferrari enthusiasts would drive across the country to see it lying there looking forlorn, particularly as GTOs broke first the 100K barrier in pricing and continued to climb into the millions. Even Innes Ireland, the man who had actually raced it, visited Kortan, recognizing the now-shabby car as his former racecar by the scrutineer's stamp on the inside of the windscreen left over from Nassau, but he was unable to talk him into selling it, though he secured a promise Kortan would call him first if he ever came of such a mind.

Kortan didn't keep the promise. It was Frank Gallogly of Englewood Cliffs, New Jersey (later to own a car business in Lime Rock, Connecticut) who broke the impasse and rescued the thoroughbred beast. It is not recorded what he paid but he only owned it for a short time and re-sold it in July 1988 to Engelbert Stieger of Switzerland (www.barchetta.cc, a Ferrari records website, records Stieger paid $4.1 million). Stieger restored it and today it is one of the most magnificent of the breed not only racing in historic events but appearing at many top concours.

Lessons to be learned here? First of all, going back to my first opportunity to buy a 250GTO, as soon as I realized it was Henry Manney III, he of the tweedy hat, I should have respected his opinion as a man who had been there (covering all the European races) and knew well of what he spoke. Of course I had read *Road & Track* for several years prior to working for the founders of the magazine on another title, but didn't really think of him as an authority. Rather, I thought of him as more of a humorist, an entertaining Yank who affected a Tweedy Brit image (signing his dispatches from races as "y'r ob'nt servant") and the man who coined the immortal description of the E-type Jag as "the greatest crumpet catcher known to man." If I would've realized that the man before me was offering the keys to a kingdom and was indeed a world class racing authority and not just a humorist, I could have, and should have, opened that briefcase full of money and seen if he was a man at all amenable to bargaining.

So, I hear you asking, what good does all this do me now? How can you find an all-time great bargain—a car that will make your fortune? I say it's never too late to start dossiers on the cars you covet. Update them religiously with last known owners/locations every few weeks, using not only the net but the phone, Fax, hell Telex (if there still is a Telex). Then if you get the money together, you can close in on your target in earnest with the latest information. Those who found that ragtag GTO (the high school/abandoned in the field car) in the Sixties obviously did that, but look at their techniques. You didn't need Sherlock Holmes. If you would have followed sports car racing teams in the '60s, particularly those racing Ferraris, you would have heard of Team Rosebud, and eventually noticed, hey, seems like they haven't been on the grid for awhile. Step one would be to contact them and ask if, by chance, they still had their race-cars? Okay, let's say they already donated the car and engines to the high school. I am here to say I think the offer of cash money plus the donation of a new school bus would've turned the trick. Joe Kortan was the hero there—he figured out precisely what the high school wanted and did the deal. It was maybe the best barn-find in Ferrari history, in light of subsequent values. Now when it came to later Ferrari hunters dealing with Kortan, that was a whole new set of problems for enthusiasts. How does one deal with true eccentricity? Frank Gallogly figured that out; and by my book, has all the smarts it takes to solve wars, let alone buy a one-time racecar sitting out in a field. Methinks the best deal to be made on the car was before Kortan got wind of it; when it was still at the high school. How would you know where Team Rosebud donated it to? A $25 classified ad with a picture would have found it, when you consider there were literally hundreds of graduates of Victoria High who knew about the car. I would have run a classified worded something like this:

FERRARI GTO: Looking for former racecar that looks like this. Formerly run by Team Rosebud. Will pay finder's fee. Contact so-and-so.

That would've found its location when the car was still cheap. There's loads of efficiency in zeroing in on the specific car you want and running ads to find it, maybe promising a reward to whoever tips you off to its location, payable only if you get the car. I cringe when I speculate on what that car is worth now, considering how I let that other one slip me back in '69 through sheer ignorance. By the time the ink has dried on this book, even that ex-Henry Manney 250GTO has no doubt nudged up another million from its 2013 assessed valuation. The Ferrari rumor mill churns with buzz that one of the 36 250GTOs changed hands privately recently for $52 million. It's getting harder to ascertain which sales are real because but no one who owns one wants to put their car through an auction and get all that attention that would focus on the sale of the most expensive car in the world. The closed-door sale (what the Brits call "private treaty") is now the norm for cars of this magnitude. We won't know if they have changed owners until the next Pebble Beach, or Amelia Island concours when we read the placard identifying the owner, and even then the displayer might be some name you never heard of, intended to throw you off the trail.

So, as much as it hurts to talk about it, there's something a barn finder can learn from my mistake in missing a 250GTO.

Chapter 30
ZORA'S ZINGER
(1963 CORVETTE GRAND SPORT)
Fooling the Brass on the 14th floor.

Back in 1962, when Zora Arkus-Duntov, the so-called "father" of the Corvette (though it was in production when he was hired on at GM), saw the A.C. Cobra and instantly he knew the Corvette's goose, racing wise, was cooked. Even though the new aerodynamic Corvette Sting Ray was coming out shortly as a '63 model, it was still 1,000 pounds more than the Cobra. So Duntov planned a sort of sneaky end run—to make and homologate (get approved as a production car) a lightweight Corvette called the Grand Sport. The plan was to have GM build 125 of them.

So it was done—on a tube frame with round tubes, and a very thin fiberglass copy of the Corvette coupe body was made. The car was to have a 377-cubic-inch side draft Weber carbureted iron block V8 rated at 550 hp. It weighed in at 1,900 pounds, 1,350 pounds less than the standard street Corvette. But only five were made when the execs on the 14th floor of GM World HQ realized ol' Zora was up to something and cancelled the program.

Why? Because way back in '57, GM President Harlow "Red" Curtice, under pressure from the media who were hyping the theme of teen deaths as a result of racing on public roads, signed an agreement with the other automakers in the American Manufacturers Association saying they would all pull out of providing any more factory participation or assistance in racing events.

Ironically, Ford gave lip service to it but still kept funneling money to independent firms like Holman and Moody, who were building NASCAR cars, and making special Fords—so somehow Ford got away with violating the ban. Chrysler also funded high performance parts by calling them "Police parts" and such, but the result of the resumption of the ban was that GM could only fund racers out the back door, shipping racers cars and engines in plain brown wrappers.

So the Grand Sports went out the factory's back door for as little as one dollar each to various racing teams. The consensus of opinion is that, of the Grand Sports, one went to Chevy dealer Dick Doane, one to Gulf Oil executive Grady Davis and three to the Mecom Racing Team run by John Mecom Jr., an oilman in Texas who also ran Ferraris and whatever interested him at the time. Davis hired Dick Thompson, a moonlighting dentist from Washington D.C., and Thompson recorded the only Grand Sport win of 1963 in an SCCA club race at Watkins Glen. Because they couldn't get the experimental aluminum block 377, the private racers of the GS cars ran mostly big iron block 427 Chevy engines. At some point the roofs were cut off the first and the second car to make them lighter, but these are still considered original Grand Sports because GM did the cutting. Management again found out Duntov was messing with them and came down on him with all fours again. (Will that boy ever learn?)

As a result of their banishment from GM, the cars never performed as well as Duntov had hoped they would because, by not having enough produced for them to be classified as "production cars" they were forced to run in the prototype class where there were lighter cars that could beat it, i.e. the Chaparral, the Porsche RS-60, and the "Birdcage" Maseratis.

Ironically, GM and Duntov got some satisfaction early on when at Nassau in 1963, supported by a cadre of GM engineers who were "on vacation," the Grand Sports raced and finished third and fourth behind two prototypes. Roger Penske returned to Nassau in 1964 with a Grand Sport and won the Nassau Trophy race, and that was the swan song for the Grand Sport.

Shelby of course developed the 427 Cobra with Ford's backing and they swamped the Grand Sports who had no development or engineering help from GM.

The cars had fantastic performance. William Jeanes, an author, quotes former Texas Chevrolet dealer Delmo Johnson, saying, "It is…the only car I ever drove that would lift the front wheels off the ground in all four gears." Johnson also said he was clocked at 205 in the car.

The one problem with the car was the front-end shape—it did lift. Johnson told Jeanes: "The front end was off the ground from 160 on up, but the road was straight so it didn't make any difference."

But even though their racing careers were cut off before they were fully developed, the Grand Sports were seen in combat at tracks like Sebring, Watkins Glen, Daytona, Nassau, Road America and Mosport. A lot of famous drivers piloted them, including Roger Penske, A.J. Foyt, Jim Hall, Dick Thompson, John Cannon, Don Yenko and Delmo Johnson.

This particular car, 002, only had a few owners. It was sold from GM to Penske to Wintersteen to John Thorne, who sold it to Ed Mueller who sold it to Jim Jaeger, that last sale in 1990. During all that time it was never restored, so was a car with its "original patina" as car restorers like to say. Finally it was restored and now makes appearances at concours and vintage races.

THE TIME TO BUY

The time to buy any of the Grand Sports was right after their racing career was over and no one thought they had any future. And if you were in Chevy's secret list of those to receive support, a production model called the Z06, one that was homologated to run in the production class, was coming in '63 so they would rather have you run that. The only direct evidence I have found of what they were going for "in period" is from *Hot Rod* magazine in April 1967. It has a small classified ad that shows the ex-George Wintersteen racing team white roadster, Grand Sport 002. The ad said the price was $4,500 without the engine and $5,500 with the 427-cubic-inch Traco-built 550-hp V8. (Today the engine alone would be worth $25,000!)

That might have seemed a lot of money back then for an old thrashed racecar, actually about the price of a new 1965 289 Cobra. When it was at an RM auction in 2009 SN 30837X-10002 bid to almost five-million dollars but failed to meet reserve.

Now sometimes old racecars get junked or taken apart for spares but it is amazing to note that all five of the original Grand Sports survive and have even been restored. It's hard to pin a value on one since they so rarely come up for sale.

Going back to the right time to buy, I knew one Porsche mechanic who went to Sebring the last day the Porsche 904GTS cars would be running as "current" cars. He had his checkbook in hand. He went up and down the line of 904 cars and, one by one, offered to buy each car when it finished the race. One owner agreed and, after the race, the car having survived, my friend paid his money (around $7,000), welded on some mufflers and drove home. The car probably increased 100-fold in price since then.

Lesson to be learned here? That the absolute dead-nuts ideal time to buy a racecar is just when the automaker that supported that team is pulling their support. The team that was racing it wants to race the new model they will build next year so the old model is suddenly of no importance. This was especially true in the '50s and '60s when vintage racing was not the powerhouse attraction it is now. It was thought of as a sport for "old fogies" with prewar cars. But the same advice works today. There's hundreds of race teams and hundreds of racecars. Every fall is the end of a season. The old cars gotta go, to make room for the new cars coming in.

Start targeting your future collectable now!

Chapter 31
THE BARONESS AND THE MERCEDES
(1936 MERCEDES 540K)
The long lost sequel to Raiders of the Lost Ark.

If this sounds too Hollywood, stop me now. For starters you got your prewar setting with a bombshell blonde Prussian baroness gadding about Europe in a rare, rare, rare jet black supercharged two seater Mercedes roadster. Then, as war clouds gather, she flees the Nazis (except for her brother who served the Reich), taking her dream car with her to America.

All this sets the stage for what became a dramatic barn find over 40 years later.

The lady was the Baroness Gisela Josephine von Krieger, by all appearances quite a looker in her day, compared by some to Greta Garbo. The car was a 540K, a Special Roadster, a straight eight, with the "K" meaning "Kompressor," or supercharger.

The place where it was "discovered" in 1989 was a storage building at an Inn, the Homestead Inn in Greenwich, Connecticut, one of the wealthiest small towns in the U.S.

I use the word "discovered" loosely, because in fact the car was never actually "lost" to its owner, who had moved to Europe, intending to come back to the Inn and collect it some day. She simply didn't get around to it.

How long had the car spent in slumber?

Oh, four decades or so. Enough for it to make the transition from "old car" to "valuable collector's item."

First some background on that particular model is in order... The 500K was introduced in 1934. That supercharged car had 160 bhp with the supercharger engaged. Then in '36 came the 5.4-liter version, the 540K, with 115 bhp normally aspirated and 180 hp with the blower engaged. The wheelbase was increased to 128 inches to make the ride better and the longer chassis allowed more elegant lines. Just 419 540K chassis were built, ending production in 1940 when the country was at war. A total of eleven body styles were created. The car is huge—17 feet long and six feet wide.

The buyer of record was actually her brother Baron Henning von Krieger, just 19-years old at the time. He paid $7,000 for it and immediately had the family crest painted on the doors (something you did, I reckon, if you were an aristocrat). His sister quickly glommed onto the car and drove it all over Europe, favoring the Riviera where she was a frequent visitor.

It was not the best time to be gallivanting around in a luxury car though. According to *Forbes* magazine, which published a story on the car, in Sept. '39 when Germany invaded Poland, the Von Kriegers were briefly placed in a French internment camp. Henning quickly returned to Germany to join the Luftwaffe, while Gisela and her mother returned to neutral Monaco to live in the Hotel de Paris, not bad digs and an appropriate setting for the dramatic car.

With her brother off fighting the war, Gisela von Krieger was neutral to pro-allied in her politics, and, according to an article by George Maley in a 2005 article in Britain's *Classic Car* magazine, she had been a society fixture in London, even attending the coronation of King George VI (The British Royal family, in fact, had German ties but only occasionally did that come to light in the press). After fleeing to Monaco, she then decamped to neutral Switzerland. The Mercedes, which was being repaired when war broke out, was shipped to her after she negotiated a Swiss visa by "feigning an illness."

Though a German through and through, Maley also wrote that she feared persecution for a romantic relationship she had with a Jewish Englishman before the war.

After the war, according to *Forbes*, the car was shipped to America on the Queen Mary, and she kept it in the City where she had it serviced at the famous Zumbach's shop. Then the Baroness relocated to Connecticut, where the car was first stored in the garage of Greenwich Cab. Co., then to the garage of the Homestead Inn, one of the Greenwich resorts where the baroness liked to spend her summers to escape the heat of the city. Her brother didn't seem to miss the car, having acquired a 1951 Lincoln, then the best America could do in a luxury car.

Eventually, though, in 1958, the Baroness decided to return to Switzerland, but as often is the case with the very rich, she left a lot of her stuff in her previous place, and thus the car sat at the Inn, patiently awaiting her return.

Her brother's death of melanoma only a year after she had moved back to Switzerland gave her a lot of responsibilities and the fact was that she just couldn't find the time to make it back.

The car slept on, oblivious to the dramas occurring in her life.

Oh, collectors knew about it. One particular enthusiast, George Maley, according to the Gooding auction house description in their catalog, made no less than seven trips to Switzerland, each time seeking to convince the Baroness to part with the car. She always turned him down, saying that she was fond of it because of the pre-war associations she had with it.

She even wrote a letter in 1986 to a Homestead Inn employee who himself had been seduced by the car's beauty and tried to buy it. Gooding Auction Co. later quoted the letter: "As long as I am still here – I won't decide anything."

She fully understood why people wanted it. In the same letter she wrote, "This love of good cars is said to be man's purest passion."

She kept her promise. After dying without a will in 1989, the Baroness left the car sitting, its future uncertain. When Gisela's body was finally discovered in her apartment in Vevey, Switzerland, that year, she was buried in a pauper's grave despite owning considerable property in London, valuable bank securities and diamond jewelry by Cartier and Van Cleef & Arpels.

Steven Heyman of the *New York Times*, writing in June 12th, 2012 issue said, "In 1989, when she died of a heart attack, she was living in Havishamian squalor, with $320,000 worth of jewels by Cartier and others – later auctioned off by Sotheby's – scattered around her filthy apartment."

David Gooding, owner of the eponymous auction firm who eventually marketed the car, said, "She really died very much alone. It was quite a tragic story. When they discovered her body, she had been dead for quite some time."

Gooding had first received a call from the von Krieger estate in 1991 (another source says 1992) when he worked for Christies auction house. According to *Forbes*, after they told him about the car, he went to see it. Of all the thousands of cars he had seen with an eye toward auctioning them, this was the one that transfixed him most. The *Forbes* reporter says he told the estate trustees: "You've got the Holy Grail. You've got something really special there."

But it took more long years, until 1994, when the estate won control of the car after some litigation, and, when they did, somehow a private collector in New Hampshire, Lee Herrington, owner of a very prestigious mail-order company, swooped in and purchased the Roadster for an unknown sum.

He sent it to restorer Chris Charlton who finished it in black and chrome over a cognac leather interior.

Flash forward another few years, by now Gooding has his own auction company, Gooding & Co. He receives a call from the very same man who had beat him to it. The car is for sale. Gooding arranges for it to go through his auction at Pebble Beach in 2012.

It was finally the right car, being rolled across the block at the right place at the right time.

It sold for $11.77 million, just short of what Gooding sold a 1957 Ferrari Testa Rossa for (roughly $16.4 million) at that same auction.

Of course, the Gooding company made a profit selling the car but the lesson learned here is—when dealing with estates, sometimes it is a problem in getting them to get them off the dime. On the other hand, maybe the market wasn't ready to pay that amount back in 1994, if Gooding could have gotten it for his employers back then. And then your heart has to go out to that poor Mercedes fan who went to Switzerland seven times! What could he have done to evoke a better response? Maybe hired a German actor to sweep the Baroness off her feet—someone like Kurt Jurgens (no, he died in '82, but someone like him, a tall imposing man exuding old world aristocratic charm).

But the biggest lesson to be learned here is one that's surprising. Some cars don't move. If you would have heard about "the old German car in the garage" at the Inn back in 1959, you still would have had another 39 years to work out a scheme to buy it.

So follow those old rumors. Some of them actually turn out to be true.

Chapter 32
THE TANKER
(1963 Z06 CORVETTE COUPE)
Sometimes you find a treasure right close to home.

Terry Michaelis, the Corvette King of Napoleon, Ohio, has bought and sold over 10,000 Corvettes in his more than 30 years with the marque. Sometimes he goes far afield to find a rare Corvette, to the West Coast, even to Europe.

Yet one of the most interesting barn finds he ever made was a rare Corvette '63 split-window right close to home (well, within two hours drive anyway). He actually bought two rare Z06 race-cars that same year, but the one he kept was the one owned and raced by Dick Lang because it had such a good "pedigree," i.e. a race history.

Dick Lang was a Chevrolet dealer and SCCA racer. His red '63 was one of the "batch built" Z06s produced in January 1963 the same week as the Delmo Johnson, Mickey Thompson, and A.W. Joslin's Z06 "tankers." Each and every one of them was made at the behest of Zora Arkus-Duntov, the European-born engineer known as "the father of the Corvette." He feared Shelby's new

Cobra, weighing 1,000 pounds less than a Corvette, would blow the Corvettes off the racetracks, and wanted to send some fast Corvettes out to the Coast to a race at Riverside to put Shelby's pesky Cobras in their place. The race was held, a Cobra blew past the Corvettes and back in Detroit, they cringed, but fortunately, the Cobra broke a stub axle and the Corvettes won—but it was a false hope as the Cobras began to catch up on the Corvettes in the 1963 season. By '64 and '65, the Corvettes were history as far as racing.

Now, about the "tanker" model—exactly 198 1963 Corvette coupes were built with the Z06 RPO option package which cost an additional $1,818.45 on top of the base 1963 Corvette coupe price of $4,038. Only one of all those cars was a convertible. The Z06 RPO was a short-lived option, only offered for '63 until the name Z06 was revived for the 2001 model year.

The 1963 RPO Z06 is nicknamed the "tanker" because of its huge 36-gallon gas tank. That was just part of the option package which consisted of a larger diameter front antiroll bar, a Positraction limited-slip rear axle, a vacuum brake booster, dual master cylinder braking, sintered-metallic brake linings within power-assisted Al-Fin drums cooled by front air scoops and vented backing plates, and larger diameter shocks and springs almost twice as stiff as those on the base Corvette. Ironically, early in production the Z06 RPO eliminated the big tank as a part of the package and lowered the price. Though the big tank was still available as an add-on $202.30 option to the Z06 package, only a total of 63 of the 199 Z06's produced had the big tank. The Z06 package also required the L84 327-cubic-inch engine option rated at 360 hp with 11.25 to 1 compression ratio.

Lang successfully took on the Shelby Cobras which, up until the introduction of the Grand Sports and Z06 Corvettes, dominated the race tracks. Lang raced his car throughout the East and Midwest and also raced the car at Daytona. In the 1963 Daytona race, Lang started on what became an enviable list of podium finishes.

But it wasn't easy. The Cobras had Ford factory support and, officially, GM wasn't supposed to be supporting racing (they had decided to start adhering again to some resolution they had signed with other automakers to not support racing, a ban they had signed way back in '57). In 1964, Lang's Corvette was the only non-Cobra car among the top five finishers at Daytona.

THE FINDING

Here's how Terry Michaelis heard of VIN 6553 back in 2011. "I had just bought a silver '63 Z06 Corvette in Michigan. At the time, I was knee deep in assembling facts on that car," recalls Michaelis. "So I ran ads in newspapers and on our website asking for information on it. Out of the blue this fellow calls me and says his father also has a 1963 'tanker' Corvette and he would consider selling it. So, considering it's only a two-hour drive, I drive over there and look at it. It's dusty, but at least stored indoors, and it's lacking the original high performance engine. But I know from owning racecars that sometimes engines last a day, or a month but racecars change their engines several times a season. The price was over $100,000 which I know would deter most people for an old car with unknown history but there were enough clues here and there—such as holes drilled for brackets to hold various race equipment, that I could tell that it was at one time a real racecar. I bought it."

Had Michaelis had an inkling earlier that the car was still existent, it should have been predictable where it would be found—less than twenty miles from Dick Lang's Chevrolet dealership. The car had been through a bit of trauma and many owners. Somebody had removed the "split" in the rear window in the '70s only to have that put back in the late '70s when it had been restored. It also had been through the hands of at least six other Ohio enthusiasts. When Michaelis found the car, it was rough and incomplete but on a car like this, the serial number is everything—Michaelis quotes the NCRS/GM shipping data report (SDR) which he ordered 3/22/2011. It showed that the car was built within the same week as Delmo Johnson, Mickey Thompson, and Joslin's Z06's: 6553 (Lang) built Thursday, January 10th, 1963; #6577 (Delmo) built Thursday. January 10th, 1963; 6669 (Joslin) built Friday, January 11th, 1963; #6844 (Mickey) built Tuesday, January 15th, 1963.

As he often does, when he buys a car missing some parts, Michaelis immediately posted an ad on his website asking for missing parts. The roll bar, brake drums, master cylinder, fuel tank and cover, the original engine and the FI unit all went someplace. But where? Maybe they were down the block, in someone else's garage. As a perfectionist, he also wanted the window sticker, the dealer invoice and car shipping paperwork, offering a $5,000 reward just for those paper items. He announced his intention in his ad: "We want to return this car to race livery."

Terry also purchased a report from the NCRS (National Corvette Restorer's Society) files which further documented the car. He praises clubs such as the NCRS and the *National Corvette RaceCar Register* for their completeness in compiling records on cars. "It makes our job of selling the car a whole lot easier," he says. Because it didn't have as strong a race history as the Lang car, Michaelis sold the silver Z06 he had bought so he could concentrate his research fully on the Lang Z06.

Michaelis' ProTeam firm sent the car and boxes of parts to Nabers Brothers in Houston for a full "no expense spared" restoration which cost over $220,000 and took a full year to complete. The car was eventually to win awards in several major shows and concours.

Lesson learned here? Though it is dramatic to think you can find that rare car in Argentina or Italy (and get a nice vacation to boot), the fact is that sometimes you don't have to make an epic journey. Sometimes it just takes a little more research into a car that once was local, starting with the last place it was seen and that's your ground zero. You move outward from there, in concentric circles. In this case the Lang Corvette was garaged less than a few short miles from the most logical place—the dealership where Dick Lang headquartered his race team.

Second lesson (and this one may come only through experience)—sometimes you have decide to buy or not without the time you would like to weigh the pros and cons. That's because the availability of the car became known to your rivals the same time you learned of it and you know that if you delay the purchase even one day more, the seller might just pick up the phone and call the next person who has expressed an interest. Terry had documented his first Z06 tanker six ways to Sunday so, at the point where he got to inspect the Lang car, he knew more than the average bear what to look for. He had an inkling it was a "right" car, but he went ahead and bought it before completely documenting it. As he says, "sometimes you just have to go with your gut."

Chapter 33
THE HARLEY EARL CORVETTE
(1963 CORVETTE ROADSTER)
When the King speaks, his minions listen.

When Harley Earl was a kid, out in California, he played in the mud of a riverbed, sculpting cars. Little did his parents realize that Harley would become the world's most instrumental man in the direction of car design while he ran GM Styling.

When Harley was hired by GM before WWII, he had already made a splash in Hollywood designing custom cars for actors and actresses.

He came to dull drab Detroit and added some color, even calling his section the "Art and Colour" division at GM when he talked GM into forming a group to affect car design in 1927. His style right from before the war was to make some special show cars to show what could be done. Among the early ones was the 1938 Buick "Y-Job." After the war, he was known as the father of the Corvette.

Earl retired in 1958 but in a remarkable act of generosity, GM kept him on as a consultant and in 1963 GM, as a sort of bonus, gifted him with a highly personalized 1963 Corvette, VIN #010323, modified to his taste by the GM design staff with some of the design cues of the XP-755 Mako Shark I Corvette.

He only drove it for two years—Harley was not nostalgic about keeping his cars. The legend is that he sold it to an Army veteran. Then there's a big hole in its history, an eight-year hole up to 1973 when a racing group purchased it perhaps without realizing that they weren't just buying a car but buying history.

Of course there had been some changes along the way. When first sold, like the similarly styled Knudsen one-off Corvette convertible, Earl's car had been equipped with a "fuelie," a fuel injected motor, but apparently maintaining that down in Florida was a problem so somewhere along the way that engine was replaced with a 300-hp carbureted engine. It did come with A/C, a rare option in 1963, with only 278 (1.29 percent) of 1963 Corvettes so favored.

Like the similar Knudsen '63 Corvette, it had some items that were previews of what was to come, as by then GM already had the '65 models "locked in" (as far as equipment and styling). Some of the features on Harley's '63 were knock-off wheels, which although they were listed as available for '63, no Corvettes were built with them after GM discovered to their chagrin that the wheels leaked. Also in the mechanicals were four-wheel discs, not scheduled until 1965. The hood was a later small block Corvette style.

A mystery is the body color. The original paperwork showed it to be Riverside red with red interior. Somewhere along the way it got changed to blue with blue interior, which in a way was good because it distinguishes it more from the Knudsen '63 Special Order Corvette.

Now there's what some would feel is an excessive amount of instrumentation in the car, not only gauges on the driver's side but duplicate gauges on the passenger side. That reflects Mr. Earl's lifelong passion for flying and getting feedback on what's happening with the engine. During the war he was famous for taking some Cadillac designers to look at the new P-38 fighter plane and they were so inspired they went back and designed tailfins for postwar Cadillacs.

The stainless steel side exhaust was the piece d'resistance of the car, straight off the Mako Shark Corvette design. GM of course did offer side exhausts as an option in '69 but they didn't sprout out of the body side as on the Mako and the Knudsen and Earl Special Order Corvettes. To accommodate the pipes exiting the engine, the battery was moved to a new position behind the passenger seat.

Harley Earl's special Corvette eventually reached full recognition as the special car that it is.

Some questioned why it was called the "Harley Earl" car when it was not created by him but by a whole team (he had some other special cars created to his own design). And, technically, you could say it wasn't even a GM show car, but created for him personally. All that criticism is but a tempest in a teapot as history is the decider on whether a car is significant and this car is more an example of the power of autodom's top executives to get what they wanted than it is of any design trend (the '63 Corvette had already been designed when this was built).

The documentation that eventually surfaced to prove it was modified by the GM styling staff insures its claim as a rare car that got special treatment for a very special pioneer in American car design.

Incidentally, this is part of a niche class of collector car which I call "personality cars" since it is thoroughly imbued with the personality of the man who ordered it. Just as with the, say, Raymond Loewy Jaguar E-type (in *Incredible Barn Finds*) it would not be a significant car if owned by Joe Schmo from Idaho. But if you are a fan of a famous designer like Raymond Loewy or Harley Earl, you can get a kick out of owning the car once driven by your hero.

THE FINDING

On this one, it is unknown how the first barn-finder who got it from Earl wrested it away, maybe just buying it as a used car from GM. On the Corvette Forum site, there are forum members who have posted tantalizing clues to the car's long sojourn when it was still lost in the sands of time. One said, "I tried to buy the blue car with the white stripe in the late seventies, early eighties. It was owned by a guy named John in Dillburg (Pennsylvania). He had bought it from a bank, repossessed. As I remember him telling it, about $1500+-. John sold it to Bob Gold for $12,050."

The famous Corvette collector, Bob McDorman, bought it from Gold, price unknown. Not that collectors were fighting each other to get it, mind you. Another forum member posted this note: "The car sat at the Carlisle fairgrounds an entire weekend with no takers. Not many people knew what a S.O. styling car was at that time. Bob bought it later from John W. and Dave W. from Dillsburg."

Terry Michaelis of Pro Team Corvette had it for a while. The

"King of Corvettes" from Napoleon, Ohio, was not only best positioned to buy it but probably had missed it several times earlier when it was still lost in the wilderness. It sold it for $980,500 in 2010 and $1.5 million in Chicago in 2013.

Lessons to be learned? Lots. First of all, the car had high visibility in the early '60s even when it wasn't a show car officially. Anybody who began tracking the car then could have kept tabs on when Earl would dispense of it and tried to find out if it could be bought from GM.

Maybe the way to find the dream car you are looking for, is to run a classified ad with a picture of the car and ask: "Do you have this Corvette?" etc.

Of course the U.S. is a big country and the problem would be where to run the ad—it helps if you have a locality where it was last seen. (See the last chapter on barn find strategies.)

This story just proves it can be done. The cars are out there. Our job is to find them.

Chapter 34
WHAT THE KINGS WANTS,
THE KING GETS
(1955 FERRARI 375 AMERICA)

One Ferrari Speciale for "the uncrowned King of Italy."

Okay, technically, he was not a king. What he was, fundamentally, was a captain of industry. The industry was cars and his grandfather, Giovanni Agnelli, was sort of the Henry Ford of Italy, the man who had put Italy on wheels. Now it's one thing to be a hired-on Captain, but it's even better if your family owns the factory. Such was the case with Giovanni "Gianni" Agnelli, Chairman of Fiat.

When he wanted a Ferrari, he wanted a special Ferrari, one which, in his drives down the Corniche highway in Cannes, it was guaranteed he wouldn't see an exact duplicate coming his way.

To show you what kind of guy Agnelli was, here's a little background. He turned 18 as the war started, was wounded twice on the Russian front, then again in North Africa, all that time on the Axis side. Well, that last one you might not want to count as a "war wound"—it happened when he and a German soldier got in a fight in some dimly-lit bar over a girl, and Agnelli took a bullet for his pains. But he loved women, so one bullet was a small price to pay. After the war, his nickname on the Cote d'Azur (French

Riviera) was "Rake of the Riviera." He and the other playboys set the pace—Porfiro Rubirosa, Gunter Sachs, Taki, all of them went through women and exotic cars with astonishing rapidity. Rich Cohen, writing about him in *WSJ* magazine, said "to be a man of elegance, you should be interested in everything: art, design, cars sports—all things that express beauty."

Hence his *unico exemplare* (unique example) of a Ferrari, a 375 America, one very special car that, decades later, caught the eye of two college professors from Orange, California, who, on the side, decided to start a Ferrari business back in the 1960s in Anaheim, California. These professors, Chuck Betz and Fred Peters, were ideally typecast for their role as Ferrari future value prognosticators because one was a professor of history, thus knew the historical import of each car they bought and the other was a professor of business, who knew how to run a business.

The earliest Ferrari designed for the road was the Tipo 166 Inter, a tuned down version of the 166 racecar that had won success on the track. From the 166 forward, Ferrari designed progressively larger cars, moving to the 195, then the 212, each of which was offered until a larger engine design was needed in order to beat the competition.

It was the 340 America which introduced the Aurelio Lampredi-designed V12, sometimes call the "long block," to the Ferrari's production chassis. This was also the first car to bear the "America" designation, which hinted at the intended market, but wasn't where all of them were sold. Progress continued on the 340 line, and it quickly became the 342 before reaching the specification of our barn find, the 375.

THE 375

The larger displacement road cars, such as the 342 and 375 America, which were a cut above say the more prosaic 250GTs, the Americas intended for a more exclusive audience. In fact there were only ten 375 Americas made.

Fundamentally they had the same basic layout as other road Ferraris of that era—your usual tube framed ladder chassis, with double wishbones upfront and an old-fashioned live axle in the rear with hydraulic drum brakes at all four corners. (Enzo was opposed to discs until an English race driver in his employ had some installed on his private Ferrari and then he loved them.) When it was introduced, aside from its luxury features, you could say the 375 didn't go much beyond the 250GT Europas except for its larger engine, the biggest Ferrari had made to that time.

It was descended from engines designed for racing, when Ferrari had to have the largest engines he could make for races like the 24 hours of Le Mans where he entered the glorious 375 Plus. But, despite its racing heritage the engine could be tamed down for use in Ferrari's most exclusive gran turismo cars. It was rated at close to 300 hp, depending upon carburetion and compression. With the 4,505-cc engine, it could top 150 mph, which was pushing it for the tires available in that era. The engine was better than the tires available and Ferraris sometimes lost races because the tires frayed while the engines still had enough in them to win the race.

THE AGNELLI SPECIALE

Usually a big wig like Agnelli might get the first of a new series, but for some reason he got the last 375. The usual 375 of that time had a body similar to the 250 Europa with the usual horizontal rectangular grille cavity. But for some reason, again maybe to make sure that everyone who saw it coming knew it was The Boss's car, it had a vertical grille.

The car had extremely high body quality. It is safe to say that Battista Pinin Farina (later his nickname and last name were combined to make "Pininfarina") was at that point trying very hard to get the majority of body contracts from Ferrari, who were still going to their rivals like Ghia, Bertone, etc. Also getting credit for the design is Francesco Martinengo of whom car designer Tom Tjaarda says, "Franco wasn't a designer per se, but an artist with a fantastic eye for proportion."

This 375 America, chassis 0355AL, made its debut at the Turin Salon in April 1955. It was obvious to all that saw it that Pinin Farina had bent over backwards to make this car special—with such features as a flat vertical rear window nestled between rear flying buttresse sail panels, a huge tempered glass sunroof; two-tone paint, forward leaning A-pillars and again that vertical fluted grille instead of the usual horizontally-themed Ferrari "eggcrate." Interior oddments included a faux woodgrain finish over the metal instrument panel and more wood on the gear shift knob, window cranks and around the chrome door release handles. Like some other Ferraris for VIPs, a chronometric rally clock was installed on the transmission tunnel.

Under the hood it was also special—the bore had been increased to 4.9 liters, making this the first road-going 4.9 Ferrari. It also boasted a distributor for each bank, and larger 42mm Weber DCZ3 carburetors were installed. The chassis changes included taller 16-inch Borrani wire wheels to make room for what were really competition drum brakes. Now it seems ridiculous but there are reports that some of the suspension components were chromed! But that makes sense if they figured Agnelli was going to be showing his car to his friends and Ferrari knew the praise of his friends for the car would cement the relationship with Ferrari (as it was, after negotiating in bad faith in 1963 to sell the production car side of operation to Ford Motor Company, Enzo Ferrari did in fact sell that part of his company to Fiat in 1969).

COLOR A BARRIER?

The Agnelli 375 was controversial because not only did it have a bottle fly green exterior but for some reason the roof was ruby red, meant to coordinate with the red leather (but looking a bit Christmas-tree-ish).

Agnelli only kept it for five years. Why? Rich people get bored easy. He sold his 375 and the car went to others who would appreciate its uniqueness. Well, maybe not all of them because by the 1990s the car was looking shabby (the cognoscenti would say, even with the paint falling off in shards, it had "a nice patina") even though it was regularly driven and fully maintained mechanically. In the late '50s after Agnelli returned it to Ferrari, they sent it to their dealer in New York, Luigi Chinetti, who sold it not once but three times (it kept coming back!). The third time Chinetti bought it back, they paid Arthur Kyle $3,500 in 1967 but finally were able to unload it to Illinois resident Edward Andrews a year later for $5,000 who kept it for ten years until it went to a Ferrari collector Wayne Golomb. Now why would Golomb sell a one-off car? Probably because he had a more significant Ferrari in mind; he is on record as owning another 375.

David Smith of Indiana was quoted on a Ferrari-themed website saying, "I remember having correspondence with Mr. Golomb around late 1984 when it was for sale for $27,000 or so." He passed it up for a car with a Colombo V12, one not nearly as distinctive, but far easier to maintain.

The car then went to European Auto Sales in Costa Mesa, California, priced at just below $50,000. That's when the two college professors, our heroes, building a collection of Ferraris, saw it and realized its potential, buying it in June 1985.

Why the car changed hands so often is inexplicable. It seems a minor quibble with a one-off car but maybe one discouraging fact to owning it was no trunk lid—and what luggage space there was could only be found behind the seats where most of the room was taken up by the spare. So if you traveled, you didn't go too far (though Agnelli of course could afford to send his luggage on ahead). Another problem was the color. This was just the beginning of the "original color" movement where, when you bought a truly historic car, you were supposed to restore it to the colors, interior and exterior, it came with when new and dark green with a red roof was probably this car's curse because nobody wanted to bring it back to that color. In fact when the professors bought it, it had been painted a deep but flawed turquoise blue.

The college professors kept it for 15 years, driving it to many a prestigious Ferrari event, such as the Copperstate 1000 and the Colorado Grand, seemingly indifferent to pleas of "why don't you restore that?" and meanwhile leaving little flakes of blue paint in their wake—which they encouraged bystanders to snap off as souvenirs! Conversely they may have unwittingly been instrumental in getting a "preservation class" started at such events as Pebble Beach concours where show-goers let the show organizers know they wanted to see unrestored cars "AS IS," especially if they were historically significant cars such as this one, rather than wait several more years to see them restored.

The professors finally sold it after 15 years of ownership to Jack Thomas, a collector who prides himself in his collection of the Ferrari "America" cars, of which there have been several series.

It was then restored and has won many awards since.

Lesson learned? Sure, it didn't look like any other Ferrari of the time, and sure, when the Professors had it the paint was flaking off it, but, y'know, sometimes ugly ducklings have a way of growing into beautiful swans. Anybody who saw this car in New York in the '50s and didn't leap for it once it was mentioned as "Agnelli's car" missed a golden opportunity. For, if you are the boss, and especially if you are Giovanni Agnelli, you get only the best.

Value now? Oh, I'd start at a couple million and go up from there.

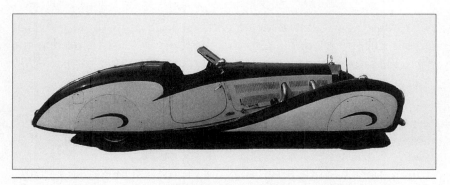

Chapter 35
SADDAM'S MERCEDES
(1935 MERCEDES 500K)
Is his 500K Mercedes truly lost in the sands of war?

When you are a dictator, especially in an oil rich country like Iraq, other countries give you things, cars, diamonds, whatnot.

So back when Saddam Hussein, or as he was known more formally Saddam Hussein Abd al-Majid al-Tikriti, was in power he got lots of loot. His two sons were ace sandbaggers as well. Their slogan was: if we want it, it's ours.

Take for example this particular classic pre-war Mercedes. Saddam stole it himself, right out of the Royal car museum.

It was thought destroyed when the U.S. bombed Iraq, but this writer has seen pictures of it taken after the American invasion.

First some background on the model...The Mercedes 500K (type W29) was a grand touring car built by Mercedes between 1934 and 1936. First exhibited at the 1934 Berlin Motor Show, it carried the internal factory designation of W29. The "K" stood for Kompressor (German for supercharger) and it was the successor to the 380 introduced only a year before.

The 500K used the same independent suspension as the 380, with a double wishbone front axle, and a double-joint swing axle at the rear. It used coil springs instead of the more common leafs. This gave it better handling and a better ride than all the previous S/SS/SSK roadsters.

It was quite a heavy car, but the 160-hp engine could get it over 100 mph.

The customers had a lot of choices, including three different chassis to choose from (eight with the short "A" chassis used as the basis for two-seater models: the Motorway Courier, or the 1936 Special Roadster which offered the highest performance).

Now back in those days you could still order a luxury car chassis and have it sent over to your favorite coachbuilder for a custom body. This car was so honored, having coachwork by Erdmann & Rossi. Actually there were two identical cars built, both with huge front fenders with the front tires completely enclosed like a Figoni et Falaschi-bodied Delahaye but then that is ruined a bit by the insertion of headlights in the leading edges of these front fenders.

Now a word about the coachbuilders—according to the website Coachbuild.com Karosserie Erdmann & Rossi dated back from 1906, when Eduard Rossi joined Willy Erdmann's company, which he'd founded in 1898. Willy Erdmann had been building horse-drawn carriages since 1898, but when car-salesman Eduard Rossi joined the company in 1906, they started to offer individualized coachwork for cars as well.

The company got through World War One by manufacturing utility vehicles. It was only after that war that they became known for designing and building bodies for luxury German automakers like Mercedes and Horch and foreign marques, like Bentley and Rolls-Royce. Their work was so respected that they became the exclusive distributor of Rolls-Royce and Bentley motorcars in Germany.

A ROYAL COMMISSION

During the 1920s and 1930s, many famous one-off designs were delivered by Erdmann and Rossi to Royals including Prince Bernhard of the Netherlands and King Ghazi of Iraq. About 200 craftsmen could build two to three bodies per week.

King Ghazi had seen an Erdmann & Rossi Mercedes roadster at an auto show in Spain in 1935 and put in an order for one. Originally the one he saw had a 2.9-liter engine, so wasn't a 500K, but the factory told him to wait and they would have that same body style put on a more powerful 500K for him.

Ghazi had been crowned King in 1933 at the tender age of 21. The same day he was appointed Admiral of the Fleet in the Royal Iraqi Navy, Field Marshal of the Royal Iraq Army, and Marshal of the Royal Iraqi Air Force. The king apparently didn't log a lot of time in his new toy which has been identified by Mercedes as order #2698 placed 5 December 1935, with engine #123705. The King was killed driving another of his cars in 1939. There are dark rumors that his "accident" was no accident when the brakes failed (we can't blame the CIA—they didn't exist yet, but he is described as having pro-Nazi sympathies).

A CAR THIEF'S TREASURES

Now flash forward at least half a century, to arch-villain Saddam, who, if you wish, can be posthumously charged with Grand Theft Auto (though one could argue as the ruler of an empire, you pretty much own whatever you want, anyhow).

Saddam's world as he knew it ended when the Americans rolled in. As everyone knows, his palace was overrun in the big American invasion of Iraq.

Problem was, he had many palaces. The one on the west bank of the Tigris River had two 40-car garages but in an internet search for pictures of the American troops examining the cars found at the palaces I only saw a couple I'd want—a Silver Cloud III, a Jaguar XK140 or 150, a Hooper-bodied Bentley, or maybe the black Packard; but the rest was dreck—a Prowler, a 1980s Zimmer (a car *Car & Driver* described as "a hokey neoclassical car built on a modern chassis, the result ranking high on the pimpmobile charts"), a London taxi, a Ford woody wagon, and dune buggies apparently driven inside the palace.

Looters made off with about 20 vehicles during the initial rush of troops in. Among the rumors left over from the invasion is that Saddam's son Uday, sometime somewhere before the Americans came, ticked off the old man and Saddam destroyed some 50 of his cars as punishment.

But the big prize, the pre-war 500K, seems to be missing.

ROYAL RESTORATION

At some point during Saddam's ownership, some say around 1986, the 500K, then yellow and black, was sent to Germany for a complete restoration with none other than the King of Jordan footing the bill. Why would the ruler of a rival country do this? Well, it might have been a favor to a relative, as in fact they were related. Also the King was a real car buff with his own museum, and he would know the right people to restore it. Also, Jordan doesn't have oil. Iraq does. Be nice to your oil supplier. While the Saddam 500K was in Germany, it is said a complete replica was made, but for whom? And on what chassis?

Anyhow, some years after the American invasion a car restorer in Orange, California, showed me a digital picture of an Erdmann & Rossi fully skirted 500K roadster in Iraq, parked in a modern underground garage.

Where this prize jewel of the crown went is anybody's guess.

Don Williams, head wheeler-dealer for the Blackhawk Collection, declared the car his favorite "in all the world" soon after he saw it being restored in Germany almost a quarter century years ago. Some say its value could be as high as $8 million.

Then there are rumors that filter in. One is that the car was on display sometime since the invasion in a German Mercedes dealership.

Much confusion was sewn when a silver look-alike appeared at the St. James Concours in London in 2013. Some reporters carelessly identified it as "the" missing King Ghazi car while others dug a little deeper and found the show car was in fact one year newer, and a copy ordered by King Hussein of Jordan on a genuine Mercedes chassis at the same time he had sent the original to be restored in Germany for Saddam. The replica body is on chassis 113640. Due to war in the Mideast and the King's subsequent illness and death (in 1999) he never got to see his copy.

But all that begs the bigger question: if and when it is found, just who does it belong to? The Saddam estate? After all, he left a wife and daughters though his car-loving sons lost their lives by duking it out with American troops. Or does it belong instead to the country of Iraq as a national treasure?

So the upshot is, if you hear of an ex-Saddam ex-King Ghazi two-seater Erdmann & Rossi 540K coming up for sale at this or that auction you will have to take the world's greatest experts to authenticate it (the serial number should be 123705), and even then maybe fight the Iraq government for ownership. (If you just have to have a Saddam car, there's also his postwar 600 landaulette which, when we last heard of it, was in storage at the Petersen Museum in Los Angeles.)

Lesson to be learned here? In many countries of the world, there are great cars in the garages of the leaders, be they Royals, duly elected officials or just plain ol' run-of-the-mill despots. Hey, leaders come and leaders go. Sometimes the cars stay in the Royal garage. Those who aspire to own some famous leader's car need to do their research well in advance of any anticipated changes in leadership. The rule is: when the shooting stops, you move in.

Warning: this is not a route for the feint of heart.

Chapter 36
WHAT THE SHAH GIVETH AWAY
(1939 BUGATTI TYPE 57)

Wherein one man's trash is another man's fortune.

One of the nice things about being royalty is that leaders of other countries give you stuff. Of course in 1939, on the eve of WWII, everyone wanted to make nice with a prince in a country that was awash in oil.

Thus Mohammed Reza Pahlavi, son of the leader of Iran, was sitting pretty in 1939 when he arranged to marry the daughter of King Forouk, of Egypt, himself a car guy. Each western power searched for a unique present to give the young Prince and France provided one of the best—a brand new Bugatti type 57SC.

First a little background on the marque…You're right if you guessed Bugatti is an Italian name. Ettore Bugatti was born in northern Italy but started building his cars in Molsheim in the Alsace region of France. Ettore Bugatti's son Jean was in charge of the design team responsible for the Bugatti 57C's (poor Jean was later killed testing a Bugatti).

The Type 57C is thought to be the best of the production Bugattis. Though not intended for racing, some racing versions of the type 57 were built and one won the 1936 French Grand Prix, and the 24-hour races at Le Mans in both 1937 and 1939!

For the prince, the French government chose Van Vooren, a French coachbuilder—but that coachbuilder seemed to steal a lot for chassis #57808 from rival coachbuilders Figoni et Falaschi, who were already building a Delahaye for the NY Worlds Fair which had the same very short windscreen that could be wound down into the body and "disappearing top," very unusual in cars built before the war (see the profile on this car in *Incredible Barn Finds*). And they all lived happily ever after. Isn't that what happens in fairy tales? Well, the real story is the Prince dumped Fouziyeh when she gave birth to a girl named Shahnaz, and you needed a boy if you wanted an heir to the throne. Their divorce finalized on October 16, 1948.

The Shah married anew (in fact he married twice more), finally produced a male heir, but that heir never got to enjoy the fruits of being a ruler because the Shah left Iran to seek medical help for cancer, at least that was the excuse other than he was being overthrown in the Revolution that took place in the 1980s.

The car was not, however, sold cheaply in the streets after the sacking of his palace as has been rumored. No, it had been bought way back in the Fifties by a very astute Dutch classic car dealer named Ruben who, ironically, according to his son, Jack Braam Ruben, thought he was buying a Bugatti Royale going by the description of "a car with a long hood."

Now the question is, was one of the six Royales missing at that time? I don't know, but the younger Mr. Ruben has published a picture of the Type 57 on a website, showing the car in Amsterdam after his father received it. The car looks much less impressive without the front wheel spats that make it so distinctive. And it didn't arrive from Iran with a Bugatti engine but some American engine, possibly a Cadillac or Packard.

The car was sold by the Royal Hunting Dept. for as little as $275, so if there was ever a time to buy a future classic this was it. Now you wonder, where was the sentimentality—I mean we're talking wedding present here.

It eventually was sold to an American who had it restored in England and then resold a couple of times until it reached magazine publisher Robert E. Petersen, who made it the cornerstone of the collection that now graces the Museum bearing his name.

You have to wonder—here was one of the most distinctive cars in the world. Why did the Shah let it go? Ah, let's say anybody who has been married a second time would understand. Odds are Wife No. 2 doesn't like to see the car given as a wedding present to Wife No. 1 around. Plus they must have blown the engine at one time or another, hence it was no longer all Bugatti once the American engine was put in.

And back in the early '50s, there just wasn't the mania for restoring cars that there is today. It was just another old car. Fortunately, some of the Shah's old cars are still there today, in a museum pieced together from what was recovered after the Revolution, including several Rolls Royces, a Bizzarrini, a one-off Chrysler by Ghia, and so forth.

It's likely that Mr. Petersen, publisher of *Motor Trend*, had seen the car in his own magazine decades earlier and, as a result, had filed it away in the back of his brain, part of a "wish list" of what he would buy if he ever started a collection. When the car became available, he bought it, though at a full restored price.

Lesson to be learned here? Rulers are given gifts—special firearms, airplanes, cars, boats—and, when you are given stuff, you just don't value it as much as if you had to pay for it. So that's part of it; then, too, as I say, it was the Fifties. It's too bad the Dutch trader didn't keep it but when you are a dealer, you turn cars over—it's what you do, and then it's on to the next one.

Chapter 37
THE BOUNTY HUNTER
(1968 CORVETTE L88)

Maybe the first "art" Corvette...ugly, but valuable.

The late pop artist Andy Warhol was not only famous for his prints of movie stars like Marilyn Monroe, occasionally he painted a real car, like a BMW M1. The few cars he painted in wild colors are known as "art cars."

Well, Terry Michaelis of Napoleon, Ohio, who runs a business called ProTeam likes art. but he collects Corvettes and retails them all over the world. This is the story of an arty Corvette he bought, not something created for art mind you, but painted in a manner reminiscent of Warhol.

Here's the story. In the car biz, buying and selling collector cars like Corvettes, you get your odd phone calls, your guys who found an old car and claim this one is the Bomb—the *ultissimo.*

Well, fact is, sometimes it is and sometimes it isn't.

When the caller says "Sixties" and "Big Block" in the same sentence, it tends to get your attention.

The caller said it was "rough." That could mean anything. That could mean non-matching numbers, a thrown-together car of junkyard parts. Or worse yet, one that was raced, hit, and repaired badly.

But Terry Michaelis didn't fall off the turnip truck yesterday. He knew that big block could also mean L88. He asked it if was an L88.

"Yessir."

At that point, sirens went off. Bells rung.

The L88 was a legendary Corvette package that first saw the light of day at Sebring in 1967, where it was entered in the 12-hour race. The L88 package included many competition components like an M22 transmission, large disc brakes, upgraded suspension and an aluminum head 427. Shortly after the race, the L88 option would be offered on production cars. It offered the most powerful engine that would ever appear in a production Corvette up until that time.

The engine itself had many special components: a new forged crank, 12.5:1 pistons, cold air induction and alloy cylinder heads.

Other changes to the car included a complete removal of all luxuries. Chevrolet removed heater, radio, air conditioning and choke. To compensate for these deletions, an F41 suspension, K66 ignition transistor, J56 power discs, G81 positraction differential and a large aluminum radiator were added.

The L88 was a racecar and Chevrolet wanted to keep them on the track. If the deletion of several creature comforts wasn't enough to discourage dillitantes, the advertising for the car rated the L88 as having less horsepower than the cheaper L71 package—Chevrolet released a figure of 430 hp at 4600 rpm. This was well below the actual peak power which was more like 600 hp at 6500 rpm.

Only twenty were made that first year. This one was the second year body style, the so-called "Mako Shark style" based on the concept car.

Michaelis bought the car for a price equivalent to several new Corvettes and began to restore it. Once it arrived back at his shop, he did some research and found out that it had a production date of April 23, 1968, and delivered new by Modern Chevrolet of Winston Salem, North Carolina (dealer code 503 in zone 16) per the official NCRS/GM shipping data records (SDR). Most importantly, he found out it was an L88 with M-22 heavy-duty transmission, and the numbers matched for chassis and engine and transmission. Further, it was one of 80 Corvettes produced with an L88 for 1968 and only one of two known Red/Red L88's.

You're sold already, right? Well, Michaelis didn't have to think five minutes about buying the car because the caller was the equally legendary Ronnie Reid Joyner. On their website ProTeam has a biographical story on Tar Heel (Mt. Aire, North Carolina) Joyner whose story sounds a little like the TV series Justified, with gunplay, fast cars and well, pretty women added. Joyner liked to race, but to hell with formal racetracks and scrutinizing and all that, he liked to do his racing on the street, mano-a-mano. He called himself the "Bounty Hunter" and he collected a lot of bounties. He bought many a fast car as he had one hard and fast rule—once a car failed him and lost a race, it was toast. He had started out with fast Fords but moved over to Chevys. His personal Corvette history, furnished by him, was:

1963 Corvette – got outrun, sold it

1964 Corvette – got outrun, sold it

1965 Corvette – got outrun, sold it

1966 Corvette – got outrun, sold it

1967 Corvette 427-435 – finally got outrun, traded in on the L88.

When he still owned that '67, Ronnie had an ear to the ground that Chevy was going to continue making these extra-mean Corvettes after '67 so he pre-ordered the 1968 L88, trading in his 1967 427 Corvette. It was a long wait, especially having to live without a Corvette until his '68 L88 arrived. It was two months into the 1969 Corvette production when his '68 L88 finally arrived by rail. The Pro Team website mentioned Ronnie off-loaded the red L88 off the train himself. He was quoted saying: "When I come off that train track, them boys said, 'you could see up underneath of it.' I come wide open. Tires were a'smokin'. It hit the ground a runnin'. Been wide open ever since, 30,000 some miles on it and they were all wide open racin'."

The most Ronnie ever won was $2,500 against a guy who owned the Corvette shop in Winston-Salem. He did have a race scheduled up in Virginia that would have had $5,000 on the table. He refused to race and they shot him and the car. Ronnie told the Pro Team reporter: "That's okay, I shot him back. Payback is hell."

When asked, "Which gave you the best run?" His answer was: "Another L88." This was in Winston-Salem against another L88. "It was close," Ronnie told Pro Team, "but I believe I was a little better driver than he was and I had better tires than he had."

Ronnie also liked to tell about the time he went up against Zack Reynolds, another infamous tar heel. "Me and Zack were friends," said Joyner. "He had a Ford 427 Cobra. His family owned the Smith-Reynolds airport in Winston-Salem. They detoured the planes landing and taking off long enough for me and Zack Reynolds to race on the airstrip and I outrun that Ford Cobra like it was tied. It wasn't for money. He wasn't a bettin' man. He carried no money. You had to buy him a damned cocoa."

Reynolds, by the way, was a real character. I once called him up and was talking for half an hour when I had to beg off to get to an appointment. A few days later I got a tape recorder in the mail. I noticed it had a tape in it. I pressed PLAY and Reynolds' voice boomed out, "As I was sayin'..."

Now with all this money on the table you kind of wonder how Joyner collected when he won. He explained that to Michaelis: "I always had a convoy; 'clan' is what they called it," he told Pro Team's reporter. "They went with me wherever we raced."

The clan was 30-40 motorcycles who were following him in a convoy behind his L88. Joyner says, "People would always pay-up when they lost."

The races were generally two miles—blow the horn to start (the other guy got to blow their horn first), starting/finishing point would be bridge to bridge, etc.

Now when Michaelis bought it, the car had non-stock humongous fender flares. Ronnie knew the mechanics at Junior Johnson's garage so got all the racing tires he wanted. He had to flare the fenders to make them fit.

THE L88 MEETS THE SAND DUNE

Cowboys have a saying for trouble, what they call a "hitch in their getalong." Well, providentially Joyner hung out at a little bar called the Hitchin' Post. He had a friend drive him home when he got a little tipsy. Only trouble was, one night he was drunk and the driver was drunk. The friend got the right driveway but kept going and sunk it into a sand dune. Ronnie recollects that the first driver "couldn't drive no how."

The Pro Team story recounts what happened after Ronnie took the wheel: "Ronnie put the car in low gear and left it there until the clutch exploded." Joyner said: "Divine providence sent most of the clutch down instead of up through the firewall because, 'It would've blown my feet off but that was the last time I drove. Right after that, I quit drinkin' so I never got it running again. I was so drunk the next morning I'd wondered where my car went… and then I seen it out there in the sand buried up."

So, okay, the car was messed up some. But Joyner figured he could restore it. He built a new garage, and hired on two different guys who each started the restoration but quit in turn. Well, maybe "restore" isn't the right word because at some point Joyner and a buddy painted it all sorts of colors like an "art car." Said Ronnie, "It looked good if you were drunk."

Eventually, Joyner figured, hell, once the car was restored, it wouldn't be the same anymore. All the character would be gone. It was at that point he called ProTeam because he knew if they restored it they would restore it the right way.

Michaelis restored it, at considerable cost, and sold it, but he admits that it will be a long time before he comes across another Corvette owner as memorable as Ronnie Reid Joyner, the Bounty Hunter.

Lesson to be learned? If you're looking for a special car, one that only a few of were built, it behooves you to pound the pavement looking for old references to people who had those cars when they were new. Now Joyner's races were unofficial to say the least but this was at least his fifth Corvette, so he was a legend in the South. But even legends have to hang it up sometime and, through Michaelis' persistence (and a scout that he had on retainer to find cars) he found the car and the numbers checked out.

Value today? Start with a million and go up from there.

Chapter 38
THE TIME CAPSULE 'VETTE
(1954 CORVETTE)
Talk about low mileage!

There's all shapes and sizes and mindsets of car guys. One rather rare type is the guy who buys new cars or almost new ones, and tools around for a while and then gets bored with it and puts it away.

Sometimes for a month, sometimes for a year, well, how about 27 years? That's the story of a 1954 Corvette that apparently spent almost three decades bricked up inside a grocery store in Brunswick, Maine, where it had been put there by the store's owner, a Mr. Richard Sampson.

Sampson was a successful but clearly eccentric man who not only built a chain of 33 grocery stores, but ran for governor and formally served as a Senator from Maine for awhile. He bought the car new and drove it until 1959 at which point, since a new store was being built for his chain in Brunswick, got the idea of having the workmen enclose his treasure in a room which was then walled off with a 4-inch thick slab of concrete. He had a porthole put into the concrete on one side so he could periodically look at it and two lights were left burning (you have to wonder how he planned to change light bulbs).

Famed historian Ken Gross first told the story run in 1976 in *Special Interest Autos*, at that time saying one of the light bulbs had burned out and the grocery store had become a sporting goods store. "By the dim light of the second bulb," wrote Gross, "the polo white Corvette can still be seen, surrounded by dust and cobwebs...The dampness in the enclosed room has already caused the car's surface to blister. The chrome and convertible top still look perfect, however."

When it was rolled out into the sunlight, Corvette people came from all over to gaze at the car in awe and wonderment. The car was dead stock original, the odometer reading a mere 2,331 actual miles. Mr. Sampson's will had stipulated that the car remain so entombed until the year 2000 (although it wasn't honored), when I guess he thought it would amaze those future folks on how high technology the Corvette was in 1954 (they were unimpressed).

UNINTERRED, ONLY TO BE PUT ON ICE AGAIN

When the store changed owners in 1982, the new owner generously gave Mr. Sampson's daughter until 1986 to move it, Mr. Sampson having given up the ghost. Four years later his daughter moved the car all the way to Daytona Beach, Florida, where it is said that she parked it in her living room for approximately the next 10 years, though other stories say it was only in her house for three years and then moved to storage. At some point though it went to a National Corvette event in Bloomington, Illinois, where it was displayed in honor of her father.

Terry Michaelis of ProTeam negotiated with Mr. Sampson's daughter, Cynthia, to buy what was probably the oldest lowest mile unrestored Corvette in the world. ProTeam did not even try to start it but took it to a Florida auction where it stalled out in bidding at $100,000.

Of course there are always skeptics. A couple such armchair critics on the website Corvette forums pointed out that a state inspection sticker in the front corner of the windshield indicated that it had not been sealed up since new (though the original stories did not claim that) but this is carping—the point was nobody had messed with it so when it was wheeled out into the sun it represented a Corvette such as they had been built and sold in '54.

Lessons to be learned here? When you hear one of those old rumors that someone has stashed away a car, be it 5, 10, 20, 30 years later, it's worth checking out to see if it is still there or perhaps been relocated by a relative if the original owner has passed on. Of course whoever bought that '54 eventually had a full restoration ahead of them but you would be surprised how some collectors will pay a bunch more in order to buy a "time capsule" car that's been totally unmolested so they won't have to spend time and money undoing the mistakes of a car that's been restored badly.

Patina sells, man, and you can bet that after 27 years, this car had world class patina!

Chapter 39
RITA'S RIDE
(1953 CADILLAC GHIA)

Just marry a prince.

This is a story of unrequited love all the way around. It occurred in the early '50s. Think film noir, mood lighting, moonlight on the ocean, diaphanous beaded gowns that are all too revealing, that sort of thing.

First, as the female lead I offer Rita Hayworth, born Margarita Carmen Cansino, to a Spanish Flamenco dancer father and Ziegfield girl mother. She was reportedly an under-age dancer at a Tijuana club when she was discovered by Fox Studios.

She became one of the hottest actresses in Hollywood. Her one-glove strip tease in the movie Gilda put her on the map. Rita was a top movie star and a popular pin-up girl during the Forties. Her second husband was famed director Orson Welles, who she married in 1943. Her career bloomed during that time, but she couldn't resist living on the edge by having a fling around 1948. Not with some ordinary Joe, mind you, but with an Ismaili prince, Aly Kahn.

Now fact was I had heard about Aly Khan since I was a teenager but back then (you might say "before Wikipedia" and even before the Internet was invented) I never actually had been able to figure out what country he was a prince of, primarily because, as I found out in 2013, the Ismaili sect of Muslims have no country or territory of their own. Prince Ali Salman Aga Khan, known as Aly Khan, was a son of Sultan Mohammed Shah, Aga Khan III, the head of the Ismaili Muslims. Aly Khan's son, born in 1957, is the current Sultan Aga Khan IV and worth about $800 million. So they are not only royalty but "come from money" (what a great old-time phrase).

Rita was also associated with the Savonuzzi Gilda project (see later in this book).

Well, an American girl doesn't meet a prince every day! She up and dumps Orson Welles and marries the prince, becoming, for a short time, a Princess. The couple had a daughter, Princess Yasmin Aga Khan. Now this is a car magazine, not a movie rag, so I must force you back to the Caddy. The Prince sees a flamboyant car at a European auto show and orders an identical one for her. Oddly, it's an American car, a series 62 Cadillac, but you can't tell that because Ghia, a famous Italian coachbuilder, has clothed it in a svelte European-shaped body. And amazingly it has quad headlamps though no one told Ghia that GM wouldn't feature those for another five years!

Ghia had built that first Cadillac on spec. Cadillac did not pay for it—Ghia was just hoping to get an assignment from Cadillac like the many they were getting from Chrysler.

Ghia was also hoping, if an automaker didn't step up with the company checkbook, that wealthy individuals would order a copy. Ironically it was Chrysler who later came a-callin' for bodywork, for the run of 55 turbine-powered cars, but that was later.

Back to the Prince. The marriage was already on the rocks when the Prince ordered the Cadillac bodied by Ghia as a present for his wife, or ex-wife. Rita had filed divorce papers in 1951, though it appears it took some time for the divorce to actually take effect. Some say the Ghia coupe was still being pounded out at Ghia when the marriage finally fell apart. If that's true, maybe the Caddy was intended as a reconciliation gift. If so, it didn't take. Her next of five marriages had already begun in 1953.

But good publicity never dies and from that point on, this design on a Cadillac is called the "Rita Hayworth Cadillac." Now sometimes you have these situations where these special cars are ordered for famous people who never quite get to them (Clark

Gable's Jensen-Ford for example), but in this case I've got one eyewitness. Your author published a blurb about this car on the website VeloceToday.com and some guy named "Hugh" posted the comment: "I saw Rita driving it in Palm Beach in December of 1954. At the time it was black with a red side insert. Shortly after seeing it, there was a Ghia Cadillac on the cover of *Road & Track* which was blue with a silver side insert. Having grown up near Detroit, I had seen several of the Ghia Chryslers, but I had no idea of what this black and red car was until I got my *Road & Track* in the mail."

Now the question is, is the black car Hugh saw the same one I saw? Which one of the two was turquoise for a time? The black one is presently in the collection of the Petersen Museum and I am hoping the chief curator lets me know, eventually (it is, admittedly, not one of life's burning questions).

THE COMEUPPANCE OF MR. SMARTY PANTS

Now this is another ultimate collector's car that I came within a hairsbreadth of owning only to be shot in the foot by nobody other than myself.

It was the early '80s. I was driving South down Highway 1, the coast road that offers occasional views of the ocean, through Encinitas, a few miles from San Diego, and I passed a used car lot.

There was an odd turquoise blue car in the front row lineup. I slammed on the brakes and went back. The salesman said, "It's a Ghia Cadillac."

Well, I knew Carrozzeria Ghia—I knew about all the Chrysler dream cars they had built and I had never heard they had done a Cadillac. I proudly announced, "Well, I know Ghia and they never did a Cadillac." (In the author's defense, there is no mention of the car in *Ghia, Ford's Carrozzeria*, published in 1985.) The more fool I.

The salesman wanted $14,000. Now it so happened that I had about $10,000 between my wife and I. We were saving for a house. It would have been a stretch but maybe the car dealer would have taken ten grand. What turned me off, and made me seriously doubt that it was an Italian carrozzeria-built car, were the three exhaust pipes per side sprouting out of the rear fenders aft of the rear wheel wells. These looked hokey as hell, very George Barrisish (sorry George!).

I thought this has to be some Hollywood custom car, certainly not a product of Ghia. And the exhaust pipes were painted a dull gold, as was all the chrome trim. More Hollywood 'crapola,' I thought.

But I had to admit the grille shape was beautiful as were the front fenders. It probably had the best front end of any Italian-bodied American car I had ever seen, despite the four headlamps.

We drove off, me feeling smug that I (the great expert) had spotted a misrepresented car. Well, I was wrong. One of the two Cadillac Ghias was later bought by Ken Behring, founder of the Blackhawk Museum in Danville, California, and restored and became a million-dollar car that appeared at many an event, including Pebble Beach. The ugly exhaust pipes I hated on the one I saw conveniently got "lost" along the way on both of the Cadillac Ghias (without seeing an in-period picture of the car as built I'll never know if they were part of the original design). I suspect they probably were original because the Touring-bodied Hudson Italia, done about the same time period, had them (although they were really receptacles for reflectors) as did the Boano-bodied Lincoln Indianapolis, though on the Lincoln their three exhausts per side sprouted out of the front fenders behind the front wheels. You can't blame the Italians for going ga-ga over exhausts. They had only to look at the prewar American greats like the Duesenberg, which had four exhausts sprouting out of the body per side for inspiration.

So I blew it. I could've had an Italian coachbuilt car (before Ford bought the coachbuilder and reduced the "Ghia" name to nothing), which was also a Royal car (always good for status in a country of commoners), or a movie star's car (well, even if it was the wrong one of the two made, Rita had one just like it).

But in the end I had nothing.

Lesson to be learned here? Pride cometh before a fall. I don't make that mistake anymore, thinking I've seen everything, and I've read everything so what somebody is showing me that doesn't compute must be misrepresented. Now I'm always willing to learn, but in this car's case, it's too late, and Rita's Ghia-Cadillac is another one that got away.

Chapter 40
DUNTOV'S DALLIANCE
(1966 CERV II CORVETTE)
Yes, you can buy engineering prototypes, but it ain't easy.

What if you were at a classic car auction and had the chance to bid on a mid-engined prototype built by GM—a car contemporaneous with the Ford GT40? You then find out that GM is blocking the sale.

Why? Because they had donated the car to a museum and thought it would remain on stage at the museum forever more.

Their lawyers, see, lose sleep thinking some old GM-built prototype will be taken out on a race track and pedal put to the metal and someone will get hurt, somewhere around 200 mph.

Well, it happened. Not the racetrack part but the buying part. The would-be buyers persevered and the great GM Corporation had to eat crow.

First some background on the major character in this drama, one snow-white haired chain-smoking French-speaking German-educated engineer named Zora Arkus-Duntov. He worked for

GM in the Fifties and Sixties, becoming known as "the father of the Corvette" (though he arrived at GM when the Corvette was already in production).

He enjoyed the status of being Chevrolet's "in house" racer even when GM was officially against racing (as a part of campaigns for auto safety). He developed several cars that looked like racecars, that ran as fast as racecars of the time but which were actually not raced.

ENTER THE CERVS

The first GM experimental car to be called a Chevrolet Engineering Research Vehicle (CERV) was a single-seater called the CERV I developed between 1959-'60—an open-wheeled single-seater racecar, with Larry Shinoda (famous later for the '63 Corvette Stingray design) and Tony Lapine doing the design.

Then there was the CERV II. You have to know that Duntov, jealous of Ford openly getting cars ready to win Le Mans, was working behind the scenes in hopes GM would do an about-face and "green light" an endurance racing team. After all, Duntov himself had competed at Le Mans, both in an Allard and a Porsche.

Duntov was indefatigable when it came to these back door racing projects. Only the year before, Duntov had championed the front-engined Corvette Grand Sport—a look-alike for the '63 Corvette using a lighter tube frame—only to get it shot down by GM management which pulled the plug at five cars (which he snuck out to racers with no sponsor money to race them).

The CERV II was his mid-engined project, but the most the public saw it was on the cover of *Motor Trend*.

The CERV II was started in early '62 and developed after the front-engined Grand Sport program was dead for sure.

The chassis was similar to that of the Ford GT40, a monocoque with steel subframe carrying the suspension and engine.

The original engine was an injected alloy block with alloy heads, overhead-cam 377-cubic-inch V8 rated at 490 hp. It had a similar cross ram intake manifold toting 58mm Weber carburetors that you saw on the Grand Sport. The compression ratio was 10.8 compression ratio, and later it was fitted with Hilborn fuel injection.

Duntov kept changing the engine and re-testing it, trying to stay abreast of racing developments in the real world. In 1970, he dropped in a ZL-1 aluminum block 427 Corvette engine rated at 550 hp. This would go 0-60 in a claimed 2.8 seconds and top

200 mph. There was no complicated "bundle of snakes" tuned exhaust as in the GT40, just vertical exhaust stacks like on some farm tractor.

Duntov had a co-conspirator in Chevy General Manager Semon "Bunkie" Knudsen, who wanted GM to get back into racing, so the specs laid down for the CERV II were coincidentally close to that of the international prototype class. For some reason they chose a 4-liter version and one experiment used special 3-valve single overhead-cam heads. There is some who are racing experts of that era who say the engine was based on that used on some '62 mid-engined Indy cars, the Harvey Aluminum Specials designed by Englishman John Crostwaite for Mickey Thompson, making the changes to Buick aluminum V8's.

Another theory credits the head designs to Englishman Sir Harry Weslake who helped develop heads associated with Ford.

At any rate, the CERV II also saw the use of titanium—a lighter, stronger metal than aluminum (you might remember the SR-71 spyplane, built largely of titanium) was speced for hubs, connecting rods, valves, and exhaust manifolds. The target weight was 1,400 pounds.

Duntov was one of the first to realize that the manual shift was a time waster, and fitted the CERV II with an automatic racing gearbox without a power-wasting hydraulic coupling.

Ironically, just as the CERV II was being built, the high brass on the 14th floor of the GM building swung the hammer to smash any racing plans but Duntov persisted in building the one car, even if it looked like GM was not going to be in racing.

The engineering of the drive system and torque converter arrangement was assigned to to GM's engineering staff/team, with Raymond Michnay in charge. His crew came up with an advanced 4-wheel drive unit. Not only was it 4WD but this was one of the first instances which would pioneer the concept of having variable power delivery to each end of the car, the amount of which varied according to speed.

The gearbox used two torque converters, with a 10-inch Powerglide converter from a Corvair placed ahead of the front wheels for the front drive portion. An 11-inch diameter Powerglide torque converter was modified so that it wouldn't reach lock-up (1:1 ratio) until about 4500 rpm, which was mounted off the rear of the engine for the rear drive. Lock-up was about 4100 rpm. Duntov specified a two-speed gearbox for each end of the car, placed behind the final drive gears, which allowed a choice of direct drive or a 1.5 to one reduction.

The car ran wide Kelsey-Hayes magnesium wheels—9.2x15 inches.

The brakes were outboard, Girling calipers widened to accept a vented rotor. The hub carriers (front and rear) were cast nodular iron with the front steering arms being forged steel. Concentric coil springs and Armstrong shock dampers were used all around.

The cars first broke the light of day in March '64, at GM's spacious Milford test track in Michigan. GM also had bought their own GT40 to test their prototype against. When the word came down from the big brass that there would be no GM racing team, the program was cut short.

But at least some famous drivers had raced it, including Jim Hall (an oilman from Midland, Texas, who had the Chaparral team), Roger Penske, and GM test driver Bob Clift.

One report was that, after its racing plans were scotched, the car was used as a testbed for a mid-Sixties super-Corvette but since no clay models exist, one has to doubt the truth of that.

Even though work stopped on the GSII, it continued on other mid-engined racecars being run by Chaparral in Texas, the team run by Jim Hall. Paul van Vaulkenburgh, a former test track engineer for GM, in his book *The Secrets of Chevrolet Racing*, goes into this extensively, describing how GM would build racecars and send them to Hall for testing against his cars on Hall's private racetrack. If GM's car was faster, Hall kept it and adopted its ideas. His Chaparrals raced against Ford's GT40s in Europe but his was a shoestring operation that only resulted in a couple of victories. One wonders if Duntov's projects were the ones meant to be seen, like the CERV II, while the real effort at Chevrolet Engineering was being put on Hall's cars behind the scenes.

By the way the Hall car should be mentioned. That was the GSII, a very similar looking car. There were two of those built, one with a steel hull, the other with an aluminum hull, and Jim Hall got to keep the aluminum-hulled one. Reports from various historians say that the car was deep-sixed by GM brass after they saw that Ford might interpret it as a threat to their GT40 program and they didn't want to go head-to-head out in public battling Ford with an endurance racer.

There was even a CERV III later on, in 1990, a more roadable car, but that was only a show car. Never raced, the CERV II ended as a show and museum piece. After that came the CERV IV show car, until finally the CERV name was retired.

THE AUCTION FRACAS

Now about that fracas...In 1989 the CERV II and its earlier single-seater cousin, the CERV I, finally went to auction for the third time.

The previous year GM had tried to forbid their sale on grounds that the company still held the title to the historic cars.

The CERV I had earlier been at the famous Barrett-Jackson auction the year before, drawing a $1.25-million bid, but that's when the lawsuit came.

Why was GM all hot and bothered?

You see, GM had donated the cars to the Briggs Cunningham Museum in 1972 (other sources say '74). But they had no contingency plans for what would happen if Cunningham up and sold his collection which he did, in one big hurry.

Miles Collier Jr., the son of an early sports car advocate in America (the Collier brothers brought some of the first sports cars to America and raced them on their private track overlooking the Hudson River in New York) bought the Cunningham collection in late 1986 after Briggs had his emergency sale, and after putting the cars he liked on display in his own Museum in Florida, Collier sold off the rest, including the CERV I and II in the fall of 1987.

An auction of the two cars was planned for Monterey, even then a hotbed of old car activity (before it became a full week of activities). But according to the *Autoweek* in a 1989 article: "GM obtained a court injunction against the plan to sell the cars in Monterey so that it could prepare a legal case claiming title to the cars. The claim was that GM had donated the cars to Cunningham as a charitable trust, with the provision that they not be sold."

The claim was documented poorly, however, based on vaguely worded stickers placed on the cars and Arkus-Duntov's recollection of undocumented restrictions against private sale. The court ruled against GM on the issue of title. During the court case an independent appraisal assessed the value of CERV I at $2 million and CERV II at $1.5 million, backdated to Dec. 31, 1986, when Collier bought it along with the whole collection.

GM was miffed by the judge's decision (you kind of wonder if the judge had ever owned a GM car that turned out to be a lemon). The car subsequently joined the collection of Mike Yager who owns Mid-America Motor Works, a supplier of Corvette parts. He had the car restored by Corvette Repair Inc. of Valley Stream, New York.

The car came up again for Auction on November 21, 2013, this time with RM Auction Co., a premier auction firm. This time the results were $1,000,000.

Lesson learned? You can win against a giant Corporation. Just because they are big doesn't mean they have all their ducks in a row. GM simply dropped the ball when they donated the cars—they didn't anticipate what would happen if Cunningham suddenly closed his museum doors. So here's a case of even when you're told "NO," you can still win, especially if the donating automaker was a little sloppy on the paperwork.

Chapter 41
A Cowboy's Cord
(1937 Cord 812)
Once lost, twice found.

Before there was Roy Rogers…Before there was Hopalong Cassidy…Before WWII, there was Tom Mix, a "white hat" in that he always played the good guy and was a good role model for kids. A cowboy star, he had actually started out as a real cowboy, and was a real lawman, and then became a stunt man in the movies. He made 348 Western films before WWII.

And he liked cars. Well, if you were an American car fan during that period the one car you wanted was the Cord, designed by Gordon Buehrig. It was a very advanced car both in styling (with hidden headlamps) and in engineering, with front-wheel drive.

The Cord company was part of the Auburn-Cord-Duesenberg empire run out of Auburn, Indiana, by Errett Lobban Cord. Cord had, by the early 1920s, become the top seller of Moon cars in Chicago and subsequently rescued the failing Auburn Automobile Company in Auburn, Indiana. In 1926, he acquired Duesenberg, a luxury car built by former racecar builders, and then decided to add a third brand, a new luxury brand, carrying his own name.

The stunning 1937 Cord model 812 was not only V8-powered, front-wheel drive, and aerodynamic, it was available in a supercharged four-seater Phaeton.

The first incarnation of it had been the model 810 in 1936. It was an instant sensation at the November 1935 New York Auto Show.

The 812's main difference between it and the earlier 810 was the supercharged engine option that became available on the 812, adapted from the Schwitzer-Cummins centrifugal supercharger used in the SJ Duesenberg.

The 810 and 812 production combined made for a total of 2,900 cars built over an 18-month period. Of these, 612 were Phaetons and only 196 were supercharged.

It is thought that Mix paid $3,000 for the car, a heady amount then when a 2-bedroom home in the suburbs was $8,000. Unfortunately, as radical as the Cord was, a few early reliability problems, including slipping out of gear and vapor lock, dampened the public's zeal for it and the dealer base shrank so rapidly that left-over and still-being-built 1936 810s were sold as 1937 812s.

THE ACCIDENT

Now back to Tom Mix. Mix actually outlasted the Cord Motor Co., which went down before the war. The accident happened in October, 1940, near his ranch in Florence, Oklahoma, when a bridge was out on the highway near his home and construction workers were attempting to rebuild it.

According to Bob White, the Scottsdale-based owner of the car who rebuilt it with his son Scott, "The accident was fatal. And not due to anything wrong with the car mechanically. The State of Arizona was putting a bridge over the wash on Highway 79 near Florence, Arizona. The workmen saw the yellow Cord coming and noted it was going really fast. Mix was fearless on a horse or in the car. The Cord is capable of over 100 mph. This wasn't his first car to crash. As the yellow speck neared the construction site, the workmen began to move aside nervously because it didn't look like he was slowing a whit. One went out on the road and tried to wave the driver down, but Mix didn't see him until it was too late. It was not a deep wash, but the car slid back and forth and turned over once into the wash. Mix was thrown out and the metal suitcases that he kept on the back seat hit him in the neck breaking it. "

There was a bit of irony there—Mix preferred to carry his money around with him, lest ex-wives glom onto it in a bank account. He may have been killed as a result of that habit—those suitcases were heavy.

The senior White is of the opinion that Mix was a heavy drinker and that, coupled with his lead foot, was the cause of his accident.

SEARCHING FOR THE WRECK

After the accident, the car changed hands many times and, at one point, in the year 1943, it was sold for a mere $100 to a man named Ray Nelson, a collector and hardware store owner in Hollywood, by an executive at RKO Studios. It had taken Nelson months calling each studio to find out who had it. The way it got to the seller was that a studio executive had loaned Mix money and Mix had signed over the car as collateral. But then the studio exec who owned it didn't start restoring it because it looked bad, maybe unsalvageable. Maybe another reason it hadn't been sold earlier was that it had no tires, as this was during the war and tires were strictly rationed. Letting nothing stop him, Nelson bought another car, removed the tires to use on the Cord and gave the tire donor car back to the owner, who thought he was crazy.

Amazingly it started right up as soon as he installed a battery.

Nelson drove it until the early '60s but, after he nearly flipped it, he worried it was an accident car and sold it. It was "driven to the ground" by indifferent owners, and changed owners until it reached a Chicago man named Dusek who liked to race trains across the desert, proving he could beat the fastest trains. (Ironically when Mix owned it he would bet airplane pilots he could beat them to a nearby city, so he would race planes, not trains!) The Chicago owner, after driving the car into the ground, left it with a mechanic in the San Fernando Valley to restore.

That mechanic took the car entirely apart—engine out, trans out, every part out, even down to taking out the window channels, and then let the car sit with the parts scattered hither and yon in the baking sun. Nelson had been called by the owner of the car for advice and when he went to the farm where the car was stored, he saw what the mechanic had done. Nelson was so exasperated he made an offer. However, the Chicago man moved the car and parts to a nearby gully and it sat, with parts pickers discovering it and picking it clean.

THE REPEAT PHONE CALL GAMBIT

But Nelson still lusted for his former car. He kept making offers for five years, calling every month, usually on a Saturday night, until he wore the Chicago man down. He finally was able to buy the car for $500 in 1966. But the two things he couldn't find among the scattered parts were the Lycoming V8 engine and the transmission (which, being a front drive car, you would have to call a transaxle). It turned out the mechanic had left both at a machine shop for rebuilding but the seller couldn't remember the name of the shop. Nelson got the phone book and luckily found the shop with his first phone call. He reclaimed the engine, which had not only been rebuilt but paid for! All he had to do to claim it was give the shop owner the serial number (the honesty back then is refreshing to hear about)!

In the restoration, Nelson kept the Continental spare on the rear bumper, similar to that on movie star Barbara Stanwyk's and singer Al Jolsen's identical cars. But then, after 20 years being involved with the Cord, Nelson died. An *Old Cars* newspaper writer said "he broke the 'death jinx' on the big yellow Cord forever."

After years of collecting Tom Mix memorabilia, Bob White bought the car in 2010 in an auction in Missouri and then he and his son, Scott, brought it straight to Kansas, to Stan Gilliland, a well-known restorer of Cords, to start a frame-off restoration going on for about a year and a half.

The White's really got into the history of the car and are still collecting pictures today. (The senior White can be reached at bw1105@yahoo.com.)

It was found that Mix had hand-tooled leather stone guards at the front of the rear fenders. After much searching, White was able to find a leather worker that could tool leather the same way and had those parts made. He also found the King of Denmark had awarded Mix two medals and, in typical TM fashion, he screwed them to the front of the hood. The originals are in the TM Museum in Dewey, Oklahoma. The Oklahoma State Historical Society, allowed the Whites to take them out and recast exact duplicates.

White stopped short of re-fabricating the metal boxes Mix carried in the trunk. "If I did make them," he said, "I'd sure as hell figure out a way to strap them in."

The White family even searched for revolvers similar to those Mix had carried in the car, in this case .357 Magnums with hand-made grips which the Whites were able to get duplicated. They aren't the same but look the same. How was it that Mix toted around revolvers? Three reasons: this was the Wild West, still mountain lions in the hills and bears in the woods. Two, he was ready to perform in stage shows so that was part of his costume. And three, he was a former Marshall in Arizona so, as such, allowed to carry a sidearm (you never know, as an ex-law officer, when you might run across a guy you put in the pokey).

The Whites take the car to many events and museums. True, at every event he goes to with the car, there are less and less people that remember Tom Mix, but he's proud to own a car owned by such a famous man.

Today the value of such a collector car can be determined by looking up the latest auction results. There was a newly restored car sold to Pebble Beach standards at RM in the late 2000s that went for over $400K and the Whites have over $600K in buying and restoring this one.

Lesson learned here? Alas, you would think when you sell a car in good condition that the new owner would treat it well, and keep it up. Well, sometimes things don't work out that way. The car was driven rough even before it got to the Chicago owner and by choosing that errant mechanic, the Chicago owner almost sealed the car's fate. It's a wonder it wasn't scrapped for one of the wartime scrap metal drives.

But Ray Nelson did not assume it had been scrapped after the wreck. A lot can be learned from his steadfastness for first in tracking down the car at the movie studio.

True, he made a mistake selling it, but I'd give Nelson kudos as a great barn finder the second time around for keeping on that Chicago owner for five long years, with monthly phone calls, before the owner caved in and allowed Nelson to be re-united with his car.

Third lesson? Bob White and his son Scott deserve praise for their diligent research efforts aimed at "bringing back" the car to the exact way it looked when it was owned by Mix in the late '30s. They have not only brought back the car, but a little lost American film history with it.

Chapter 42
GIUGIARO DOES AN ASTON
(1960 ASTON MARTIN DB4 GT JET COUPE)
Sometimes it's the odd one that appreciates the most.

Racecars were fetching a lot more at the major auctions than car show one-offs. The idea was that, you buy a racecar, you're lucky—you get one with history. You buy a show car, a one-off (*esemple unico* in Italian), what do you get—a momentary bauble; a flavor of the moment as it were; a design that came and went, mostly forgotten.

Well this 1960 Aston Martin DB4 GT Bertone Jet coupe, chassis 0201L, Engine no. 370/-201/GT was sold at a May 2013 Bonhams auction for the top-dollar sum of 3,249,500 GBP ($4,928,697 USD) which is more than some Aston Martin DB4GT's go for even with some racing history.

There is a reason for this—this particular car was the last DB4 GT chassis, and the last of any series is worth more than the ones in the middle.

First a little bit about the Aston Martin DB4 GT as a model... "DB" means "David Brown," he being the owner of Aston after WWII. The DB4GT was introduced as the competition version of the DB4 sports saloon. First launched at the London Motor Show in 1958, the Aston Martin DB4 was a direct challenge to Ferrari.

It had an all-new steel platform chassis with disc brakes all around, and a race-developed twin-cam six-cylinder 3.7-liter engine, all clothed in a perfectly proportioned aluminum body designed and built by Carrozzeria Touring of Milan.

Engineered by Harold Beech, the immensely strong platform-type chassis had Touring's Superleggera body which used a lightweight tubular structure to support hand-formed aluminum body panels. The front suspension employed unequal-length wishbones while the rear was live axle located by Watts linkage.

But the factory quickly realized they needed a lightweight version for racing, that model, the DB4GT, making its debut at the 1959 London Motor Show. The lightweights had 5 inches chopped out of the wheelbase and replaced the rear seats with a luggage platform on all but a small number of cars. Even the bodywork at 18-gauge was thinner aluminum, which contributed to 200 pounds (91kg) less weight than in the street model.

The engine was mightily tweaked, boasting a twin-plug cylinder head and triple Weber 45DCOE carburetors, and a rating of 302 bhp at 6,000 rpm, a big jump over the standard car's claimed 240 hp. Maximum speed of 153 mph was reached during testing with a 0-60 mph time of 6.1 seconds.

The Comp version had a few changes from the touring car, such as faired-in headlamps with Perspex covers, a feature later made standard on the DB5 and DB6. The rear screen and quarter windows were Perspex (plexiglass) on many examples; bumper over-riders were deleted and the wind-down windows were frame-less within the doors. Twin Monza quick-fill competition fuel fillers were added atop the rear fenders, and a large-capacity fuel tank mounted flat in the boot. GTs were fitted as standard with lightweight Borrani 42-spoke wire wheels with alloy rims and three-ear 'knock-offs.'

Piloted by the likes of Roy Salvadori, Stirling Moss, Jim Clark and Innes Ireland, the DB4GT model did well. Only 30 were produced in left-hand drive configuration.

The Aston Martin DB4GT was another variant, bodied in Italy by Zagato, and those have become the most sought after of the DB4GT cars.

A BRIEF TIME IN THE SPOTLIGHT

This particular car, chassis 0201L, was ordered by Bertone to be the carrozzeria's show car for the 1961 Geneva Motor Show. The design

Giugiaro had put on paper wasn't just a bolt-on, the whole wheelbase had to be shortened five inches. The body that went on was steel even though someone somewhere is saying it was 200 pounds lighter than the aluminum-bodied production car (possible, when you consider the weight savings of cutting out five inches of length).

The car did its time at the auto show where it was celebrated (though some seem to think the Giugiaro-designed Bertone-bodied split grille Ferrari 250T swb coupe a more memorable design, done the same year).

The engine was tweaked a bit, still an inline six twin-cam displacing 3.7 liters but producing 302 bhp (225 kW) at 6,000 rpm as a result of switching to three Webers, a sizable jump from the standard 240 bhp (179 kW) output. The car would go 0-60 mph in 6.1 seconds and top end was 153 mph.

UPSTAGED BY THE E-TYPE

One reason the Jet coupe did not get much publicity at the time it was first shown was because it had the misfortune of being unveiled in 1961 at the Geneva show just as Jaguar rolled out the E-type, which was arguably a more seductive shape at less than a third the price of an Aston Martin. So the press sung the praises of the Jag and the Aston was ignored. Hey, timing is everything.

And then the Aston disappeared into the sands of time. Some say it was in Beirut, not the place to toodle around in with a valuable one-off car. Then it went to America where it didn't fare too well. An engine fire scorched the bonnet and engine compartment and then, through poor storage, the steel body rusted.

THE RESCUE

Who should rescue it? None other than the Chairman of Aston Martin at the time, Victor Gauntlett. He brought it back to Blighty and had his shop re-do it, which involved much rust repair and hand fabrication of various one-off bits.

The car was midway through restoration when Hans-Peter Weidmann discovered it and bought it in 1988 and the car was finished for him. He drove it quite a bit, accumulating 35,000 miles, one time telling *OCTANE* magazine that he did 950 miles in one day across the U.S. and part of Canada.

When Weidmann passed on, the family brought it to Bonhams in 2013, who fetched that extraordinary amount.

Your author feels the outsize amount, more than some DB4GTZ cars were selling for at the time, was due to the fact that it is an example of "early Giugiaro," i.e. the work of then young designer Giorgetto Giugiaro, who toiled at the boards at Bertone while still in his 20s, creating a surfeit of memorable designs. Other one-off Giugiaro cars like the Maserati Boomerang, have also fetched large amounts because they are one-offs that were well-remembered show cars.

Lesson to be learned here? One-off show cars, however obscure, can be good long-range bets. That's because a lot of those scrambling to buy a factory racecar, particularly a Zagato-bodied DB4GTZ, walked right on by this show car, figuring it just to be a show car bauble. Also in this case Giugiaro was steadily becoming ever more famous, and is now recognized as the most brilliant designer of the Sixties to come out of Italy. Lesson No. 2: Buying a car that has had a fire sounds scary but the truth is there are different levels of fire damage. Maybe the fire in this was confined to the engine compartment. True, some of the small trim parts were irreplaceable, which means you can get them made again but it's going to cost an arm and a leg. But remember, it sold for almost $5 million, and I'm sure there was enough profit in there to re-make all the little parts that had to be fabricated.

Now it's possible the general public wouldn't have known about this car sitting in obscurity and you can't get any higher at a car company than to be its chairman, so it's logical that all news funneled to the man at the top. Odds are, once this book is published, I'll find out that others knew of the car sitting around in America, in the back of some shop with not one enthusiast who saw it willing to tackle a car that was an edition of one, with no spare body parts and a blackened lump under the bonnet. I'm just saying that sometimes it's worth the risk to buy a damaged car. Not only did Hans-Peter buy it but it sounds like he had a lot of fun with it. I envy first his "eye" for recognizing the car's pedigree and then the fun he had in driving a one-off Giugiaro grand touring creation built on such a great race-bred platform. He drove it further than most any barn find purebred I've heard of. I would venture to say he got full use of it (take that, you fellows who are scared to take your classic car out for fear of "road rash").

Lesson learned here? Don't pass up those "ugly ducklings"—the one-offs that people pass up on their way to pay full boot for a racecar with history. Sometimes the "ugly ducklings" grow more beautiful in time, as this Aston certainly did.

Chapter 43
LIFE IN A BUBBLE
(1947 ROLLS ROYCE SILVER WRAITH)

Hey, if it's good enough for the Queen...

Of all the fascinating people who have owned fascinating cars (you notice this book has no Chevy Vegas), one of the guys who I would have liked to hung out with for awhile was Nubar Gulbenkian (1900-'72). He was an Armenian-born playboy tycoon who lived in the Ritz Hotel in London. His money came from the family oil business (which owned five percent of BP's shares) and he was a well-known figure about town, corpulent, bearded and mustached, wearing three-piece suits, always a fresh orchid in his buttonhole and using a monocle and silver-topped cane.

You would expect a natty gentleman like that to order a bespoke (hand-built to one's tastes) Roller. And you knew it would be a splendorous thing.

And it was.

Yet his 1956 Silver Wraith sat in the basement of a sleazy bar on the French Riviera for years, not in the parking garage but right inside the nightclub itself where it served as not much more than a quaint place for people to sit while imbibing overpriced cocktails.

Finally, it was saved by a connoisseur.

But I digress. First a little background on the Wraith which is a word synonymous with "Ghost," which was a prior Rolls model. The Silver Wraith was the first post-war Rolls-Royce and was made at the Crewe factory from 1946 to 1959.

The first cars had a 127-inch (3226 mm) wheelbase chassis based on the pre-war Wraith with coil sprung independent front suspension and semi-elliptic leafs in the rear with a live axle. The engine was also based on the pre-war Wraith, but had a new cylinder head with overhead inlet valves and side exhaust valves and initially a capacity of 4,257 cc. From 1951 this was bumped up to 4,566 cc and in 1954 to 4,887 cc on only the long-wheelbase models. The braking system was a hybrid hydro-mechanical system with hydraulic fronts and mechanical rears.

The long, 133-inch (3,378 mm) wheelbase chassis was announced in 1951, and 639 were made until 1959. The last short-wheelbase cars were made in 1953. At first you could only order it with a four-speed manual but finally a General Motors automatic was put on the option list in 1952.

The Wraiths were built in the final years of the coachbuilders, who were essentially tailors in metal. You bought your luxury car in "chassis only" form, and it was shipped to the coachbuilder of your choice, usually an English coachbuilder, but on occasion one went to Italian or French coachbuilders. Most of them were "formal" limousines in style but a few were sedanca de villes (open over the chauffeur area) or much more rare, landaulettes (the rear area open with a canvas roof).

Now back to my main man, Nubar. It was said he liked big, fast, expensive cars and, after owning many rapid pre-war sports cars, he had acquired a taste for Rolls-Royces in the post-war years. He had a chauffeur named Wooster, but would often take the wheel himself or urge his driver to drive ever faster from the back seat. There was one such memorable event in the late 1940s when he instructed his chauffeur to drive his Buick Super from Estoril to Sintra, all the while contesting for the lead against a Jaguar SS100 driven by the then-youthful racecar driver Alan Clark. To gauge their progress in these impromptu contests of speed, he even had a second speedometer fitted in the rear compartment.

Naturally his Rolls-Royces, of which he ordered one at a time, were as flamboyant as he was. The first, christened Pantechnicon, was built in 1947 and looked like, as one wag said: "the unfortunate progeny of a liaison between a Rolls and a Wehrmacht Panzer tank" with its faired-in front wheels and armored-car-like front grille. There was at least a traditional sliding roof over the chauffeur's compartment—a recurring theme on Nubar's cars. Rolls-Royce was not very happy about his taste in regards to that particular car and even the coachbuilder Hooper hesitated to have their name attached to it, but they needed the work, so they built it to Nubar's specifications.

Gulbenkian redeemed himself with his later commissions on Rolls chassis, which are credits to the design continuity of the marque.

His next, built in 1952, was a four-door cabriolet that was also used by the Queen on a visit to Nigeria. (Note to barn-finders: check in the garages of African rulers in nations once allied with Britain—every damn one of them had to have a car worthy of Royal transport in case the Queen scheduled a visit.)

He replaced that with his third Hooper Sedanca Deville with full, sage-green, lizard-skin trim—and that included covering the steering wheel and grab handles modeled to look like lizard tails. In 1987 it starred as Uncle Monty's car in the cult film *Withnail and I*.

This chapter is about the car he had built for wafting about on roads overlooking the sea on the French Riviera. Again it was a Wraith, LELW74, built in 1956, again by Hooper, and fitted at his request with a transparent Perspex hardtop strangely reminiscent of FAB1 from Thunderbirds (given a 1950s pastel paint-job, you could imagine it being owned by Lady Penelope's mother).

Gulbenkian planned to use the car only on the Côte d'Azur, so inside the hardtop was an electrically-operated sun shade that, along with the air-conditioning, kept the interior at a reasonable temperature. One source says he hated to be in confined spaces but since his other chauffeured Rolls did not have this top, this author is inclined to think that the real reason for a see-through top was that he wanted to be recognized on the Riviera rain or shine. Normally, the only other customer for Perspex tops on a Roller were assorted Royals so they could wave to the commoners.

The car also had electric windows, a stereo radio and even a television set—quite something in 1956.

After Gulbenkian sold the car in 1968, it appeared in a film called *Les Félins* (released as *The Love Cage* in the U.K.) with Alain Delon and American actress/occasional anti-war activist Jane

Fonda. It may have already belonged at that time to a Nice night-club owner called René Gourdon.

Gourdon was, like Gulbenkian, a man who treasured being seen living in the lap of luxury. To make quite certain he was seen, and remembered, he had the already flamboyant car painted fly yellow and planned to rent it for film work, although it isn't clear what other films, if any, it was featured in. By the 1980s it had fallen into disuse and he parked it in the basement of his nightclub in Nice so customers could sit in it, much as other night clubs have parts of London buses, Filipino Jeepneys, etc.

James Crickmay of Frank Dale's, a famous and well respected classic Rolls Royce dealer in England, whose employer owned two previous Gulbenkian Rolls Royces, told a magazine editor in 2007 precisely how it was found:

"About 10 years ago we got a call from our French agent to say he'd found this funny Rolls-Royce that was bricked up in the base-ment of a nightclub. We checked the chassis number and discov-ered it was a Gulbenkian car. He made an offer, it was accepted and he literally went with a sledgehammer and some chains, knocked the wall down and dragged it out. He changed the plugs, put some petrol in and it started!" The Frenchman decided he wanted to restore the car and had the mechanics and the body totally redone, along with a new Perspex hardtop that turned out to be too small. "The car has come to us for a re-trim with new leather and to have the wood sorted out," says Crickmay. "Like all the Gulbenkian cars, the wood is covered in leather." (It is rare in RR history that someone doesn't like the carefully grain-matched woods.)

By the time they were ready to sell it, the yellow paint was gone, replaced by dark blue and silver gray. Apparently they also received the Lalique glass bonnet mascot of a reclining nymph—but had to re-do the suede trim. Fortunately the TV set had been lost which was probably a good thing.

Frank Dale offered the car for a time and the salesman said that the owner could consider selling the car for a minimum of least £150,000 when completely restored.

But what of Gulbenkian? He had a few more special-bodied Rolls-Royces built but by the mid-1960s was looking for some-thing a bit more practical, but still different. So, in 1965, he had a special taxi constructed to his own design, one that looked Austin in front but Rolls Royce razor-edge roof in the back!

Bonhams in the U.K. had the Wraith, tastefully repainted in gray and blue, for sale in 2008 for what they estimated would be $370,000 to $420,000. This writer wrote Bonhams to find out what it sold for but, alas, even in its more demure color scheme, it didn't sell. (Hey, Bonhams, go back to yellow!)

Regardless of its more recent adventures, it's still a lesson in barn finding to be learned in that the finder didn't take "No" for an answer.

What lesson? Sometime you will no doubt hear of a luxury car or a sports car or a racecar that's in in a very unusual place—atop a roof, walled up in a building, or, in this case, the basement of a nightclub with no obvious garage door. Kudos to the Frank Dale representative who first realized the car's pedigree, bid on it, paid for it and, sleeves rolled up and sledgehammer in hand, knocked down the walls that held this car prisoner.

Don't let a few bricks deter you—beyond lies treasure, m'lad.

Chapter 44
THE "BUNKIE" KNUDSEN CORVETTE
(1963 CORVETTE CONVERTIBLE)

Again, executive priviledge...

B ack in the Sixties, Detroit auto executives, those at the very top anyway, could have just about anything they wanted on their own personal cars. Lamb's wool carpeting? A little extra chrome? Polished aluminum parts? Yessir, yessir, three bags full.

Semon "Bunkie" Knudsen was a powerful GM executive, the General Manager of Chevrolet at the time they were coming out with the '63 Corvette. He wanted a Corvette but liked the styling of the side pipes on the Shark prototype that had been done earlier and asked that his car have those pipes. So the styling department at GM did a car similar to a Chicago Auto Show Corvette, but this car has an earlier SN (148) which indicates to Corvette experts that it was already in service when it was modified by the Engineering garage.

The car was found by Corvette Restorer Werner Meier, who actually worked for GM on prototype before going out on his own to restore Corvettes.

The barn find goes back to the early 1980s. The Knudsen convertible had, amazingly, passed through the hands of no less than six owners in the Detroit area, each time being thrashed as a daily driver, by the time he found it. It had not only been sitting forlorn in a garage but the people who owned it were using it as a stairstep to stand on while they accessed possessions stored in the shelves above it.

The frame was rusty, the paint cracked and faded and the interior worn out. And, oh, as found, it was undrivable.

A BARN FINDER STRIKES GOLD

Fortunately for the Corvette world, the car still had enough special features to first catch the ear and eyes of Wally Abella, a Corvette collector in Detroit, who suspected that this car had to be more than just some Joe Blow-customized 'Vette. He had started restoring it but then decided it was going to take too much special knowledge. He didn't know if he was repairing someone's custom or a special car from GM. Around 1984, he asked Meier to come over and look at it and tell him the news, either good or bad. Meier assured him that it was indeed a one-time show car, and offered to trade a 1971 Corvette, straight up, for the dilapidated historic '63 roadster. Once he got the '63 back to his shop, Meier saw that he had a very special car indeed.

Now comes the bad news. Hardly anything on the car was normal so you couldn't buy stock parts for it. Everything damaged or missing would have to be hand-made.

It took Werner Meier three years to restore it. The biggest job was the unique exhaust system, which he made fully functional. That took eight different craftsmen, including Werner's father, to fabricate!

The interior also had a lot of special trim. The seats, for instance, were re-shaped to reflect 1964-type, while the upholstery was done over in white leather with maroon accent stripes (not available on other '63 Corvettes). The interior also featured the floor grilles that were typical of styling cars built in that era. What are floor grilles for? Well, Michigan is a state with a lot of snow in winter which looks real pretty until it turns to slush. When you get in the car, you want to rub the shoes on a grille to get the sludge off, otherwise you are driving the car with 3-inch thick shoe soles! The door panels were naugahyde with stainless steel plates and crossed flag emblems, while the steering wheel was not only wood but had unique dual spokes featuring two types of wood inlays! The console was a preview of what would come on the production car in 1964. The instrumentation, in fact, was 1964, and Werner determined that, while Knudsen was using the car as a driver, the prototype parts were installed in his personal car.

And since the car had started out in life as a "fuelie" (fuel injection) roadster, that meant to be "correct" it had to be a fuelie again.

The engine, fortunately, was left relatively stock as far as content but it had a whole lot of prettying up done at GM styling, such as various parts of either chrome or crinkle (some call it "wrinkle") finished in place of cast aluminum surfaces. Of course when we're talking those special pipes, the engine bay had to be modified to make way for the special pipes, including trimming the heater box for clearance and relocating the battery to the trunk.

Knudsen had a favorite color red, called "Firefrost red" (the Mecum auction company called it "rose pearl") and insisted that color with white Le Mans-type stripes, be applied to all his cars, which included a Nova, a Corvair, and an Impala, all convertibles. The special Corvette was actually his wife's daily driver, and, as a privileged executive wife, she could drive it with "M" plates (manufacturer's plates). GM records show the car was turned back in to GM about 1967.

Now was the car actually shown, though built as a twin to the Chicago Auto Show car? Researchers don't agree on that. But it is a close match to the Harley Earl personal '63 Corvette and the Chicago Auto Show cars so, even if it didn't make it to a show, it's documented as a GM Styling special. (Incidentally GM discourages executives from custom ordering cars today, but it is still done in recent times such as the Corvette for Don Runkle.)

In '64 Mrs. Knudsen got another special Corvette, a '64 with not only six taillights but a domed hood announcing something that wouldn't come until 1965—a 396-cubic-inch near-production version of the engine Hot Rod magazine called "Chevy's Mystery V8" when they saw it at Daytona in early 1963. Unlike the production 396 first made available near the end of the '65 model run, this one had hydraulic instead of solid lifters. It was mated to a Powerglide. While that sounds like it would have made a pretty macho machine, those who would covet have to live with the fact that, to be technically correct to its original when-owned-by-the-Knudsens condition, it would have to be painted Pink Pearl. Oh the ignominy of being NCRS correct!

Lesson to be learned here? First of all, Detroit is where Chrysler, Ford and GM were located for almost 100 years so it makes sense as a place to look for very special cars built for executives. Secondly, there are those who have bought very special cars as they changed ownership many times but who didn't have the knowledge to know how special they were, thus they may be amendable to a trade. Third, it takes a heap of hand fabrication to make a special car special again but in the end it could be worth it. The '63 Bunkie Knudsen roadster sold at the Mecum auction in 2010 for over $400,000.

Chapter 45
THE PROTOTYPE IN DAVEY'S LOCKER
(1956 CHRYSLER NORSEMAN)

Hey, ships sink...get over it.

"It was a dark and stormy night." Sorry for the cliché but seems like the best adventure stories always start out that way. Well, this is an adventure story involving an American automaker, an Italian coachbuilder and a wee mistake in navigation in two ships at sea, a mistake that led to death and disaster, and maybe the destruction of our barn find target. First a little background on the American auto industry, such as it was in the Fifties…There was, at the time, a certain glamor to having a prototype bodied in Italy. Chrysler could tell you about that. In the Fifties, they had nearly 40 prototypes, then called "dream cars," bodied by Ghia in Italy. Ford, too, had the occasional dream car built in Italy such as the Lincoln Indianapolis show car (Carrozzeria Boano) and the Lincoln Futura show car, bodied by Carrozzzeria Ghia (later to become, courtesy of George Barris, the Batmobile). Though Chrysler never put an all-Italian design into production, they did put in an order with Ghia in the '60s for 55 turbine cars used to raise public awareness of the cars. But mostly the Italian connection gave them something exotic to show at auto shows, something to lord over the total domestically built fare from other Detroit automakers.

Still, there was one potential problem with having cars designed in America built in Italy—there's a sizable ocean inbetween. And best not to forget the old saying: "There's many a slip 'tween the cup and the lip." You get open ocean and bad stuff can happen, like the ship sinks. That happened to Chrysler in '56.

However, first things first—before we get into the fate of Chrysler's Norseman dream car, we owe a little background on the designer. He was Virgil Exner Sr., an urbane white-haired chain-smoking sophisticate who headed up Chrysler Styling. He had already designed a number of one-off show cars that were built in Italy and in 1956 was anticipating the arrival of another, a four-seater coupe. Ghia was chosen to build the car because they could build a car from the ground up, working from drawings done back in Detroit.

Now, about the car—it was called the Norseman, a futuristic two-door coupe. This was not just a pushmobile with no engine, no indeed. This was a running driving vehicle. The powerplant was a 235-hp, 331-cubic-inch Hemi but not the 300C engine. One expert claims that it had a torsion bar suspension in front, which would have been experimental at the time. The trick part of the design was what you could call a "cantilevered" roof, attached to the body only at the rear, at the C-pillars. There were no A-pillars, no B-pillars, side pillars, and the front of the roof rested only lightly on a fully frameless windshield (the Department of Transportation might have something to say about that today). And there was a powered sunroof as well. There were no vent windows which gave a sexy look that was to sweep the industry years later (and force you to buy air conditioning). Another weird feature of the car was the rear window was retractable, an idea later used on the Mercury Turnpike Cruiser and the Lincoln Continental Mk. III. It also had bucket seats for all four passengers, something daring in a bench seat nation, and also a feature a few years later in the Ghia-built Chrysler turbine cars. Anyhow Exner's parade was rained on a bit when he heard that the ship carrying the car from Italy had a bit of a problem off Massachusetts. It sank.

ERRANT SHIPS AT SEA

A personal note here…As it happens, that same summer, I was on the same ocean, also on a cruise ship, and remember that lifeboat drill, thinking: "What a waste of time—ships don't sink anymore. That was back in the era of the Titanic."

Well, I was wrong. Now, about that accident…It was a dark

night (though I confess, I don't know how stormy) around 11 p.m. on Wednesday July 25, 1956, when the SS Andrea Doria, en route from Italy, was plowed into by an outbound ship, the Stockholm, off Nantucket, Massachusetts. The Andrea Doria went down. A total of 52 people died. The collision took place after the Andrea Dorea had come almost 4,000 miles from Italy, with only 50 miles left to reach New York. The Andrea Dorea took almost 11 hours to sink so there was time to disembark survivors. The Stockholm, with a huge hole in her hull, managed to hobble back to port. Now, the question for a really adventurous barn finder is: can I go for it? The answer is that the ship isn't that deep, at 160 feet (50 meters)—but despite that apparently reachable depth, it is beyond the scope of "recreational diving" in that it would take mixed gases and staged decompression to reach it. At least five divers have died trying to work the wreck, so much so that its danger level is described as "the Mt. Everest of shipwrecks."

Suffice to say that it is deteriorating as we speak, losing its shape as entire decks rust and slide off. Ironically this may eventually make the Norseman easier to reach, but this author sees the only possibility of reaching the car by a robot /drone salvage machine which may have yet to be invented.

The problems in finding the Norseman are many: the ship landed on its side, so presumably all the cargo in the hold shifted and the car may be buried under tons of debris (there were eight other cars being shipped as well). Then, too, there is the problem of corrosion. The car was steel-bodied but even if it were aluminum-bodied, the ocean can deteriorate aluminum.

Then, too, and I know this will hurt Norseman fans, but, from the side view, the Norseman looks like an ordinary production Chrysler so it's not like you would be saving some priceless moment in car design (I think the Chrysler prototype worth saving is the Atlantic, a much newer prototype but a brilliant exercise in retro-art deco styling).

There's a rich irony to this story. According to historian David W. Temple, Virgil Exner Sr. was in the hospital when the ship went down and wasn't told at first because he had just undergone a delicate operation. When his son, Virgil Exner Jr., finally told him, his father's reaction was surprising. While it would have been nice if the car could at least have had a chance to be seen by the millions of Americans who went to auto shows, the senior Exner thought it was cool that one of his creations, by virtue of the sinking, didn't have to wait to achieve legendary status.

Chapter 46
THE THORNDYKE SPECIAL
(1965 APOLLO 5000 COUPE)
Sometimes old movie cars make it back to civilization.

Now it happens that Hollywood occasionally has cars in their movies that are real and sometimes they have cars that they build just for a movie (*Chitty, Chitty Bang-Bang*, for instance), cars that never existed as real brands you could once buy in a showroom.

Well, this is a story about a real car, one invented and marketed in America, but ironically it's more famous as a "car character" in a Hollywood movie than it is as a marque because the marque itself is so obscure with less than 100 built. You could say the car was a copy of the Pininfarina-designed Ferrari 275GTB except that the Ferrari 275GTB was still several years into the future when the Apollo first appeared in 1961, meaning it was the Italian coach-builder Pininfarina inspired by Apollo rather than the other way around—the big guys copying the little guys, so to speak.

Here's a thumbnail sketch of Apollo history:

Three friends and university grads from the Oakland, California, area—Milt Brown, Ron Plescia and Newt Davis—up and decide one day to build a car with European style and American reliability. Plescia, who went to Art Center College of Design down in Los Angeles, penned a svelte body shape and Brown created a chassis powered by an aluminum Buick V8 and Corvette transmission. Davis was in charge of raising capital for the fledgling company.

The car was built in two series, the first had the 215-cubic-inch Buick aluminum block engine called the 3500 series and the second series a bored-out version of that same engine, now with 300 cubic inches, which were called Apollo 5000 models.

Anyway, the way the cars came to be buit in Italy was pure serendipity. Milt Brown was in Europe attending a Grand Prix, when he met Frank Reisner, a free-lance Hungarian engineer who, in 1959, had set up shop building racecars in Modena. Milt explained that he was a car designer and Reisner replied that, well, whaddya know, small world, he happened to be building cars in Torino under the name of "Intermeccanica." Soon a deal was struck for Reisner's firm to build a prototype to Plescia's design and later the design was revised for production by the famed ex-Bertone chief designer, Franco Scaglione (pronounced SCAL-YONI)—designer of the Alfa Romeo BAT showcars, the Alfa Giulietta Sprint and Sprint Speciale, and the Arnolt-Bristol, to name just a few. I always refer to him as the "mercurial" Franco Scaglione because he would be on the car scene and then disappear for months or years.

The Apollo GT received favorable press, but had the misfortune of coming out just when the Jaguar E-type was becoming widespread and they just couldn't compete with it. The Jag was good-looking, fast, and Jaguar had dealers coast-to-coast. Production of Apollos stopped after 88 cars were built, due to lack of financing.

Now we come to the movie star role that leads directly to this particular barn find. In the Disney comedy *The Love Bug*, about a VW named Herbie who wanted to be a racecar, there were several cars "cast" to race against the bug. The Apollo was called the "Thorndyke Special" and driven by a villain named Peter Thorndyke, played by English actor David Tomlinson. Throughout the whole movie the Apollo was Herbie's four-wheeled nemesis.

The way the Apollo was picked was that Southern California racecar mechanic and stunt man Max Balchowsky was hired by the film's director, Robert Stevenson, to come up with most of the cars for the racing scenes and, among the cars the director mentioned was the Apollo. Max was able to pick up two Apollo

GT coupes. There were 76 coupes built and 11 roadsters plus one prototype 2-plus-2.

Max was well known in racing circles as the builder/driver/owner of a series of cars called "Ol Yeller" which were fearsome contraptions made out of old junk parts but somehow regularly beat racing Ferraris and Maseratis. That could also be due to the fact he picked such notables to drive as Carroll Shelby, Bob Bondurant and Dan Gurney.

Max upgraded the Apollo's front brakes, shocks, engine/transmission mounts and body/chassis mounts. The engine was also balanced and blueprinted and a chrome roll bar installed. The car was painted in Max's signature pale yellow with black racing stripes. The reason two identical cars were needed was, in the event one was smashed during filming, the whole movie set would not have to be shut down while it was rebuilt—they could just roll out the identical car.

Now I'm here to tell you that the movie and TV folk are not very respectful of keeping cars intact in films. Their goal is to get the action up on the screen, devil take the hindmost. Thus, one of the two Apollos was apparently cut open from the driver's side front fender to the 'B' post, cutting away the entire 'A' post and part of the roof. That was so that the car could be used for interior shots and that car was probably scrapped after filming due to the extensive damage.

The second car, the one that is the subject of this chapter, survived multiple collisions with trees, fences, mudholes and of course Herbie, that pesky wanna-be racing beetle. The Thorndyke Special was then painted blue and sold into the Los Angeles area. It then disappeared from view, its show biz career over.

A HUNTER FINDS HIS PREY

Decades pass. During which time, intermittingly, our hero, John Barron, was looking for an Apollo, inspired by the *Road & Track* story on the car he had read as a lad. He would find first one, and then another, but the price was never the right match for his income at the time. Fast forward to 2004. "I was surfing Ebay one evening when I saw an auction for an Apollo GT," recalls Barron. "The car was accurately described as a 'total basket case' that needed a new door skin, floors and firewall replaced. All mechanical components needed to be restored."

"The rear window was missing, the wheels needed rebuilding, the tires were shot and the seats and interior were missing. If this had been a dog, it would have been missing its tail, had its ear chewed off and had a severe case of Mange."

But Barron had been bit years earlier. "I couldn't help myself," he told the author. "I pushed the bid button and a week later, being the only person in North America crazy enough to bid on the car, I was the new owner of Apollo #52."

The seller did not mention the car's illustrious role as a star of the silver screen and Barron was unaware of the film.

The starting bid won the eBay auction at $6,000 but amazingly the seller said he would deliver it anywhere in the Continental U.S. so Barron took him up on it and had him deliver it to Port Huron, Michigan about an hour Northwest of Detroit. The car came with a new windshield worth $1,000, and a rechromed set of bumpers worth $1,500. Plus it would have cost $1,000 to ship it and that was included so in a way Barron was getting a great bargain.

It was not an easy restoration. "Slowly I began to work on the car," he told your author. "All the while wondering who could inflict so much damage on such a rare car? The nose was severely damaged and badly repaired, the passenger side front and rear fenders were covered with multiple dents and numerous holes from a slide hammer. The right doorskin had been replaced with an ill-fitting sheet of galvanized steel and then covered up by an inch and a half thick coat of bondo. What horrors had this rare car endured? I was about to find out."

"A friend had bought me a copy of the *The Love Bug* movie and while watching the various collisions between Herbie and the 'Thorndyke Special' I began to suspect that I was the owner not only of a genuine Apollo but of one of the two movie cars. Subsequent investigation confirmed that."

Once he realized he had a movie car, Barron's goal was redefined—he would now resurrect the only surviving Apollo GT from the movie. The restoration included rebuilding the engine and transmission, making a new right door, and he lucked out when a rear window became available when a fellow who owned one of 76 coupes decided to make his car a clone of the 11 original convertible Apollos built.

Now one would think it would be a pretty lonely world for an

Apollo owner with less than 100 built and far less than 100 out and about. But Barron was surprised to receive an invitation to join 17 other owners to celebrate the 50th anniversary of the Apollo GT at the Concorso Italiano in Monterey. Among the luminaries expected were Milt Brown, the man who created the Apollo, Ron Plescia, the man who designed the prototype, Paula Reisner, the widow of Frank Reisner, who still runs Intermeccanica from Canada, and finally George Finley, who was Apollo sales manager back in the day. Fired with the goal of attending the reunion with the finished Thorndyke, er Apollo, Barron continued his restoration with renewed purpose, finishing the car just hours before the transport was due to arrive to take the car from Toronto to the Monterey Peninsula. Barron treasures that moment he drove across the review stand at Concorso Italiano.

"All of a sudden the 3,000-plus man hours I had spent restoring the car were forgotten," says Barron, "That replaced with the thrill of sharing my passion for these cars with all those spectators in the stands. Mission accomplished!"

Lesson to be learned here? You can in fact find treasure on eBay but you have to know what you are looking for, or at. In this case, John Barron had been carrying a tiny lit flame for the marque for 40 some years and needed only to find an Apollo for sale at the right price to ignite that flicker of flame into a full blown conflagration. I say prepare your "dream shopping list" now and check all available resources (including eBay) on a regular schedule, say once a month, to see if anything on your target list has popped up.

Chapter 47
A PORSCHE WHAT?
(1952 PORSCHE AMERICA ROADSTER)
Sometimes it's just too rare to believe.

Now the truth is that cars are bought for a lot of cockama-
mie reasons. Some women like the color. Some men like the
faded racing number on the side that gives them a little of that
former-race-car macho. Some fall in love with the sound of the
engine. Yadda-yadda.

But this is a story about a couple that bought a car merely because
of the year it was made. The story goes back to 1976, to a New
Jersey couple. That was the year Donna Paterek, wife of John, gave
him a book on Porsches for Christmas. In looking through the
book, wifie notices that the Porsche America Roadster came into
being in 1952. And that it was rare, with less than 20 made.

She turned to her husband and said something to him to the
effect of: "Hey, this car was made the same year as me, we should
get one."

Not easy. A lot of die-hard Porsche 356 owners had only vaguely
heard of it and not seen it.

A word about the history of the model…Porsche had been in
production since 1950 with the pre-A cars, which ended their run

in 1955 with the "A" model. The America was sort of an oddball in the system, coming along in '52 and dying in '52 with only 20 built (some say only 15).

What got the car built was the dynamic backing of Max Hoffman, Porsche's importer to America, who wanted an open car for America. The body was aluminum, built by a supplier called Gläser. It was the last car Gläser built—they went bankrupt when Porsche stopped ordering. One of the unusual features was that the front windshield was split and could be removed, saving another 120 pounds for racing. There were no side windows and the doors were hollow. When the Speedster came along in '54, the America was quickly forgotten as the Speedster was better looking, and more developed plus being built by a more reliable supplier (and cheaper for Porsche to build because of the steel body).

Now back to the search. The Patereks began advertising to find one in *Porsche Panorama*, a Porsche club magazine, but at first the results were slim. One person offered a wheel, another a shift knob but that was a long way from an actual car.

Meanwhile, they steamed ahead on the restoration of their second Porsche (a 1962 356B coupe) which they drove to the 1979 Porsche Parade. During the concours, a friend named Stu French happened to meet a young lady with a 356 for sale. He was surprised to see that the faded crumpled picture she showed was of an America Roadster. Her father had been the owner and she was selling it for her Dad's (the original owner) estate. The two hit it off well so French called the Patereks and told them he'd found their dream car. The Patereks got in touch with the lady and there was an agreement made to trade the America, SN12317, for the Paterek's 1962 356-B Coupe.

John and Donna agreed to drive to Mariana, Pennsylvania, a town south of Pittsburgh, to see the car the next weekend. There was only one problem—Donna was 8 months pregnant with their first child. They made the trip in a more comfortable 1966 Porsche 912, as it was a long trip from New Jersey but well worth it. They obviously loved the America with its original tires and its original reading of 8,400 miles on the clock. They decided to go home and think about it. Soon after the birth of their son Andrew, they called back and said they would take it.

There were some changes in the deal, however. The seller decided she no longer wanted a Porsche but would rather have cash. The

Patereks had to decide how much they could spare with a new baby in the house. They decided they had to have it, so a price of $15,000 was agreed upon and John went back to Mariana to pick up the car.

The America was brought back to New Jersey and not much happened to it for about a year. John disassembled the engine, found a bent intake valve, and gave the car a valve job. The car was repainted Ivory, replacing the original Gray it had been finished in at the factory. That was only the first repainting. Another repainting came when John totally disassembled the car, and took it to the 1981 Porsche Parade where it won the Peoples Choice award.

Eventually the car became an awards winner at many events, such as Meadowbrook, Greenwich, Amelia Island, Louis Vuitton and Pebble Beach.

Finally, after owning it more than 26 years, it was sold, and to the Patereks that brought the car full circle. It now resides in Germany in the collection owned by Wolfgang Porsche. Yes, that Wolfgang Porsche. Oh by the way, it finally broke the 10,000-mile mark and in what better way—with a man named Porsche at the wheel.

Lesson to be learned? Rarity within a given marque is almost a guaranteed appreciation builder. Once the Patereks realized the car (whose existence they had discovered in a book) was that rare, they targeted one. After targeting, they diligently spread the word amongst all their Porsche friends to be on the lookout for just that model. After they found one, they were willing to sacrifice a more common model (a 356B) to obtain a much rarer one and indeed, ended up making some financial sacrifices to get it, but in the end it was worth it as they became recognized throughout the Porsche world as owners and restorers of a very rare car.

Chapter 48
SUGARMAN'S FOLLY
(1967 GHIA 450/SS)
Sometimes you have to get downright down and dirty.

A lot of guys read car magazines. But few are so inspired by a picture of a car that they jump off the sofa and say, "I'm going to go into the car business and build that car."

Yet it happened to Burt Sugarman, a Hollywood music producer, way back in the Sixties.

The car that inspired him was a Fiat G230S Coupe, a one-off lime green car based on Fiat's 2100 sedan chassis that was shown at the 1960 Turin show. The coupe made the cover of *Road & Track*, and also made a personal appearance at Geneva and Paris motor-shows. It survives today, in point of fact.

Sugarman contacted Ghia Carrozzeria in Italy and said he wanted to make a car in that body style in quantity, to import to America and, oh, would they mind terribly making it in a convertible and, oh, yes, he would like them fitted with a Chrysler 273-cubic-inch V8?

This wasn't some one-off car for one man he was talking about, but a production run. By the mid-'60s Ghia had pretty much stopped bodying cars for individuals. It had become so expensive you had to be an automaker to afford Italian coachbuilders. (There are still coachbuilt cars being built for private customers today, though, for instance Pininfarina did a couple of Rolls Royce Phantom drophead coupes at the cost of at least $2-million each.)

But back to the good old days of 1966…At the Turin International Auto Show of 1966 there stood Sugarman's convertible by Ghia. The design is sort of timeless (except for the quad headlamp grille which was copied later by Ford for the Torino) and an excellent example of the more restrained work of Giorgetto Giugiaro while he was at Ghia (after his first job at Carrozzeria Bertone). Sugarman knew Europeans were impressed by engine size so since the 273-cubic-inch Barracuda S engine was 4.5 liters, he called it the 450/SS which sounded oh-so-much larger. The chassis were hand-made of square section tubing though some reports say it was a Plymouth Barracuda chassis (unlikely since the Barracuda was a unitized car). The 235-hp engine was mated to either a 3-speed Chrysler Torqueflyte and though they talk about a manual shift, this author has heard of only one such car being made. An option was a lift-off hardtop.

The dashboard looked a lot like Giugiaro's design for the Maserati Ghibli, and no wonder—same coachbuilder, same designer and both cars done at about the same time. The upholstery was leather.

Sugarman's ambitions of being a car builder ran into the harsh reality that his pricetag of $11,000 in the U.S., necessary if he planned to make a profit, was a tad too high—more than twice the price of a Corvette with a larger V8 engine.

Although some would like to hope that this was a high performance car like the Cobra (a European chassis with American V8), they forget that the Ghia was steel-bodied, so the body weighed hundreds of pounds more than the 289 Cobra with its eggshell-thin alloy body. The Ghia 450/SS had disc brakes only on the front where the Cobra had them on all four wheels, and the 273 V8, though it sounded tough on the Barracuda "S," wasn't really a high performance engine like the 289 K-code Ford V8 in the Cobra.

What hurt Sugarman, too, was having one showroom nationwide, in Beverly Hills. While that was where the money was, he could've reached out to more enclaves of the rich, say, Palm Beach, Florida or even Palm Springs, California, because the old money moves further out once people retire.

Maybe Sugarman was thinking of emulating the success of the Dual-Ghia, a plush Ghia-bodied Chrysler from a few years earlier built by Gene Casaroll's Dual Motors out in Detroit. Those cars had been briefly popular with movie stars, such as the "Rat Pack" (Sinatra, Dean Martin, Sammy Davis Jr.). But if Sugarman had looked at Dual-Ghia's history more objectively he would have found out that

Casaroll lost his shirt on that car, losing money on every damn one of them he made—reportedly by being too much of a perfectionist, such as re-painting each car several times, etc.

Then, too, back in those days small volume car importers were completely at the mercy of magazines like *Road & Track*. Those who read such magazines might have noticed that, whenever it was a small company like Sugarman's firm (or Jensen with the Interceptor, etc.), the cars were criticized much more than the cars made by large companies who were prone to buying large full-page color ads. The Ghia 450/SS was not praised much by the car magazines.

Those who have been following the cars since the 52 were imported to America say they believe just half of them are still out there. Now that Giugiaro is much more famous and Ghia no more, they are considerably more appreciated now than they were back in the Sixties.

A registrar of 450/SS, who I had a long conversation with on the phone, said that one shouldn't worry that Sugarman lost a lot of money on his Italian adventure. For one thing he didn't have to put any money up front—he paid for each car only when it hit the dock in New York. Plus he was selling Maseratis and Excaliburs at the time, and the Ghias were just a little frosting on the cake. He later went on to a show business career (record producer, TV and film producer), is no longer into car collecting, and when last heard of, was jetting off to Montana to go skiing (and he's over 70!).

MY GHIA ADVENTURE

I bought one, not for me, but in my role as a semi-pro "barn hunter" for a collector with commercial real estate investments in The Big Apple. He liked that particular model, and already had three of them, almost enough to be a "market maker" (a Wall street term, meaning if you have enough of a firm's stock and you do something with it, your move alone could affect the market price for that stock).

So I advertised, I think in an *Auto Trader*, for one and a lady from Studio City (right across from Universal City studios) calls me up and says she has one but she is a film editor on deadline to finish cutting a movie, and could I wait until Saturday? She must have told me the price, which I forget now, some 30 years later, but I think it was $40,000. At any rate, I tell the client. He is a player for the car so he Fed-Exes a cashier's check made out to her and I think I faxed a copy to the lady.

But no way in hell was I going to wait until Saturday. On Thursday night, once I had said check in hand, I show up at her home at night with a flatbed truck. Now flatbeds are handy things. You don't have to worry if the car you barn-found turns over. You have to understand, this was a rare Italian car with a cheaper-than-dirt American engine. Thus I didn't care if the engine worked. I didn't care if it was rusty. By the way, rusty California is not like rusty New York. I didn't even care if mice had taken up residence in the upholstery (see last chapter for advice on car condition).

So I knock on the door and she comes out red-faced and angry, saying, "You weren't supposed to come until Saturday." The truck is blocking her road from neighbor use. It is running, and diesels are N-O-I-S-Y. So she sighs, snatches the check, signs off the title and hands me with the keys. "Five minutes," I tell her and within 5 minutes I am, as promised, on my way down the hill with the car.

Friday night I get a call from a guy who is angry that I "broke the rules" by coming early though she had said Saturday was going to be her sell-the-car day. Turns out the guy was a pressman at the *LA Times*. He set the type in the classified ads section that ran each Sunday and thus got to see the ads for precious collector vehicles before anyone in the public saw them. He went around on Friday nights buying the cars he had typeset the ads for. So I was supposed to feel sorry for this semi-professional claim jumper?

And whoever said there were "rules" anyway—isn't the motto of the SAS, "who dares wins"?

Of course I didn't want to re-sell the car for a higher price. I was only the conduit between the seller and the buyer in New York. It wasn't mine to sell.

Lessons to be learned here? No. 1: Your job is to buy the car. Don't let any rules of nicety stand in your way.

No. 2: You can create a climate of acceptance for your offer by presenting a cashier's check in person that has already been faxed to the seller beforehand so they can check on its authenticity with their banker.

No. 3: You can create an artificial "burden" by having a big noisy truck blocking traffic in front of the seller's house. They might say "move that sonovabitch" or they might just hand you the keys and title to get you to go away, which is exactly what happened in my case.

I think of that one as the one time I won over the *LA Times* pressman.

Chapter 49
OF ROLLERS AND BENTLEYS
(1961 BENTLEY CONTINENTAL, RR SC
DHC, BENTLEY MK. VI)
Wherein your author was a little slow on the draw.

Coming from Detroit, I rarely saw a Rolls Royce until I got to California in 1969. Working in West Hollywood on Sunset strip for *Motor Trend*, I soon began to see them every day and learned the intricacies of properly referring to them. For instance, you did not, if you wanted to be prim and proper, call a Rolls Royce ragtop a "ragtop" (the horrors) or even a convertible but instead you called it a "Dhc," which means "drop head coupe" and is the British way of designating a convertible (the "dh" meaning drop the head, the "head" being the roof). Are we all simpatico now?

The first story is about a Silver Cloud drophead coupe, either a six-cylinder or a V8 (you couldn't tell when one was driving by if it was a SCI or SCII because the SCII had single headlights but used the same body as the SCI which only came with a six-cylinder).

At the time I spotted this car, around 1970-'72, I am at lunch at one of the outdoor restaurants populating the strip and this guy sails by in a sand-and-sable Silver Cloud Rolls Royce convertible (oops, drophead coupe), top down, and he's got a couple of small-size but dappled jungle cats industriously chewing away at the red Connolly hide.

At the wheel of the Roller is a tall handsome guy with black curly hair. I know I've seen him on TV. I ask my buddy, salesman Ed Durston, who worked over at a nearby used car lot specializing in Rolls Royces who that dude with the cats is and he says: "That's Gardner McKay." I then remembered seeing him on a TV show where a guy sails a large sailing vessel hither and yon, you know the type of show, guy has his hairy chest showing, sleeves rolled up, muscles bulging, yelling out commands like "furl the mainsail" and such. The series was called *Adventures in Paradise*. Well the series by then had been off the air for years, but there was Gardner, sailing along in that Roller looking like he owned the world. Durston gave me a hint he lives up in the Hollywood Hills in an area called Mt. Olympus and even the name of the street, and said he'd like to see if I could get the car. So in my off-time I began searching the hills and finally I spot the same car in a garage with two Facel Vegas (French luxury cars with American Chrysler V8 power). All three are in tacky condition, dents and all. I go back to the office and marshal my resources and figure I can come up with about $12,000—which at the time was exceeding my year's salary. Fortunately the garage was right at the curb and the garage door left open so I didn't have to confront his jungle cats. The man that beat me to the car told me over four decades later that the actor had raised African lions, a cheetah, ocelots and mountain lions on his sizable lot. Now all this would be considered unusual where I am from, Michigan, but hey, this was Beverly Hills where you damn well expect something unusual. When I discovered the treasure trove in the garage, I wrote McKay a note and Xeroxed a copy of a check made out to him for $12,000, drove over there and put it in his mailbox. I noticed another business envelope in there from an independent dealer in Rolls Royces and Bentleys. I stymied the impulse to take that letter out, take it home, steam it open, and see if I was being outbid. Anyhow I don't get an answer to my note.

A few days later I see that same independent dealer in Rolls and Bentleys driving the car and I ask him "Hey, buddy, I made an offer on that car. I saw a letter in his mailbox from you—how much did you offer?" It was a mere one thousand more than I offered. About this time you're thinking: "You should've ditched his letter." Yeah, why didn't I? I could have put it back in his mailbox the day after I made my deal—maybe it's a lesser penalty for only holding up someone's mail for a day or two. Ah, the moral ambiguities that beset the barn hunter. I lost. And decades later the same dealer hinted the car may have also belonged to Tony Curtis (a.k.a. Bernie Schwartz), a much more celebrated actor—though when I found an RRSCI dhc on the net claiming to be an ex-Tony Curtis, it is red, not the color I remember (maybe ol' Tony owned more than one Roller). Well, today the car is worth, let's say up to half-a-million bucks depending on which celebrity it really belonged to.

THE BENTLEY SEDANCA DE VILLE

So that almost ended my Rolls-Bentley adventures. But I can't forget the Bentley Sedanca de Ville, in Santa Monica, that near miss occurring about the same time. Now first I have to explain the French phrase "Sedanca de Ville." That translates to "town car." The body style is where the chauffeur's seat is uncovered, open to the sky and the rear part, for the Lords and Ladies, is closed. There is a slide-out roof panel for the chauffeur, though, in case the weather changes.

It was either an R-type or Mk. VI, I can't remember which, but the body style was wrought by British coachbuilder Gurney-Nutting. It might have even had fake "landau irons," which were chromed pieces of steel simulating the giant springs on the side of some prewar convertible tops, springs that folded up when the top was folded. For some reason, even though the rear roof on this car was sold, the landau irons simulated the old hinges of a folding top. So this was a case where the entire body was "coachbuilt" of aluminum, a big step up from what Rolls and Bentley called "the standard steel saloon." The first Gurney Nutting designs went all the way back to the first car they showed at the London Motor Show in October 1920. At one time the Duke of Windsor (the very same one who handed in his crown so he could marry an American divorcee—go figure) ordered a car built by them and that greatly increased their popularity (the guy was a style leader, witness the "Windsor" knot in your necktie). However, the demand for bespoke one-off bodies faded away fast in the post-war years and their last gasp was in 1948, when they showed two cars built on the Bentley Mark VI chassis. This could have been one of those cars, but I didn't know there may have been as few as two Gurney-Nutting Mk. VI sedancas until 43 years later!

I first saw it parked outside a bar in Santa Monica on Ocean Boulevard, looking a mite decrepit. I stopped and asked the bartender whose car it was and he said "mine" and since it had flat tires I figured it hadn't run for some time.

"How much do you want for it?" I asked.

"Three thousand," he said. That was when a nice clean standard steel four-door Bentley Mk. VI saloon was worth about $4,000-6,000. "What's it going to take to get it running?" I asked.

"A new battery," he replied. I left thinking "Yeah, sure, that's what owners of derelict cars always say."

Looking back I think I should have called his bluff, and pulled out the old jumper cables and started her up. But I didn't. Today I think the car would be worth in excess of $150,000 to $200,000 depending on the quality of restoration, and on how many of that body style on that chassis type that Gurney-Nutting actually did. I know coachbuilt Rolls and Bentleys are worth far far more than standard steel saloons (yes, the Brits call four-door sedans "saloons," don't ask me why). So long story short, only two days later on Sunset I see the same independent Rolls-Bentley dealer driving the same Bentley Sedanca de Ville I saw in Santa Monica and asked, "What did it take to get that car running?"

He replied, "I charged the battery."

A BENTLEY DHC SLAB SIDE

So that ended my Rolls and Bentley adventures. I couldn't beat the local expert, who had eyes and ears everywhere. Well, come to think about it, there was one other one, a dhc Bentley Continental S1 that I actually barn-found and brokered without my nemesis finding out. I am sure he had his tentacles out looking for it, but I used a bit of ingenuity to find the car.

First, the car, a slab-sided Bentley Continental S2…Rolls-Bentley aficionados refer to this model as the Mulliner Park Ward (combined name of what was once two separate and distinguished coachbuilders). Rolls-Royce acquired Mulliner in 1959 and merged it with Park Ward, which they had owned since 1939, forming Mulliner-Park Ward in 1961. This new entity was no longer an independent company and they were tightly focused on Rolls-Royce and Bentley, though I seem to remember Mulliner bodying a little known marque (in America), the Alvis. The Bentley I found had a Silver Cloud/Bentley S-type chassis but was clothed in an all-aluminum body that had slab sides and huge tailfins with three taillights per side not unlike a (gasp!) DeSoto.

Now exactly why this most British of British cars (except for an automatic sourced from the U.S.!) looked like a big ol' American car was a mystery to no doubt all concerned. Maybe the regular Rolls-Bentley designer, John Polwhele Blatchley, was busy and thought this Norwegian chap, Wilhelm Koren, had some original ideas. Original ideas—hell, Koren threw out the baby with the bathwater and dispensed with the total tradition of Rolls and Bentley up to that point, going for a minimalist design which actually, if you study it, had what the website rrab.com calls "an impeccable harmony of clear lines and balanced proportions." (Even if it did look like, from the rear, a damn DeSoto.)

In other words Koren's design grew on you. Now the one I found was extremely rare, being the single headlight model because the last one, the S3, had slanted dual headlamps on each side, unfortunately referred to colloquially as "Chinese eye" models. It was available as a drophead and as a fixed head coupé (what the Brits call a two-door hardtop) and clients could also order such coachwork to be erected on the chassis of the Rolls-Royce Silver Cloud III, where sadly the Rolls angular grille shell didn't quite look as good as the more rounded Bentley grille did on the S2 and S3.

(A sad note about Koren. According to the website rrab.com he hated the long wait before a new car was launched, which in RR and Bentley's case could be a decade or more, and switched occupations to architect, leaving slabside fans bereft that he would never again design a car.)

The car had been spotted for me by a carpenter in Manhattan Beach who I met when visiting a German friend who stayed with him while he was in town to buy cars to take back to Europe.

"You like Rolls and Bentleys?" the carpenter asked. I said "yes."

"Well, if you walk along the Venice beach on the sidewalk and look in the basement of each apartment house that has an underground garage you'll eventually come to one where you can see this old Rolls or Bentley convertible. It's covered with dust and I think there's cats living in it."

I did so, and within a few hours found the car. There was no clue who owned the car and the garage door, of welded bars, was only operable by remote control. Being a free lance writer, who should have been pounding away at the typewriter (this might have been in the days before computers), I was too busy to stand there all day so I had this friend at the time who was totally broke so I paid him $20 a day to stand there at the garage entrance and ask each and every person who drove in and out whose Bentley that was. After two days he had an answer and I called my customer in New York (at that time I was already a bird-dog barn finder for a wealthy building owner in Manhattan) who sent a cashier's check for $36,000-$40,000 or thereabouts (again, memory fades) made out to the owner's name. These cars sold so rarely I didn't know what they were worth but this one could have a frozen engine and the interior looked kind of shabby—not only was there a family of cats inside it but you can guess with the car parked top down and ocean dew settling on the interior each night it wasn't pretty. I put a note in the person's mailbox who had been identified as the owner and a couple days later was invited up to meet the owner, who was a Texas cowpoke who was a day trader in the stock market. His way of making a living was to jump into the market in the morning with a bundle of thousands and then to sell out just before the close of market each day, hopefully at a profit (I later lost $40,000 this way so I don't recommend it as a way to make a living). He said he bought the car in Texas and just didn't drive it anymore but couldn't guarantee it would start. I told him no problem and he got the title and it had the name of a ranch on it (no, not Southfork) and when we got down to the car I could see it had Texas plates. I handed him the cashier's check, he gave me the keys and title and I tried to get it out of the garage with my Honda Accord and burned out the clutch in the process, but eventually a tow truck towed it out and up onto the flatbed. When it got to New York I heard all my customer did was change the oil, put a new battery in it and it started right up. Today those dhc Mulliner Park Ward dhc's in LHD (left hand drive) have to be worth $150,000 to $200,000 restored, maybe more. I was paid my finder's fee and never did find that carpenter again (Mike, you find me, I owe ya). There are several lessons to be learned here. First, on the TV star's Silver Cloud I dhc, I should have had more in reserve and asked for a chance to outbid any other offers. Second, the letter in the mailbox—well, I won't go into what I should have done there, the Post Office might object (I could have at least held the envelope up to the sun). As far as the Sedanca de ville Bentley, that was stupidity writ large. I had $3,000, I could have taken the battery out of my own car on the spot to test the bartender's claim. Lesson learned there: don't be pessimistic, sometimes it is what it is. It could be that all that's wrong with a car is exactly what the owner says is wrong with it. I was too skeptical and someone else got a car that could have changed my life.

As regards the slab-sided Bentley Continental found in Venice Beach, after the deal was done and the car on the way to New York City, I neglected to go back and pay the carpenter a finder's fee for the tip, on the basis my usual commission was $1,000 but in this case had been only $500 (this was decades ago). I later heard the carpenter had moved and the only mutual friend we had didn't know where to, so that could be why he never called me with another tip.

Oh, I can't leave this subject area without telling a second happy story where I advertised in a local paper for a Rolls or a Bentley and was contacted by a local realtor with a SC III, lhd in the favorite two-tone sand-and-sable paint scheme. I drove out to Marina Del Rey, saw a mint car, drove it, and got a dealer on an island off the Georgia coast to subsequently send a cashier's check for $25K. Today these Cloud 3's are worth about $135,000 up for a left hooker (used car dealer slang for a left hand drive car). I remember the guy didn't send me my commission for over a month and I had to nag him about it—such is the life of an itinerant barn-finder.

If you ask, dear reader, am I now cured from pursuing Rollers and Bentleys yet? Well, almost. You know that SEARCH function on Google, where you select images? Well, I can't remember exactly what I typed in 2013, "Bentley Continental" or "Bentley Mulliner" or what, but one day I typed a couple words similar to that and these Bentley pictures start filling the screen, page after page. Now every one of these cars looked to be at a show or event except for one. That one car was pictured sitting in a garage, somewhat dust covered. It looked like a two-door that had some sort of Mickey Mouse vinyl top glommed onto it, maybe by some tasteless Yank. It had California plates, which I could read clearly, so clearly that I could see it had last been registered in 2004. I'm not exactly sure of the model but it had a trunk lid handle that consisted of two graceful chrome curves with a rectangular flat-faced trunk release button. I knew that bootlid handle was a style particular to "James Young" (a British coachbuilder). Today such a car would be worth, oh, $150,000 restored.

Now I'm thinking—how many other Bentley guys have seen this same picture? Then there's the matter of tracking the plate to its owner. Some years ago, after an actress was killed by a "fan" (he told the court that he was either going to ask for her autograph or kill her—he hadn't quite decided when he was ringing her doorbell) who had bought her address from the California DMV for $3 after spotting her driving her car and wrote down the plate number. After that fiasco, a law was passed where, if you ask for an address to a plate, that request is first sent to the owner to approve whether or not that information should be released. Of course, there are ways but I'm not in the position to buy now, and if you read the last chapter you will become acquainted with my rule: don't approach the car owner until you have the money in hand.

But again that illustrates my oft-said warning that the internet is both your friend and your enemy. Thanks to the net I now know that Bentley is out there (or was in 2004). But the downside to Google image shopping is that so will everybody else who manages to type exactly the right phrase into the search engine.

Chapter 50
DER DOPPLEGANGER
(1952 C-TYPE JAGUAR)
Sometimes there is a pretender to the throne.

Sometimes you have to fight for your car's pedigree.

With Jaguars, the most famous one is probably the E-type introduced in 1961, its lines echoed in the new F-type.

But there were significant racing Jaguars before that, most notably the C-type and the D-type. The D-type though a pure racer, was also offered as a street car known as the XK-SS.

This is about a C-type barn find. It's a story of a historic car with a lot of twists and turns so fasten your seat belt tight!

First of all, more about the type…Only 53 were made so it is a rare model to begin with. Even the D-type, with 87 made, was more numerous. The C-type in Jaguar history is of huge importance—it delivered the marque their first Le Mans 24 Hours win and spawned a lot of competition, Mercedes deciding to make their own sports car, the 300SL, after seeing Jaguar win.

One particular Jaguar collector in the U.S., Terry Larson, has made it his mission to write Registers for the C-type and D-type, not only because he has owned both but because he thinks history is important.

Now it so happens that, after several years of recording where cars were, Larson was able to account for every single one of the C-types except for one. And there was a reason for that. It was a racecar that went out there, but never raced at Le Mans, nor was ever piloted by Moss or any other legendary driver.

No, instead it was sold to a part-time hobbyist racer who raced it at small events. Jaguar was happy with such a sale because they needed to penetrate the byways of America too, and to them a win at Mansfield, Louisiana, by an amateur was just as important to them that their cars be at Sebring or Bridgehampton.

This particular car, the one that escaped Larson's net for so long, SN XKC 023 began on September 22, 1952, when it was assembled at the Jaguar factory. It was shipped to their West Coast U.S. Importer, Charles Hornburg, in Los Angeles, on November 28, 1952, and was from there forwarded to the authorized dealer in Seattle, Washington, Joe Henderson. In those days, you didn't send a special truck to pick up a car even if it was a racecar so the car, after unloading in Portland, was driven on the road to Seattle in freezing weather. The poor bloke that volunteered to drive it had the thrill of his life but having no license plates and those damn yellow headlights, his bravado earned him a ticket, later dismissed in court.

Soon after the dealer took delivery, it was fitted with the new Weslake competition head (designed by the famed British engine tuner Harry Weslake) featuring larger valves and higher performance cams. The car then ran some West Coast events including Seattle's Mayfair 100 miles race. There it was piloted by Hollywood screenwriter and producer, 1955 Emmy-Award-Winner (Best Written Comedy Material) Jack Douglas who finished 2nd in that event and later bought the car. There was a brouhaha about the price, though and Henderson took off the Weslake head, which went over to his friend who had driven the car from Portland.

Over the next couple of years, Douglas ran it at other California venues including Bakersfield and Santa Barbara. Douglas was often pictured at these events with his lady friend, famous actress Mitzi Gaynor, sitting on XKC023's fender (I vaguely remember her—I think I was a teenager discovering sports cars and women about that time, but of course now I like sports cars more).

BAD STUFF HAPPENS

Could life get any better than racing a factory racecar and having a movie star girlfriend? Apparently not. But into every life, some rain must fall. On July 10, 1955, Douglas rolled the car over some hay bales at the treacherous Torrey Pines course near San Diego, that moment immortalized in a sequence of pictures published in *Road & Track*.

As often happens with crunched racecars, the owners get impatient and while the C-type was laid up, Douglas moved on to a newer D-Type which he took delivery of in New York and drove cross-country to his home in California.

In January 1956, Douglas sold the C-type car to his race mechanic John Cesar Critchlow for $2,000. Critchlow was so eager to be a race driver that, back in '51 when he was just 17, he lied about his age, got a Competition license, and managed to place 2nd in his first race, driving an MG-TD in Salt Lake City.

Douglas may have regretted he sold his C-type to the cheeky Critchlow at Santa Barbara when Critchlow beat him in the C-type as Douglas was driving the newer D-type. (I guess Douglas never heard the old racer's rule: never sell a competitor one of your racecars if he has a chance of beating you in a race.)

Critchlow, being a mechanic, had modified the car, welding the spider gears in the differential to maximize traction out of the corners, an old dirt track trick. He also threw out the carburetors, going instead for the new Hilborn constant-flow fuel injection. This crude system, favored by American hot rodders, gave you lots of torque but was always malfunctioning.

He had his own crash in the car at the Paramount Ranch Races (run on a movie set located in the Malibu mountains) after brake fluid leaking onto one of the rear brakes sent him into a spin, and down the shoulder bank where he found himself trapped under the car with the engine still running. He wanted to shut the car off but had one hand trapped under the car. He still managed, though, to stall out the engine.

THE DISAPPEARANCE

Now we come to the part where the car disappears. Oh, it was still there, out and about, but just didn't look like a C-type for a while. After this second crash, the C-type frame was still straight and true but the body was hopelessly wrinkled.

Ces figured he couldn't afford a new body so he sold the C-type to his employer, Horwath Motors, who also didn't want to spring for a C-type body so they threw on a Devin fiberglass body (one of the first kit cars) which, ironically, was smaller so once it was laid on there needed to be some fiberglass work to fill out the body to cover the car.

Then Ces went off to the U.S. Army, during which time his employer traded the Devin-Jag (yes I know that phrase hurts the purists even to hear it) to a painter who would paint the front of their business. And then the painter traded it in turn to a man named Frank Schierenbeck in exchange for fixing the painter's truck plus $1,000 in cash.

Schierenbeck, owner of Car Services Imported of Costa Mesa, California, in Orange County, knew Jags backwards and forwards, and deep-sixed the hot rod Hillborn injection system, replacing it with the original SU carbs. He ran the car at Orange County airport in 1963, recording 165 mph. He not only ran the car in local SCCA events but, amazingly, had been able to street register it in 1962. At that time it was common to run racecars on the road and when this author arrived in California in 1969, I saw Ferrari 250Ps and suchlike tooling down the streets being driven as regular cars, still with Le Mans racing numbers on the side.

Now when you go to register a car for street use that had previously only been on the track, there is the problem of no prior registration to show the Department of Motor Vehicles (DMV). So Schierenbeck was able to get a California DMV Title (commonly referred to as a "pink slip"because of their pink color) with an assigned number. In early 1974, having had enough of the crowding of Los Angeles and seeking a new adventure, Schierenbeck moved first to Idaho and then to Alaska, leaving the Devin-bodied C-type stored in his parent's garage.

ENTER FROM STAGE LEFT...THE BAD NEPHEW

Now a truly nasty turn comes in the car's history. While his uncle was far off, his nephew (and you can't blame the kid for that) up and takes the car out of the garage and enters it in a few races. When Frank found out, he hit the roof. Reportedly out of revenge, the nephew partly disassembled the car and when Schierenbeck returned from Alaska in 1981, he moved the car out of temptation's reach to his new home at Oroville in Northern California where it joined a number of partially complete XKs.

Meanwhile, interest in '50s racing Jaguars was ratcheting upward because of events like the Monterey Historics. Before Monterey was started by Steve Earle, vintage car races in the U.S. were thought of as primarily for prewar cars. The success of the Monterey Historics changed that and from 1970 on, the race among collectors was to find the racecars of the '50s and '60s and put them back on the track.

Even Frank Schierenbeck began to wonder if he had a treasure under that kit car body. After he found the original chassis number on the frame, in 1997, he took the car back to the DMV, had them inspect the frame to find the serial number, and amend their paperwork so that the chassis number would be reflected on a replacement title. In value alone, that move probably increased its value 100-fold.

UNMASKING THE REPLICA

Ah, but there was a threat to his claim to that chassis number. Now here's where the story takes a few sharp turns. Hang on here—we're coming to the esses! The original 023 had been thought long lost so long ago that somehow the serial number XKC 023 had found its way onto a replica.

Just to confuse the car's pedigree even more, the body of the original 023 had been following its own destiny. What had once been thought unrepairable in '57 after the car was wrecked had been in storage. Finally in the mid-'70s, the original panels along with some new spares and a factory replacement chassis were put together by a Californian to build what is called a "Special," a hand-made car. That car was sold to Canadian collector Jim Dale, who was under the impression he had bought the real XKC023. He persisted in thinking he had the original car for nearly 24 years.

THE REAL CAR EMERGES

Now we return to the tireless detective work of Arizona C-type and D-type expert, Terry Larson. When the Canadian heard about the discovery of the real chassis of 023 in the Schierenbeck garage, he contacted Arizona Jaguar expert Terry Larson to find out if it was true—was there really another car with the same serial number?

Sadly it was true and, worse, the Devin-bodied car was the real one. The Canadian's dream of having a million-dollar racecar out in his garage was dashed.

But in what this author commends as a most exemplary and honorable twist, Dale agreed to sell his car to Terry Larson for what would be a replica price so that the original bits on his replica could be reunited with the real 023. In effect he sold the C-type registered as 023 as a now-acknowledged replica so that the real 023 could be more judged fully authentic.

Are you following?

The replica's real 023 parts such as the grille, instrument panel, doors and body tags, were refitted on the original.

Larson, who had flown to Northern California to inspect the real chassis of XKC023, subsequently wrote: "It was a very complete chassis: engine, suspension, brakes, rear axle, frame etc… We're not talking a few little bits, we're talking about everything you need to drive down the road. Even though, as I said, some numbers were missing, but the numbers on the engine block and the top cover of the gearbox matched the original records."

Larson actually had known Frank Schierenbeck for more than a decade and talked to him on the phone on and off for almost 10 years before he actually made his first visit to Oroville, California, to see the car. He hadn't expected to see so many of XKC023 original components. An important part of the authenticity puzzle was also found in one of the two original chassis numbers, found on the front cross member. Though it is true such a number could have been added to a spare chassis later in its life, Larson had seen the font used on other factory cars and it matched. Having vetted the true 023, Larson bought the car for his Swiss client, friend and fellow enthusiast Christian J. Jenny, and it was shipped to Arizona so Larson could take it completely apart and restore it and began uniting of the car with its wayward parts.

He found that second chassis number only after the plastic Devin body was removed. The body was already off when he first saw the chassis. He saw a bracket which was needed to hold the Devin body on had been welded over the place where he expected to see the second chasiss number stamping. He carefully cut at it and peeled this bracket off and saw the number. From that point there was no question it was the genuine article.

At that point he felt like an archeologist at King Tut's tomb, you know one of those guys using a camel's hair brush to dust centuries of dirt off a valuable and fragile relic.

This was so Indiana Jones. In fact in 1999 *Autoweek* ran a cover story featuring a very Indiana Jones-looking Terry Larson, car detective.

Larson had worked on no less than fifteen C-types. If you are into expensive vintage racing cars you almost have to go to someone with that deep of a background because they can replicate the techniques in use at the factory many decades before. Ironically, because the cars were built by hand at the factory, each car is just a little bit different from the next one. The body was one of the biggest problems—the body panels that remained with XKC 023 since new were the original floor pans, footwell panels, propshaft cover and tunnel cover which still had the original Harduras trim on it.

The car got a full restoration. Among the new parts installed were the radiator, electrical harness and systems along with XK-150 disc brakes to replace the original drums although those remained with the car. This was not a modern update, as many original C-Type were so converted in the late 50s using parts available from the dealerships.

Fortunately after all this time, the car still had only 12,763 miles. To his credit, Frank Schierenbeck had prepared it for storage properly, covering the engine's internals with grease.

Once they had the "spares car" unmasked as a replica, the original bonnet and tail section Terry already had were sent to RS Panels in Coventry where the body was rebuilt and trial-fitted to the chassis.

Those who are not in the events like Pebble Beach are probably not aware how important it is to authenticate a car of this caliber. In this case, the whole chassis was sent to the factory, not only to make sure the new body would fit but to submit the chassis for inspection by U.K. experts.

Was it cleaned up first? Surprisingly not. To preserve as many details as possible it was sent, uncleaned and rusty, with part of the welded bracket left on the shock tower. Ironically, among the British experts called in to inspect it was the same man who had built the previously mentioned high quality replica, but who is recognized as one the leading C-Type experts. All the judges agreed on the chassis' authenticity.

After the new body was built, everything was then shipped back to Arizona where the rebuilt components where reinstalled. The final touch was to paint it red, the same color it had been when new over half a century earlier.

A really nice touch, one that truly warms the cockles of my heart, was in inviting Norman Dewis, the former factory test driver back when the car was new, to come in and inspect the chassis and Dewis dutifully signed it off on the fuel tank as "Inspected and passed by Norman Dewis." XKC 023 was of course, the same car he had inspected and test driven on Nov. 3, 1952, in Coventry, before it was dispatched to the U.S.

Finished in late 2000, the car was then taken to a number of events, including an 800-mile tour with other C-types.

In January 2001, XKC 023 was shipped to Switzerland to Terry Larson's friend and client Christian who already had an extensive collection of significant Jaguars including the 1935 SS90 Prototype, two SS100s, an alloy-XK120, and more cars, some of which had been restored by Larson.

Lesson to be learned here? Even if you find a historic car hiding under a nondescript body, be forewarned—you may have to fight off "pretenders to the throne" who, in the real car's long absence form the scene, have adopted the real chassis' identity for a replica because the original was missing so long it was presumed destroyed. It's like some of those '50s sword-fighting B-movies where the real heir to the throne is somehow thrust into the role of being a commoner but fights his way back to resume his rightful throne. C-type 023 is a car that has now resumed its rightful title. Kudos to Terry Larson for staying on the track of the missing C-type, finding it and helping to authenticate it so once again it can represent Jaguar's glorious racing history.

Chapter 51
BARN FINDING STRATEGIES

IN SUM

Let's say, or hope, you are inspired by what you read so far. You are ready to make an investment in a barn find. Let's discuss some tried-and-true methodologies.

TARGET ACQUISITION

In the military, before they start on a mission, they do research—what's the anti-aircraft like? How close do we need to be? What kind of bomb load do we need? Yadda yadda.

It's the same here. You first have to decide on a target, do some threat assessment, and then make plans for the raid.

NARROW DOWN YOUR TARGETS

First I would say the challenge is to throw a lasso around a reach-able target. You can't just say "Bugatti Type 37" if the last one you read about sold for a million dollars if you only have, say $20,000. But if you choose a reasonable target, say "Porsche 356" or "E-type Jaguar," even though there are some going for over $100K, there are some still in the barns, or which have reached decrepit status that can still be found within your price range.

WHY NARROW YOUR SEARCH?

The chief reason for confining your search to only two or three marques is time. Unless you are retired and have all kinds of time, the search can probably only be a hobby for you. Therefore you can only devote a few hours a week.

I would say, in any one category, say Porsche 356 models, or MG T-series, it would take about ten hours a week of research just to keep abreast of who's got what, where some cars might be, what the cars are selling for in various states of condition, what shops have parts, etc. If you choose three marques to follow that would be three times ten hours a week. Choose too many marques to keep tabs on and it starts to add up to almost a full time job.

START A DATA BASE

A"data base" sounds fancy but all it is, fundamentally, is a collection of facts that you update periodically. It's your data and you are basing it in one place (I would even keep some on a thumb drive in case your computer goes all wonky on you). You could start by going to a swap meet and buying lots of old *HEMMINGS* and other magazines about old cars, and cutting or photocopying privately-placed ads. It doesn't matter how old the ads are, it's a starting point. That's why it's called a "base," it's where you started, your base camp. Besides, this book is full of examples of cars that were still where they were last seen, 10, 20, 30 or more years ago. So those old ads can at least be a base.

Far more valuable, though, are the old club rosters from different clubs. Let's say there was an early Porsche club in your area. You have decided on a 356 Porsche as your target car. You join the club, and advertise in the club newsletter you want to buy a stack of old club newsletters as complete as possible, right back to the start of the club. Odds are you go back through those and find cars to add to the database. I did this with the Ferrari Owners Club. I joined, and one day when I noticed I had a '77 directory and a '78. I compared and found ten people had dropped out within that year. I wrote them each a form letter and noted they dropped out and asked them, "Gee, do you still, by chance, have your Ferrari and if so, is it for sale?"

I bought two or three that way.

MAINTAIN A CURRENT ASKING PRICE DATA BASE

I like to think, as a well-read reader of magazines and websites, that I am current with the current going prices of various cars on my be-on-the-lookout list (cops call that a BOLO list). Well, I got a shocker in October 2013 when I went to the website of a business called European Collectibles in Costa Mesa, California, to see what they were selling 356 Porsches for. I had last owned a 356 Convertible D more than 20 years ago which I sold for $6,000 so I had no idea what 356s wer e going for now. I almost fell off my chair when I saw their current inventory. Here's a sampling from their website in October 23,2013:

1958 Porsche 356 A T2 Speedster. Silver Metallic/Black. $339,500

1959 Porsche 356A 1600GS Carrera Coupe . Ruby Red/Black. $510,000

1959 Porsche 356A Cabriolet. Red/Black. $100,000

1959 Porsche 356A Convertible D. Fjord Green/Tan. $275,000

1959 Porsche 356A Convertible D. Ruby Red/Black. $149,950

1959 Porsche 356A Convertible D. Meissen Blue/Red. $235,000

1959 Porsche 356A T2 Cabriolet. Red/Black. $108,500

1960 Porsche 356B T5 Roadster. Black/Black. $89,950

1961 Porsche 356 B Roadster. Fjord Green/Black. $159,950

1962 Porsche 356B T6 Coupe. Red/Tan. $50,000

1962 Porsche 356B T6 Twin Grill Roadster. Light Ivory/Fawn. $224,950

1963 Porsche 356 B Super Cabriolet. Signal Red/Tan. $129,950

1963 Porsche 356B T6 Super-90 Cabriolet. Red/Black. $149,500

1964 Porsche 356 C Carrera 2000 GS Sunroof Coupe. Silver/Black. $575,000

1964 Porsche 356 C Coupe. Burgundy/Grey. $54,950

1964 Porsche 356C Cabriolet. Light Ivory/Red. $159,500

1965 Porsche 356 C Cabriolet. Black/Red Wine. $157,500

Until I checked the prices of that shop's cars, I had no idea that Porsche 356s were now going, in some cases, for more than V12 Ferraris. And, boy am I mad that I saw a 356 coupe a few months ago parked outside a middle class apartment house and didn't stop to put a note on the windshield. I had no idea that a dead stock 356 coupe of any year could be a $50,000 car! This underlines why I advise narrowing your search to two or three marques because part and parcel of being an expert on various marques is keeping track with current asking prices so you don't pass them by like I did on that 356 coupe.

THE INTERNET

Now those newcomers to barn finding think, "Hey, this is easy, I'll just sit there at Starbucks and troll the net and find cars." Sounds nice, right? But the problem is (and I know you youngins will have a hard time grasping this) not everything ever published is posted up on the net. If no one posted it, it's not there, pure and simple. Say the club roster for Cobra owners for a club based in Grosse Pointe, Michigan that was established prior to the formation of the Shelby American Automobile Club (SAAC). I have that roster. It is not posted on the internet. I ran off a few and sold them and one owner wrote me back in 2012 to report that, that out of the fifty or so members listed, three of them still own their cars and that roster was at least 40 years old! So to a Cobra collector, that document is worth its weight in gold...

ESTABLISH A GAME PLAN

There are several reasons you might want to be a barn finder. Here's where you have to be honest with yourself and not let your enthusiasm carry you too far down the road.

For instance, one objective might just be to have something fun to drive on occasion. Nothing wrong with that. There are some 8,000-feet tall mountains within sight of my SoCal base. I yearn for a sports car that I can drive up there for breakfast on a early Saturday morning. That would be reason enough to own the car. One British car magazine columnist recently started out his column in a car magazine by asking something philosophical like

"What's the purpose of life?" and then answered his own question by saying that, as far as he was concerned, something like "driving a sports car, top down, on a sunny morning on a country road" goes a long way toward answering that question.

Now I can add another dimension to that ambition by saying "fun to drive" and a car you could eventually sell at a profit. That puts a different spin on it, because you then have to do some research to separate out the cars that are too plentiful (Mazda Miatas) from those that are potential investments (Triumph TR-3) by virtue of being old, collectible and far rarer. The older car will be 100 times harder to find but is appreciating because they are nearly 50 years old but are zooming up in price.

Another level, and this takes more money, more advance planning and a willing partner (if you're married). That is establishing the parameters: "fun to drive, and something I can sell at a profit at an investment level."

Ah, that word "investment" makes it a horse of a different color. That means, going back to my introduction, that the car has to be able to be sold for what you would have made in profit on your typical land or stock investment, something like, say, pick a round number—$100,000. True, there are plenty of cars you can buy, drive for five years and sell for exactly what you bought it for, like a '65 Mustang convertible, but will that amount of profit make a measurable difference in your life? Can you take that profit and put a down payment on a house? Not off a Miata, or a '65 Mustang (unless it's a Shelby GT350).

My requirement of the barn find being "investment grade" is what separates the men from the boys so to speak. Some people just luck out—they buy an old car not knowing what they have. But if you've done your research right and found the right car, your investment grade profit potential is almost tangible from the very moment you buy it. For instance, back when I was in the Iso Bizzarrini Owner's Club in the'70s, a friend bought a Bizzarrini GT5300 Strada for well under $10,000. It was a running driving car at the time, but back then clean samples of the marque were only going for $12,000 or so. He had no competition, no one else knew about the car. The tip had come in from a high school girl who he had graduated with who remembered he liked that brand and had called him out of the blue with a tip about the car. He hasn't restored it and now it's thirty or more years later. But by picking the right car, he made an investment that really paid off because in July 2013 I checked the RM auction at Monterey to see what's coming up. A Bizzarrini GT5300 Strada, estimated at $550,000-$750,000. A very good appreciation curve compared to best Dow Jones averages. Now admittedly that price they go for now is for a fully-restored car but now that auctions are occasionally feature barn-find cars, i.e. "as found," even an unrestored version of the right car can go for huge dollars if you buy the right car in the beginning.

PERILS OF THE INTERNET

Every day on the internet, I read lots of forums, dozens of them— Alfa forums, Ferrari forums, Jaguar forums, Corvette forums. Every once in a while you read about some boob who has just discovered a barn find car and immediately begins asking a lot of questions about the car he has found. This is good in that he can find out the car's significance, for instance if it was a racecar, who raced it, was it ever crashed, etc.

But there's a downside to this—a nasty peril attached to this "easy research" you can do by picking the brains of forumites. That danger is, if you haven't secured the car—haven't got it actually in point of fact strapped down to your car trailer and the keys, signed-off title and Bill of Sale securely in hand—that your innocent queries as to the value and or history that you post on the net could tip off your competition from the second you press the SEND button and you could inadvertently launch your rivals on missions to buy it out from under you.

You can see this mistake happening every day right on the forums. Kind of reminds me when, as a kid, I made the mistake of throwing a hot dog into a pool of alligators at the Detroit zoo. They sleepily sniffed at it and then, a second later, there was this wild thrashing as they all fought for that one hot dog.

"But I have a code name on the net and nobody knows what city I found it in" I can hear you saying. How dumb are we? Most websites, when you have your forum handle, also say under that handle what city you are in, or the time zone, so if a rival has done lots of research on that marque, say Porsche 356 Carrera, etc. all you have do is say "Hey guys, I found an old Porsche Carrera near my house and think you are safe imparting that information but they see that you live in Riverside, California, and then they check their records for 356 Carreras last known to be domiciled in Riverside and BAM, they got the car you probably found and are on the horn in seconds to the owner to outbid you. Or say you are dumb enough to list the SN. How many of your rival barn-finders have good databases like old car club rosters? They can look up that SN and conclude: "Oh, yeah, he must have found the Davis car. Maybe ol' man Davis is finally ready to sell. I'll call someone local and see if they can go over there and see if it's still available."

So do not, repeat, do not input your find onto the net until it's yours. You have to, research the car first on paper, then plan your attack. You can do the detailed history search of who owned it before owner-by-owner after the car is yours. But for God's sake don't announce your find until it's yours, on the flatbed, and you've got the signed-off title and keys in hand.

THE EXECUTION

Back in the 1980s I bought several cars, some for me and some for a wealthy collectors, including one from New York who I met at a Ferrari meet in Virginia who regularly was a "player" for the cars I found, from Bentleys to Ferraris. He liked the fact I was married to an airline employee in the "Marry Me, Fly Free" days. I could pop around the country to look at cars, receiving a commission if I bought one.

One thing I learned was that you have to approach the car owner only when you are 100-percent ready to buy. There is a double-important reason to combine approaching and buying almost simultaneously today and that is the damned internet.

Back when I was doing this, in the '80s, a lot of people weren't internet savvy. But now even granmas living in old cabins without electricity or running water can be counted on to have a grandson or neighbor kid somewhere who knows the net and they can always call him and say "Sonny, can you please check for Granny what E-type Jags are going for these days?"

What you want to do is line up your cash offer, and when I say cash I don't mean actual bills (too dangerous to carry around) but I mean cashier's checks and be ready to present that (actually a Xerox of it) to the owner on first contact. Give them a time limit for your offer. Say it's Wednesday when you get them the copy. You say "Y'know, I'm losing a lot of interest on that amount every day I keep it tied up in that check, so I'd appreciate it if you can let me know by Friday so I can turn the check back in." That's their deadline. Two days. Immediately they began thinking of the interest they can be making if the money's in their account instead.

When I did this regularly, I had a whole list of flatbed tow drivers ready to come at a moment's call if it was accepted. So what about fake cashier's checks? They are around. But what you do is get the owner a photocopy of the check and invite them "to take that down the road to their banker to make sure that check is real." I found bankers to be very co-operative. They want that money in their bank so they call New York or wherever to make sure it's a real cashier's check and began to lean on the car owner for you.

Compress that period as tight as you can because nowadays with the internet, the car owner might get to that search engine and you're doomed if they see their same model of car being offered at a higher price, even though they might be looking at what a restored one sold for, not that piece of ca ca they got in the garage.

INSPECTING THE OWNER/SELLER

Now I realize you might be a car guy, and totally interested in checking out the car's serial number, the number on this part and that to make sure it's not a "put together" car (put together of parts from dozens of cars). But recently after I found a rare Italian car being offered by a man who had just sold his business, I passed the word to a friend looking for that car and told him: "You know, I'd check out the owners too." It didn't take him five minutes of searching on the net to find out that there was some government agency filing insider-trading laws against the car's seller and, depending on which way the legal winds blow, the car might be among the assets if the seller's assets were confiscated.

Ironically that doesn't mean it wasn't a real car as opposed to a replica. The seller, however shaky his personal life, could have bought it for a legitimate price when he was awash in cash. It recalls the Ferrari 250GTO that the government seized from a drug dealer and sold. It was a legitimate Ferrari 250GTO. It so happened that the drug dealer had good taste in cars. But all this warning is to remember what the seller told you—where he got the car, who the previous owner got it from, establish a chain of ownership if you can. And find out what you can about the seller, and look them up on the net to see how legitimately they are regarded in the business community. You might be the last person that they scam before going off to the pokey!

A side note here. If the seller's assets are seized by a court, there may be a possibility of applying to the State, if they seize the assets, or to whoever wins the assets. Maybe they don't like old cars and will be only too happy to receive an offer.

INSPECTING THE CAR

Forget inspections. If you picked the right car, condition is irrelevant. I have to laugh when I remember the time I took my retired airline pilot friend to look at a Ferrari 250GT Lusso in the San Fernando Valley about 20 years ago. At that time Lussos were worth like $40-50K and he already had two of them in his garage but was willing to go look at it for kicks because it was advertised at some ridiculously low price like $31K. When we got there the car was a mess, half painted, half in primer, mostly missing interior, rust in the floorpans and such and he began inspecting it and at the same time, calling out the flaws he found, like a medical examiner on one of those TV shows examining a murder victim and all the while calling out all the damage. He was looking under the hood and finding this missing and that missing, and meanwhile the owner –who had advertised in the *LA Times*—was getting phone calls on his cell phone at the rate of one a minute, and people were outbidding us on the phone, sight unseen. Soon the car was up to $40,000 and my buddy was still picking away at the car like he had all damn day. Well, last time I looked Lussos were at $450,000-600,000. With today's market, if you find a car that's enjoying a healthy appreciation curve like a rocket you can't waste time picking the car apart on the details. I figured later that his quibbling was costing me—a potential buyer—a thousand dollars a minute! Of course that is the absolute worst buying situation, answering an ad in the newspaper because then all your rivals know about the ad too. What you want it to find cars no one knows about. Then, temporarily, you have no competition. And don't take my buddy. For God's sake don't take him. He quibbleth too much.

FAKE SALES

Now that we, as an audience, are cued by reality TV shows (some of which are, horrors, scripted) as to what can be found out there in the hustings, we like to think all estate sales are genuine estate sales. I'm here to tell you that one time I flew to Texas (admittedly on my then applicable Marry-Me-Fly-Free card) for an estate auction that would have house furnishings and an E-type Jag. When I got there I noticed: 1.) the E-Jag was not at the house yet 2.) the silverware in the kitchen was still bagged with thrift shop labels. When the estate sellers themselves showed up, I recognized them as a pair of brothers who liked to buy Aston Martins and who had even left one DB4 in my driveway for a week (I snuck it out on a couple of joy rides, feeling like James ("Shaken not stirred") Bond. I said "If I would have known it was you, I would have known it was a set-up" but they just laughed. Their theory was, if people thought the car was part of a house's contents being sold instead of just a car at a car dealers, it might be a real steal. So try to check out who is holding the sale, what's their reputation, before you buy that plane ticket.

OWNER PROFILING

During the unpleasantness known as WWII, they used to publish "spotter's guides" so that civilians, in, say Cleveland, could look up in the sky and spot those Messerschmitt 262s coming in at 3 o'clock.

We of the car collecting field could use a Spotter's Guide as well. That's because by far the hardest part about collecting old cars is in separating the owners from their machinery. After decades at this trade, (between other more legitimate occupations) I noticed that owners fall into many classifiable categories and that each category requires another approach angle. You have to fly under the radar. You have to find out what they need and satisfy that need. Here's the categories (I remain open to suggestions of new categories from readers...):

THE HOARDER

The hoarder is the kind of guy to whom buying and holding is everything; he talks about it but he actually never plans on taking a car out of his hoard and restoring it or even taking it to an event because then they, whoever "they" is, will know he has it. He is a loner, and scared of selling for fear he won't get what's due to him for keeping the parts all those years. One way to deal with this type is bring him something else that he wants, and suggest a trade plus cash. After all, they have to pay the rent. The cash part will go toward the rent, the car part will go into their hoard. The hardest hoarders to deal with are single guys (no wife nagging them to sell the car) who are self-employed (if they figured out how to make the house payment and taxes, they can pretty much exist on 99-cent burgers).

THE FLIPPER

These guys are slippery dudes (Hey, I've been one) who buy a car and pass it on to a new owner without bothering to change the title, get it registered, etc. These guys are best approached with cash so they can be paper-free the whole way ("What car? I don't remember that one") but beware when I say "cash" I mean a cashier's check they cash at the bank with you and the car's outside on your flatbed before they are handed the check. These guys go for paperless transactions so that they were never there, capisce?

THE PROCRASTINATOR

These are well-meaning guys, but let's face it, they have other responsibilities in life (wife, children, mortgage, medical bills) so can never quite get up to or around to restoring that car, even though they have the spare parts stacked all around (and maybe on top of) the car. The way to deal with them is The Flatbed Method. You pull up in the flatbed, leaving the engine running, hand the wife the cashier's check and invite her to go to the bank with it and cash it as she hands you the signed off title. Then you go back to the car and yank it out. Most of these guys will guiltily give in, knowing deep in their heart that they never would have gotten around to it.

THE TRADER

These are guys who see themselves as mini-Donald Trumps, empire-builders. They like what they have but they can't help but indulge in the thrill of acquiring more. I remember a young college lad I knew about 30 plus years ago who had inherited money from a rich aunt and immediately bought a used Ferrari Daytona. He then met a car dealer from Monterey who convinced him that five cars were surely better than one and traded him five cars for the Daytona. Today Daytona's are worth about $400,000 up and those five cars, well, one was a 308GT4 but the others would probably be worth a few dollars as scrap metal. Still, some guys go for the one-becomes-many gambit. (More about trades later…)

THE NEW CAR WANNA-BE

This is a variation on the procrastinator. A lot of guys buy an old car but never get around to restoring it or even making it drivable. You determine how much his old car is worth then drive him to a new car lot, or one with late-model used cars, and give him the keys to a snazzy ready-to-drive gleaming car (I find a red convertible usually works best) and say, "This is yours today if you let me take in trade that old what-it-is you never got around to."

THE WOULD-BE RACER

This phrase covers about everybody who likes motorsports. Now some guys buy a dead stock street car and say "I'm going to make this a racer."Well, it turns out that they have no idea on how much that's going to cost. One Cobra collector I know told me of a guy that who beat him to a genuine AC Cobra street car, a 289. Upon acquiring it, the man announced, "Ah'm going to be a racer." My friend convinced him that what he bought was a long way from a racecar (say along factory comp 289 specs, circa 1964) and hell, if racing was what he wanted to do, he'd find him a replica Cobra already race-equipped, roll bar, comp seat belts, the whole nine yards, ready to go, no waiting. The deal was done. Never mind that what he has is not vintage anymore, maybe the would-be racer just wanted it for club events where they don't mind a replica. Of course, at some future auction five or ten years down the road there will be a vast difference in value between the two cars, but wanna-be racers want to race NOW. Get it?

THE WIDOW

This is most times a good buy situation—if you can reach the widow directly and not have to suffer through dealing with intermediaries. The usual situation is that the widow endured her husband tinkering with his toys out in the garage for God knows how many decades and now, with his passing, she can clean out the garage. Be sure to emphasize that not only will you buy that old derelict car with four flat tires, you will clean out the garage completely in a single day, taking everything in one fell swoop (because you never know where all the parts are) You can sort the junk out later, even if it's at a dumpster a mile away from her house. Tell her that you will not only clean the garage but paint the floor a gleaming white! That oughta swing the deal!

THE KEEPER OF THE FLAME

I've used this one a few times myself. This is where the owner has gotten to a certain point, or aged himself out from working on cars; or lost his connections for parts and or specialized mechanics he trusts; or his wife has given what is known in old car circles as The Order: The Car Must Go. But she didn't understand--he was building the car as a tribute to the glory of ol'whatsiz name (substitute here the name of some designer, engineer, racer or personality). Your pitch to the car owner is that you, and you alone, will take up the cause in his stead. Yes, indeedy, you will pick up that blood-stained flag and charge forward in defense of the cause. Not only that, when you finish the car you will come back and take him for a ride in it (even if your real plan to sell it a week later).

BANKRUPTCY ATTORNIES

A lot of these guys are handed a house, cars and personal effects to auction off and their bread is buttered on the side of those owed the money so they want that stuff sold quickly, sometimes at pennies on the dollar. Since cars are rather large and take space and some care, they might want to divest of those first (after the house) so here's a deal where you might have to buy five cars to get the single one you really want.

GUM'INT AGENCIES

The DEA, the IRS and a few other government agencies are wont to grab your stuff when you do something against the law and they get to your stuff before you can get a good lawyer. These are among the most highly motivated of sellers because often they don't have a clue as to what they're selling, they just know the brand name, and want to get rid of it before something breaks and they have go to a mechanic who doesn't care if they are the U.S. gum'mint, they gotta pay that $130/hr. hourly service rate. Ironically, some of the confiscated cars might be grey market but when I asked the DEA agent in charge about a Ferrari Boxer at a DEA auction she just said "Don't worry about it" which I interpreted to mean "hey, we will make that particular car okay if you buy it."

And don't say, "They will just have late model stuff" as one of the most famous cars ever confiscated by the Feds was a genuine Ferrari 250GTO. Now you might say "Well, maybe they'll hang onto those cars that are appreciating, in case they go higher." Wrong-Oh. They want the money yesterday so once it goes on the block, they will take the highest bid. The government is not into used car investments.

THE LIFE STYLE UPGRADER

Now there comes a time in life when a man has to put away the toys of a child and upgrade so that he looks more successful. I.e. "to put on the dog" so to speak. So let's say some guy has some tatty old racecar (which you have determined ran at Le Mans, Daytona or Sebring) and it is lacking the engine, trans, blahblah, so you say to him "What say we go shopping for a late model Whatsiz and go full boat" and, after exposure to it, he begins to like the idea of a car that's actually streetable, a car that has air conditioning and automatic and GPS and eight speakers, and cooling units for the seats and God knows what other gadgets. Be sure to show the new car to his wife and let her drive it. No contest once you do that. I particularly remember the hairdresser in Southern California that was persuaded to take a couple late model Mercedes in trade for a Ferrari 365GTB/4 Daytona Competition coupe. Today the Fazazz might be worth a million, the old Mercedes not so much.

Last but not least there is…

THE NUMBERS GUY

This would be the guy who has poured money into some car, wrongly estimating what kind of funding it would take to get it (back) to some destination, ranging from making it a relatively dependable but fun daily driver to what is known in the field as a "cosmetic" resto, to—top of the world ma—the full "frame-off, concours-level, 100 point car." The way to this guy is to sidestep his constant listings of all he's done to the car and point to the cashier's check with his name on it and say "H-E-L-L-O, this is what I'm offering today, right now, this minute." He might decide to reach for the check and thus, with a great sense of relief, step out of the collector car market with most of his body parts intact.

STORAGE

I can't emphasize enough how important it is to have storage lined up beforeyou buy a barn find. Why? Because the best barn finds, the biggest bargains, are not running. The owner has died; or lost interest or can't afford to fix the car. So they are willing to let it go. Maybe you can't afford to fix it either but if it has a good appreciation prediction, that doesn't matter, the important thing is to buy the car when its' available.

But then you have to have a place to park it. I suggest a family-owned rural house because, in the city, there are many regulations against parking non-running non–registered cars. Some municipalities will ticket a car even if it's on private property in your driveway. Then too, there's much greater potential of damage occurring while it's sitting outside in a driveway. I remember finding a Rolls Royce SCIII Mulliner Park ward coupe in Orange County parked in a driveway where some kids had thrown a brick through the back window. That back window would probably set you back $3,000—if you could find one for a car they made probably less than 200 of nearly a half-century ago. The owner could have rented a garage to park it in for less than that a year.

And if it's owned by your family, the country place won't charge your rent or tow the car out the minute you are late with the rent. In this book, remember the gullwing chapter? Both times I sold my gullwing because I didn't have a place to park it. That one experience is a searing nightmare—finding treasure but unable to keep it. Ironically there was a family farm in my family, one that almost half a century later is still there today, in 2014. I should have availed myself of the opportunity to stow it there. Woulda, coulda, shoulda, that's my motto.

RE-MARKETING THE CAR

Now if your main reason for buying the car is flipping it, i.e. re-selling it for a quick profit, there's nothing wrong with that, except that then you can't take advantage of the long range gradual appreciation that will occur if you bought the right car. You could start this type of sale as soon as you have it on the flatbed truck—e-mailing pictures to a forum and saying "I found this car, etc." but there's a couple reasons why this is might be a bad idea—if the car has some damage or history you don't know about, the forumites might let the whole world know (as in my second gullwing, it had been hit hard in front, which I didn't know; such knowledge posted on the net would have de-valued the car mightily if the whole world knew).

I would at least wait at least until it's cleaned up a little, sitting on four tires filled with air, and photographed against a nice background.

LONG RANGE MARKETING

A running driving car is worth a whole lot more to some people than a car whose engine hasn't turned over for years. It could be, for appreciation potential, you bought a Ferrari and can't afford the $25,000 or so minimum to rebuild a V-12 (and that's one that doesn't need new heads, a new crank, etc.) That cost of getting a car running has to figure in which car you target. It is possible to re-sell a car without getting it running but a whole lot more difficult to schlep it around. You might narrow down your choices to cars whose engines and drivetrains you can afford to fix. Say, for instance in my friend's Bizzarrini, that's a 327 Chevy V8. Junkyards are full of them. Those engines were sold by the millions. So now, even though they are half-million dollars cars they have engines that can be bought for the price of one Ferrari V12 piston!

Going back to the path I would follow, I would get the car running, and driving and that means going through the fuel system, braking system, gas tank replacement, gauges, exhaust system, etc.

Then before doing any of the cosmetics, if your goal is shorter range appreciation, contact auction companies and see if they would take it as an unrestored barn find. Surprisingly even the fanciest auction companies, like Gooding, occasionally do that. Why would they want to sell a car with faded paint, and cracked upholstery? Because the new trend is that some of their most discerning buyers don't want a car that was restored improperly by somebody else, painted the wrong color, upholstered to the wrong pattern, or had parts replaced willy-nilly with some incorrect parts. They want to be the one to decide the colors of the exterior and interior etc. So why should they pay for a car that's been done all wrong and have to un-do what's incorrect?

MEDIA CHOICE FOR YOUR "CARS WANTED" ADS

Now I'm going to discuss which media to choose if you place a Cars Wanted ad. What you want, in a barn find situation, is to find media that reaches out to the people who are not in the old car buying/selling hobby. Those car-hip people (I know, some of your best friends…yadda yadda) are your enemies, temporarily. What you want to look at is small community newspapers. And what areas would you choose? Well, there's two theories about that. One is to choose only affluent areas—like say Palos Verdes peninsula in Los Angeles, a piece of land that juts out into the Pacific full of million dollar houses. How many of those affluent folks have some treasure tucked away? And you run a small ad, maybe with a small picture of a somewhat distressed old car and say something vague like:

SPORTS CAR WANTED

Jaguar, Aston Martin. Okay if non-running, broken, missing parts, rusty, flat tires. Paying cash. Send picture to _____ (your code name like BRIT CAR FAN and address).

Now the first thing you are going to say is: "Why hide behind a code name?" First of all, if you use your real name, that would tip off your competition that it's you who are looking and next week you can guarantee that their ad will be there too, maybe even a bigger ad then you are running. Secondly I hear you asking why not put in an e-mail address? Same reason plus you want people who are not into e-mail. Plus if they send a picture, you can cross out the license plate and e-mail that picture to a potential buyer if you are short of the money you think it will take to you to buy it yourself (however, be forewarned, that there's the peril existent there that they will immediately post that picture on a forum and a rival will guess whose car it is and go there and buy it).

Another opposite tack is to go the complete other direction and advertise in retirement communities, way out in the inland empire of Southern California, up in Oregon, Florida, Arizona and the like. A lot of car collectors who drove these cars when they were new back in the Fifties and Sixties have moved out to rural areas where they took their treasures with them but subsequently found there's no skilled mechanics there, no parts, etc. So you could work the deserts one month, the mountains the next, etc. A lot of those retirees go out to the sticks with grand plans to work on their car in retirement but, y'know, sometimes when you're 70, 75, just sittin'on the porch seems a more relaxed way to go than getting out in that garage under a car that could fall off the jack and squash you flatter'n a June bug. Plans change when you're in your golden years…

THINK OUTSIDE THE BOX

Yet another idea is run ads in publications you think are read by the people who would own that kind of car. Say some newspaper called *Airplane Trader*, or *Drag Boat News*. Airplane guys like sports cars, have plenty of hanger space and might need to sell that old car to get the airplane past the next FAA inspection. Drag boaters buy cars just for their engines and let the car's sit, such as one that bought an L88 Corvette in the Sixties and did just that. So plunk down that $15-20 and reach outside the car field to other guys that like machines—airplanes, boats, cars, it's all part of the same continuum.

FOREIGN COUNTRIES

In a word—Don't. That's the safest advice I can give. I know, I know, you want to be like the guy in *Raiders of the Lost Ark*, going into the jungle and coming out with jewels but I'm saying, after researching over 100 barn finds between the first volume of *Incredible Barn Finds* (still available, check Enthusiastbooks.com) and this one, that there are plenty of cars right here right here in the U.S. that are fast appreciating and you won't have to go through customs, freight forwarding, and all that. But if you do insist going overseas, you want that excitement of the hunt plus a trip abroad, I would first establish some relationship there with someone on some inexpensive parts so at least you have a contact there. I recently talked to a museum owner in central California who told me he helped a man in South America sell an old American car found down there, and once that worked out well for all concerned, the American asked "Say can you look for this old Alfa that's supposed to be down there?"

The man looked, the car was found and bought for the American by the South American. So it's far getter to go to a foreign country where you already have contacts than to go in blind with the word SUCKER tattooed on your forehead.

JOIN A CAR CLUB

I joined the Ferrari Owner's Club back in the'80s before I had a Ferrari. Meanwhile I was looking for one. (to read about the Ferrari I bought from a movie producer, see *Incredible Barn Finds* from Enthusiast Books). Go to the club's shows, and volunteer to do things like write articles for the newsletter. Be useful. Bring something to the table. Eventually you may meet some of the older members who have cars they want to get rid of; cars they don't have time or storage space for.

START YOUR OWN DAMN CAR CLUB

Let's say you are all turned on by a particular model of car. But you can't find many other owners. Maybe the solution is to start your own car club. I did that once, called the Bizzarrini Owner's Register or some such and suddenly had 10-15 owners. I then felt guilty I didn't own one at the time and abandoned the club but it sure smoked a lot of cars out of the woodwork I hadn't heard of previously when I'd been in the Iso-Bizzarrini Owner's club.

DISPLAY AT A CONCOURS

Now some concours are not as fussy as others. Pebble Beach, well, that's a toughie. You have to have something pretty damn special to get in there. But there are run-what-you-brung local shows. If you have a clean sample of anything, enter it at one of those informal shows. Be hail fellow well met, bring coffee for everyone and snacks, and deck chairs and jawbone about what you are looking for. Figure all displayers of cars at car shows are car collectors. Maybe in conversation you'll hear about what you're looking for. When I had my 12-cylinder Ferrari, I would enter concours in a non-judged capacity. I would see the judges arriving at the car, clipboards in hand ready to mark me off for the dead fly in the rear window ledge but then I'd say, "Good morning, fellas, I'm just here for the ambiance." I'd enjoy the show, make lots of friends and not have to worry about points off for that dead fly (hey, he was an Italian fly).

Here's some other strategies:

TROLL RICH NEIGHBORHOODS ON WEEKENDS

This is a tip I got from Tom Cotter, who has written three books on barn finds (and one on motorcycle finds). He wrote; "Search on weekends, when garage doors are often open as homeowners do yard work." That's true, most wealthy folks keep the garage doors closed during the week but on weekends the garage doors are open. Have a digital camera with a long lens and stop and shoot a picture driving by. You can evaluate what was caught in the pixels later. Sometimes it's only a car under a tarp but hopefully there's enough fender showing to guess what it is. I know a guy who barn-found a Rolls Royce SCI dhc in an open garage in Palm Springs by only seeing the taillight!

DEAD ENDS

I got this one from Tom Cotter as well (*Cobra in the Barn*, etc.) Why would a dead-end road, one posted "No Outlet" be more likely to have a treasure? Because no one takes a dead end road if they can help it. So if there's a treasure in that driveway who's going to come across it? Nobody but that guy that goes the extra mile. When I lived in Riverside, California, at the end of my street, in the very last house before you hit the foothills, was a guy with a prewar Rolls Royce with gold plated trim. But only the people who went to the end of the street would have the chance to see it, and that's only when it was out of the barn...

FREQUENT MECHANIC'S SHOPS

One of the treasures I bought, a Ferrari GTC/4, I first saw at a mechanic's shop in West Hollywood. I didn't buy it until months later when I saw it again at a used car lot and managed to get the owner's name off the registration papers in the glove compartment.

My advice is to make the acquaintance of a mechanic in the brand you are targeting and drop by on occasion and take some snack food for him and shoot the breeze. Give him a tip about cars you find that are outside of your target area. Odds are he will reciprocate the favor.

THE TRADE

You would be surprised how many widows, or fellows who have had medical maladies set in at an older age after retirement, would be willing to trade that old car in their garage, the one covered with dust, for a spiffy new one or slightly used one , one that's low mileage under warranty. I would maintain good relations with used car sales managers in case that route looks like it would swing the deal. I remember a guy with a Competition Ferrari Daytona, a car that's now worth half a million to a million depending on racing history, being happy to trade it for two spiffy almost new Mercedes 450SEL sedans or maybe it was one sedan and one 450SL. You can't blame him, the Competition Ferrari was really too much car for shopping (like taking a .44 magnum to hunt rabbits) but there's a sterling example of how you first find out what they want and then get them what they want. That might involve taking them to the new car dealer and picking out a car right then, doing the old swapperini right there. You hand them the keys and title to the new car once they do the same to you for their old dusty car, the one with four flat tires.

I just read another story like that, in *Classic Motorsports* magazine recent magazine by John Webber, about a guy named Billy Weaver, who, in 2011, found a mint condition one-owner 289 Cobra (with only 9300 miles on the clock!) that had been bought by a mechanic at a Ford dealer new back in the Sixties, driven a few thousand miles and then put in the garage for what I call The Deep Sleep. The barn finder found it by going what I call The Old Rumor Route (listen to those old rumors!) where someone, in casual conversation, said something to the effect of "Ya' know, back in my home town there was a mechanic who worked for a Ford dealer who bought a Cobra when they first came out and far as I know, he's still got it."

Weaver didn't waste any time—he looked up the name of the mechanic and damned if the family name wasn't still there—hey, it was a podunk town out in nowhereland. Well, turns out the mechanic had died only two years before Weaver got the tip but his son had inherited the car and wouldn't 'cha know the son's penchant was not for an old-fashioned Cobra but one of them hot new Ford Boss 302s. Well, here's where fortune shined on the buyer, who was in fact a new car dealer. He was able to find a Boss in short order and bring it to the son, keys in the ignition, and all the Cobra owner had to do was sign on the dotted line. Maybe some additional funds changed hands but the point is that he was tracking a nearly 50-year old rumor and damned if it wasn't true! Plus the trade gambit worked—I'll trade you my nice new shiny car, warranted mind you, for that old car that hasn't run in God knows how many years. By the way, last time I looked small block Cobras were goin' for, oh, $600K up. That's $600,000!

USED CAR LOTS

Now on the face of it, this sounds like a totally useless tip. I can hear you asking: "But wouldn't a dealer know what a car is worth?"

Of course they know. But that doesn't mean that they have the money in hand to fix up the cars that need work. They take a lot of cars in on trade and sometimes they are in such a hurry to move the more expensive one out the door that they take in trade a car that needs more work than the seller let on. I know an exotic car dealer in West Hollywood that, in recent years, had a Mulliiner Park Ward slab-side Bentley "Chinese eye" dhc (drophead coupe). Of course they knew that they could fetch $160K once it was restored but they were loathe to put the money into it that it needed to get it to that price level. The truth could be that maybe they bought it for too high a price and are "buried" in it, so were reluctant to put in even one more dollar. In such a case, they could be amendable to an offer to sell it AS IS. So I would suggest dropping by these places on occasion, shooting the bull (always remember to bring food), and give them tips on cars and parts you heard of and maybe someday they will need some car-buying money and offer you that old car parked way at the back covered with dust that you showed an interest in.

Just the other day I was looking at a foreign magazine and saw an L88 Corvette for sale. I immediately e-mailed the ad to a classic Corvette dealer I know (probably in this book) and said "you are the guy for this car." Now probably it's overpriced but the dealer over on the French Riviera in France may be scared of the car; he probably knows Ferraris and Maseratis and Lancias and Porsches but doesn't know

Corvettes and my guy knows Corvettes backwards and forwards. I don't expect a finder's fee if my buddy buys it but, if I ever have to unload a Corvette quick that I had to buy as part of a package deal, maybe he'll take my call. (By the way, it didn't take him 5 minutes to find out it was not an L88.)

THE INSIDER CONNECTION

There's a Mustang accessories guy in San Diego named J. Biddle who told me that one day his gardener saw a Shelby in his driveway and said "You know, Mr. Biddle, there's another house I work at down the road, they got a Shelby too." Well, wouldn't cha know, Biddle ambles down there one fine morning and finds a red '66 Shelby in their driveway. And, wouldn't cha know, the owners had been wondering, "How do we get rid of this car?"

Glory be!

So I'd make flyers and give them to delivery guys, landscapers, roofers, pool cleaners and all those people who are granted entree onto private property. They are your eyes and ears. Keep them happy.

THE PARTS ROUTE

Cars are made of parts. I'd say something like 15,000 on a Porsche 356 but hey, maybe 50,000 on a new Lexus (not to mention 50 or some computers on the new Lexus). In this book there should be a chapter about two brothers out of New York State that spend all their time searching for/and selling Porsche 356 parts and maybe occasionally 911 parts. It was on a buying trip to check out a 911 that they didn't buy that they caught wind of some 356 parts for sale in Pennsylvania. They checked out that lead and, though it took a crowbar to pry them loose from the seller, got not only the parts but a '55 Speedster that the guy had over at a hot rod shop to be restored…a car never finished. So here's an idea. If you don't have enough to buy the car of your dream, one way to make great connections on who has the actual cars is to start stockpiling the parts for your dream car. They bought and sold 356 parts so it was only a matter of time before they'd be directed to someone who had a car buried amid the parts. And of course, an example with new parts is ace Cobra collector Lynn Park who for many years had a shop selling replica Cobra wheels. Now it so happens that these replicas would work on real Cobras as well. So every once in a while he'd get a phone call from an owner of an old Cobra who would inquire about the new wheels and, after the caller was bowled over as to how much new wheels cost, Lynn would sometimes be able to work his way around to the possibility of selling the old car so they wouldn't need the wheels. Park finally sold that business but you wonder how many mice his "cheese" brought in.

REGIOINAL AIRPORTS

Why small airports? Because airports have hangers. You can squeeze a helluva lot of cars into an airplane hanger. One time I used to hang out with a wealthy Italian living in West Los Angeles who would rent a hanger wherever he was in the U.S. for a few months and then buy a bunch of collector cars and park them. He would rarely go back. When he died, I wonder if his relatives even knew which airports his cars were at? Or what cars he owned? Hey, it happens. It's all a matter of scale. To you and me, maybe a Maserati Ghibli Spyder is a world-class investment. To a guy with $150 million, that car could be just about as important as his next pair of Gucci shoes.

ESTATE ATTORNEYS

When people die or are hospitalized or incarcerated, what happens to their stuff?

It is inherited. Step two, attorneys are often asked by the families—"how can we get rid of this stuff?" So I would find a low cost weekly attorneys' newspaper and place the same small space classified ads. By the way when an attorney answers, don't be Mr. All Facts and tell them the market for such a car; how they've been climbing in value, etc. That is not your job. You are the buyer, remember? Keep your pie hole shut and hand them the cashier's check. (For an example, back in the '80s, when I bought that Ferrari from the movie producer, the same model that I could find cosmetically restored was fetching $45,000. I paid $19K for his tacky one, but I did not say to him "Say, you know, if you fixed this up, good ones are goin' for $45K.") It is not your job to educate the owner. His job as a movie producer was taking all of his time. He did not want to be a used car fixer-upper. Your job is to separate him from his car.

TOW TRUCK OPERATORS

Who knows more what's at people's houses than tow truck opera-tors? Have flyers ready showing what kinds of cars you want and every time you see an operator at a coffee shop, buy him a drink or order of fries and say: 'Hey, you see sumpthin', call me. I'll make it worth your while. "They might remember the house they were at a month or a year or ten years ago. It can't hurt and when you find that barn find you may need a tow quickly. Send them a Christmas card as well…

CRAIGSLIST

Craigslist is like the internet; it can be your friend and it can be your worst enemy. The trouble with posting a "cars wanted" ad there is that a rival may see your ad and immediately post their own ad, offering a better deal. I say printed community newspapers and shopping papers are better. Go old school. There you have more chance of a minor miracle occurring, I have seen it happen. It goes like this—the fact is that some people do not even know what they have. For instance, there was a guy who advertised a kit car on eBay with a Devin body but included in his ad a picture of the frame without the body on it and someone recognized it as an early Ferrari chassis, a car that when restored will be a million dollar plus car. The tip was passed on to a San Diego Ferrari expert who bought it on eBay for just over $26,000 (see *Incredible Barn Finds*). So in that case you wouldn't have snagged it by advertising "WANTED Old Ferrari" but maybe got it by running the headline "WANTED: Kit car built on old sports car chassis."

DON'T SHOW UP WITH A DAMN ENTOURAGE

That can spoil your deal as you overwhelm the seller. One time, decades ago, I went with the famed auction maven Rick Cole to a house in Monterey Park, California where the owner had a gullwing Mercedes. We took $10,000 in cash, in a briefcase, not recommended (see discussion of payment), but what turned the gullwing owner off was that we arrived with three guys, thereby not only intimidating the gullwing owner but suddenly three guys made the old car he had tucked away seem that much more important and valuable. His grown children were there and they immediately sensed we were trying to rob the family jewels. The way I should have done it was to go alone, making the whole thing casual and low key.

Like taking the money out of a battered wallet and saying "This is as much as I could get, can we do the deal?" Then once I get the signed-off title and key and the car out on the street, they I call my two buddies. To come with the tow truck. Now, true, I had to rope in investors because I didn't have the money but now I would approach it a different way, saying to the same investors. "You sit in that coffee shop, or park around the corner and I'll call you the moment I've got the title and keys in hand."

THE TRENDS

Now in one way what the trend is right now doesn't matter because tastes change and trends change. A lot of it is due to outside circumstances, maybe even outside of the hobby. When one of those young princes in England (I forget which one, those Royals proliferate like rabbits) borrowed Prince Charles' Aston Martin convertible and was photographed driving his bride around, I am sure the cachet of old Aston Martin convertibles—already on an upward tangent—took a big jump with that one little jaunt in front of millions. Or a certain car could be featured in a movie and suddenly another thousand collectors want that car (like the modified Dodge Daytona featured in those *Fast and Furious* movies).

Here's some trends I've been watching:

RESTOMODS

These are cars that look old at a distance and may be using an old car's bodywork but underneath they have the chassis or at least the drivetrain, suspension and brakes form a much newer car. The trouble with these are is that they are essentially custom cars and oftentimes customs only are beautiful in the eye of the beholder. But hey, they make great driving cars; they are fast, won't overheat, often have air conditioning. So if you want the glamor and style of an old car but the convenience of a new one, this might be the way to go. It's just that, as investment-grade vehicles, they are too hard to calculate appreciation because each individual car is different; and it matters too who did the work—Chip Foose or some backyard welder learning how to weld for the first time on your car!

KIT CARS

Don't even think about it. If you are a kit car guy, you aren't really an old car guy. You're a guy that wants to look like an old car guy without the pain. Say, for instance the guy who has an inflatable dummy of Pamela Lee Anderson. It looks like her—you could even drive around with inflatable Pamela in the passenger seat. But it's not the same thing. Sure, from a distance a kit car can look like a Ferrari or MG-TD or Porsche Speedster but even if you have a great engine and drivetrain they are and will always be a copy. I'd rather have a beat-up dented genuine made-in-Zuffenhausen Porsche Speedster than the cleanest kit car version in the world because I would know that other Porsche 356 fans are hunting for a real one. That being said, it's always worth asking that question: "What's that kit car based on?" If they say "some old sports car" that should ring a bell in your head, about the guy I described in *Incredible Barn Finds* who found the purebred Ferrari chassis under a Devin kit car body. In this book there's a Jaguar C-type that was bought, yes, again under a Devin body. It could be the case that the owner of the kit car doesn't know what he has and you do. (Gee, why does my kit car frame say "Fratelli Maserati"on it?) I also ran across a kit car in Alhambra, California, with a Porsche 4-cam engine in it. Right now I think a 4-cam four-cylinder Carrera engine from the Fifties would be worth about $75,000 or about twenty times the value of a VW-based kit dune buggy! Once again, a diamond in a pile of ten-a-penny rhinestones.

CUSTOM CARS

I know, Pebble Beach had a class for them a few years ago which gave them some respectability and there are some famous ones, like the Hirohata Merc (chopped top Mercury) or Godzilla, a Cadillac built for a rock star, but I was just looking at a website of hot rods and customs and, though I scrolled through page after page after page, I realized that these were all cars that, like some kids, qualify for the phrase "nobody loves them but their mother." Some may have superb workmanship but they are cars with no known value, unless you want to tote up the cost of parts and labor and reward the builder for that. So customs are more to be considered for their entertainment value as retro-nostalgia objects d'art but are not good investments appreciation-wise. I may eat my words on that but that's my opinion. I think the day Ed "Big Daddy" Roth's hot rods go for pre-'60 Ferrari V-12 money is never going to come.

RE-CREATIONS

Boy, some people who are not even in the words business really know how to bend words calling them "Tribute Cars" or "Continuation Cars" but what they really are is "customs" by another name. They often weren't built the year they are purporting to be, yet the DMV is some States are so greedy they collude with their owners and allow a guy with a car built in 2009 to register it as a 1932 Ford or 1966 Cobra, defying reality but making the State some money. The sad thing is when you meet an owner of a re-created car who has even gone so far as to adopt the serial number of the real car that no longer exists, and you hear them constantly refer to their re-creation by the serial number of a car that was destroyed long ago. That's like taking your girlfriend to a plastic surgeon and paying to make her look like

Marilyn Monroe and insist that everybody call her "Marilyn."

Then some ignorant newbie reporter writes a report of cars at events and says the old "whatsiz" car was there, using that SN number, thereby twisting history a little bit further. When these re-creations are sold using appropriated numbers it seems like the FBI would have jurisdiction but they probably are too busy catching terrorists to bother with cloned classics.

BURNED CARS

I know with a modern car, burned means crunch it. With all those computers, (up to 50 on a top of the line Mercedes) burned means everything important has been fried. But talking early pre-computer cars, you could burn a car like a Ferrari PF Spyder down to the frame rails and because it's rare and because it's a Ferrari (and because in the case I am thinking of, the engine was someplace else) you could rebuild it. So go look at those burned cars. It might have only been an engine fire and the rest of the car is intact. One man's "bad fire" is another man's light roasting. There's another case in *Incredible Barn Finds* where two college professors in Orange, California, bought an old Ferrari for under $4,000 that was described as "burned out." It turned out someone had tossed a match into the interior. The seats and door panels were burned. Last time I checked that car had sold restored for $16 million.

RACECARS WITH DOCUMENTED HISTORY

There are many racing events now for vintage cars. Or even con-cours for racecars or with racecar classes. But the event promoters are getting picky. Whereas in the old days they might have allowed a car to enter that, back in its original era, had only been a street car with no record of racing, now they might ask "Where did this car race? Do you have proof?"

That makes a huge difference. Now you see these vintage racers at Monterey and at the Le Mans Classic and so forth where the owners can open up an album and point to a picture and say "There it is at Sebring in '66" and so forth. So I would say, two cars being the same make and model, and in about the same state of dis-repair, I'd go for the one where the seller has all sorts of documentation that it was once a part of so-and-so's racing team, etc. Now sometimes that's not what the seller has, but take pictures and get on the net and look. I found a Porsche 911 racecar at a Porsche shop in Riverside, Califor-nia, and it had numbers on it in roundels on the doors, a roll bar, the whole nine yards of racing equipment but the shop didn't know its racing history. If I were a player for this car, I would discreetly try to find out its history and then make an offer. My hope would be that further research would reveal —bingo—it once belonged to a racer or a team that subsequently became world famous. Your big mistake would be to go on a Porsche website and post a picture of the car and ask, "Does anyone know the history of this car?" Your rivals would be there to buy it before the day is out. You have to be discreet in your inquiries.

FAMOUS OWNER TRIBUTE CARS

I had to coin that phrase. I don't like it, but it comes close to describing the appeal of some cars. Let's say you are a fan of Raymond Loewy the great mid-century industrial designer. He rebodied several of his own cars, including a Jaguar E-type (*Incredible Barn Finds*) and a BMW 507. Neither car is beautiful but, damn it, if you like Raymond Loewy's work, what better way to pay a tribute to the man that to own a car he designed?

Same with Tom Tjaarda, the American designer in Italy who designed the production Pantera but many one-off cars before that including the Corvette Rondine. I think owning a car he designed is a tribute to Tom. And there's Franco Scaglione, another great designer whose work I admire. As more and more of these great designers get known, there's more people that can say "I bought it because I like Giugiaro" (or whoever they say).

CELEBRITY CARS

Now in this case, the reason people want these cars isn't because they are connected with an engineer or designer but a celebrity who owned them. The "Tom Mix" Cord. The "Steve McQueen" Ferrari Lusso. I knew one East coast native who wanted an E-type Jag roadster because he particularly had memories of a svelte East Coast lady who, in their youth, gadded about in such a car. He would have killed to own that car; the one she sat in.

MILITARY VEHICLES

There are clubs devoted just to this; the members not only show old Jeeps, half tracks, etc. but even dress in military uniforms (though they are a bit pudgy compared to the original occupants of such clothing). But I have even seen a German G4 550 military truck at a concours in Orange County, restored to the nines. So gradually these may become collectable. One thing you can say about military vehicles, though, is that they can take a lot of knocks compared to your average collector car (though there is the matter of what the cops are going to say about those working machine guns).

LATE MODEL RARITIES

Now sometimes automakers go into making a new car and think they got the cat's pajamas when in fact they have a DOG.

Now I can't say the Pontiac Solstice was a dog but the alternately styled Saturn Sky sold half as many roadsters so that makes it twice as rare. On the other hand Pontiac went and introduced a coupe version with a removable roof panel only a few months before Pontiac as a Division slipped beneath the waves. Leaving roughly 1200 coupes out there in America in the hands of owners. They are now worth, used-car wise, about twice what a roadster is. So there's an almost-new car (in collector's terms eight years is nothing) that won't go down in value. Another possibility is the Chrysler Crosfire SRT-6. This was an American car built on a Mercedes SLK chassis. It had "art deco" styling in some respects, not beautiful but interesting. But the only thing that would make me consider it is that they sold only about 2000 of the SRT-6 version worldwide. You talk a small production number like that and you're talking collectible. And there's probably still parts and body panels on Chrysler dealers' shelves, unlike an old car found buried under bird poop in a barn.

In considering a modern car as a future collectible, you have to be in it for the long haul, because it could be decades before you'll see an uptick in value. But there's signs some high-end ones go up quicker than the middle class offerings. Take the case of the '05-'06 Ford GTs. Ford made 4,038 of them, the two years combined. They will become investment grade if Ford fails to make another car in the same niche (200-mph mid-engined car). Ford, having nervously survived the threat of bankruptcy a few years ago, refuses to make another in that vein. It's nine years ago they stopped. Once we get to 15 years since the last one, I predict the '05-'06 Ford GTs will began to look like "the last Ford supercar" from Ford (unless you want to count Shelby Mustangs, and I am a bit dubious about modern Shelbys).

But in general, there's not many cars built after the year 2000 that you can buy that are guaranteed appreciators. You can count the ones so anointed in the last ten years on one hand.

A LAST WORD: THE VIRTUES OF BUYING CLEAN

The cars are out there, waiting. First, though, a last-minute warning…Much of the foregoing involves buying cars in various states of distress, some actually found in barns, so you can get a bargain by fixing them up and selling them at a hoped-for-profit (all the while humming the depression-era song "There'll be a pie in the sky-bye-and-bye").

The trouble with buying cars half-finished is that, during your period of ownership, the cost of parts and labor might have escalated faster than the car so you could put $30,000 worth of work into a car and then check the market prices when done only to find out you produced a perfectly-turned-out $20,000 car!

What you should do, if you are not mechanically inclined (I admit I owned two gullwings, two Alfa Sprint Speciales, a 12-cylinder Ferrari and a 356 Porsche and have yet to actually change a spark plug!) is shop for the best of that model you can find. Upon falling in love with a particular model, you should spend more time looking for the very best finished example you can find, know what the market value is, and then plunk down the cash, and thereby skip all the blood, sweat and tears attendant to all the cosmetic or serious restoration.

There's one huge undeniable advantage to buying ready-to-go (a variation of Meals-Ready-to-Eat) and that you can take advantage of all the events you can drive your treasure to right now, not someday far in the future "when the car's done." Look at it this way, coming up is Monterey Car Week 2014. Miss that and it will not happen again. Oh of course there will be a 2015 Monterey Car Week but not with all the same cars or the same people. If your car is not done, not drivable, you'll miss event after event…. I'd rather have the memories of those events I was able to drive to in my prize than skinned knuckles and a car that never quite done…so if you pick the right car, one that appreciates, it will eventually become a barn find vis-à-vis what you paid for it and what you can sell it for. Of course the downside of this philosophy is that you will have to pay a lot more for the car than if you buy a project car covered with dirt and mouse poop. I'm just saying…my memories of owning old cars are a lot better with the cars that were running and driving when I bought them than the cars that needed everything.

Good hunting!

HOW YOU CAN CONTRIBUTE YOUR FAVORITE BARN FIND STORY TO THE NEXT BOOK:

Yes, I know you've been following this subject for years and what I want to hear about is your favorites—the ones you talk about when meeting with car buddies at a barbeque, after about the third beer, both cars you've found yourself or cars you've heard about that others found or even cars you just read about in the newspaper or online. If it's a good story, I'd sure like to hear it and consider it as a candidate for the next book. But before you send your letter, please allow me to re-iterate the requirements for likely candidates:

1.) the car has to be worth at least $100,000 when finished

2.) you have to give us some idea of how it was found; how the barn finder got wind of it

3.) the information you send has to have a hint of what was paid for it at the time it was found, and in what year and what country the transaction was made.

For instance in the "to do" hopper I have a candidate for a story—an Alfa SSZ barn found in Oregon by a classic car dealer in Switzerland. Now so far I dragged out of his aide how he found it—tip from an Alfa collector—but there's still no hint of what amount was paid when it was found. So as far as I am concerned, there's still no story there. (And shame on you journalists who run 3-page features lavishing praise on a barn-find but leaving out both those salient facts! You guys are in the sure-is-pretty school of automotive journalism.)

You can send your nomination in the form of a photocopy of the newspaper clipping or of a print-out off the net, and even a photo on a disc (if it's a car you personally found).

But please don't send anything you can't afford to lose because I'm researching candidates for Book 3 so I can't return any discs or even answer each letter. Think of your input as your contribution to barn-find lore in general—a story that in your view is just too good to go unheard. If you come up with a good enough example, you may see a whole chapter devoted to it in the next volume. And if you are a car-related business such as being upholsterers, car painters, body-men, mechanics, dealers, auction companies, etc. feel free to tell us the story of the greatest barn find you ever had something to do with and we will be happy to mention your business (do not fail to note, for instance, the forward to this book is written by one of the best car finders in the Corvette world; a man who I knew for 40 years but only recently realized he tells a doggone good story).

Here's the address. Remember nothing can be returned.

Wallace Wyss
Enthusiast Books
1830A Hanley Road
Hudson, WI 54016

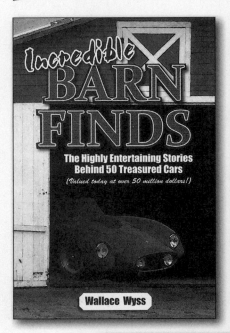
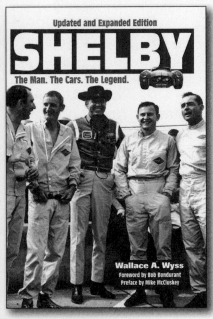